CW00376780

Copyright © 2019 by
Alex Cem

FIRST EDITION

www.alexcem.com

Contents Page

Introduction

If you were on your deathbed, and you had only a minute left to advise your loved ones how to live their lives, what would you say? I am sure you would say something along the lines of the following: "Life is short. Do what you want to do with your life," or "Find what you love to do, and do it as often and with as much joy as you can," or "Don't be so harsh on yourself. You can only do your best in life," or "Give as much as you can. Love your friends and family will all you have." The problem is most people do not live their lives this way. There are many reasons for this such as our conditioning, our limiting beliefs, our egos, pressures that society place upon us, the hustle and bustle of the 21st century and so on. Whilst we live in probably the most peaceful time in history, stress, pressure, depression and anxiety are at an all-time high, and there are no signs of slowing down. It is more important than ever before to truly work on yourself internally, so that you can be the best version of yourself, so that you can love more, earn more, share more and experience the beauties of life as much as possible. Once we know what really matters to us, then we can begin to devise a list of goals, an action plan, and a way of living that will enable us to achieve our purpose.

Fortunately, in this book, I am going to show you how to take control of your life, how to think, feel, act and live, so that you can make the most of your skills and strengths whilst avoiding the pitfalls that most people not only fall into but live without even knowing it. This book breaks mental, emotions and physical processes down into a granular level, so that you can dissect yourself, and transform yourself into the best possible you. I truly believe that this book can change your life. The principles in this book are universal, and pertinent to anyone, at any stage in life, who wants to take their inner power, happiness and success to the highest level. Not only will you develop yourself dramatically, but also you will inspire those around you, and you will have a stronger influence on people, regardless of how close they are to you, because of your newly formed mental, emotional and physical attributes. I look forward to hearing about all the new joys and pleasures that this book brings to you, so please do get in touch.

Whilst it is very difficult to measure fortitude, happiness and success (as these definitions are highly subjective), I believe that my voice is one worthy of acceptance and trust. I have studied successful and happy people for as long as I can remember. Moreover, I have become fascinated with how successful, powerful and happy people think. Most of people's success and happiness derive from what takes place inside. I am referring to how they think, how they react, what they do and why they do them. Also, I believe that we can link people's smaller successes to their larger successes, and so we will explore the seemingly innocuous things these happy individuals do to make the most of their lives.

Furthermore, whilst much of the information in the book are scientifically proven, many of the things outlined are also based on my opinion. Feel free to agree with some notions, and disagree with others. As long as you take many insightful ideas and information from this book, then I am happy to have served you. Additionally, I would say that I qualify in these areas as I am an extremely happy person: I experience mostly joyful, peaceful and energetic states, and I quickly manage to change my state whenever I experience any negative emotions. In addition, I have developed some beautiful relationships with family and friends; I have a very accepting, grateful and supportive relationship with myself and spiritually speaking. I have learned the importance of giving, and I support many wonderful charities: no one is ever self-actualised unless they give of their time, energy and finances to people in need. Also, I am constantly improving in terms of wealth: I run a successful business, and I continue to grow many investments. In summary, the teachings in this book are things that I apply within my own life, and I know the joy they bring me. I hope you also prosper and live abundantly both inside and outside.

Whilst I can certainly claim to be a successful, happy person with high self-esteem, this was not always the case. The three most important things to me (relationships, health and wealth) used to be my weaknesses. In particular, I used to be an overweight and unfit person, and after years of training and conditioning my mind to perceive food and exercise differently, I now have a completely natural, strong and attractive body. Moreover, I used to be solely an average employee who firstly was not overly passionate about my work and secondly struggling to live the kind of luxurious lifestyle I wanted; I am now a leader in my business and career (with different forms of passive income), and I now own a diverse portfolio consisting of property, stocks and commodities. Additionally, I used to take things personally, and I felt like I could never accomplish my dreams. Today, I am so grateful about how optimistically I react to things (whether rejections or making mistakes), and I am so fortunate that I get to serve people like you who are clearly motivated to bettering themselves. These successes would not be possible without a growth mindset, and a love of learning and developing my skills but also how my thoughts and emotions work together. Most importantly, I am now in a position where I give to several charities consistently ranging from Save the Children to Cancer Research to Water Aid among others. Proudly, I am now in a position where I not only look after myself, but I have the energy and aptitude to support my family on so many levels. At the end of this book, you will feel capable of becoming an even better and successful human being (regardless of how successful and happy you already are).

Why did I decide to write this book? I have met, and studied, the lives of people from all walks of life, and I have come to realise that there are certain things we can do in order to maximise our potential, and truly feel powerful, happy and successful. Some people are successful, yet they lack any feelings of sustained happiness. Others feel power in terms of position at work or within their family, yet they do not feel like in control of their lives. This book has been created to end the frustration and disappointment people frequently endure in their lives. This book not only outlines the things that make individuals feel powerful, happy and successful, but it is a meticulous guide that breaks down what happens internally (so that they can also improve their external world) and why they happen. The purpose of this book is to empower you to appreciate what you have, and to learn about the tools you can utilise to become even more powerful, happy and successful.

We live in a world that is becoming ever more complicated, where the stakes are higher and patience is lower. Our busy lifestyles result in many issues that ruin our ability to feel truly happy. Technological advancements, increasing demands in the workplace, and impatient people make it harder than ever to work on yourself. We must know how we operate, what we can do and why we should do them.

You will need to read this book several times if you are to become an even more emotionally intelligent, knowledgeable and happier person. Learn how to direct your thoughts. Understand how your emotions work. Utilise the metaphors and stories, so that you can paint your own art, and live your dream story. You will soon notice how your relationships begin to improve. You will notice how you begin to attract greater wealth. We will explore how to embed quality, supportive habits. You will notice your self-esteem improve drastically as a result of your increasing self-acceptance and self-appreciation. Your relationships with your partner, children, siblings, colleagues etc. will improve, and you will be in a position to positively affect them. You will be their role model (even more so if you already are). You will notice how things do not bother you like they used to bother you.

You will be able to change your mood more quickly, and shift your focus toward more empowering notions. I am truly grateful to be part of this journey with you. I promise to give you the knowledge needed to direct your thoughts, emotions and actions to areas that will fulfil you. All I need is your commitment and determination to adhere to the notions and principles outlined in this book. Your energy is essential, and you need to take action as of now. Time does not wait for anyone. Contemplate why you want to make this change? Whom are you doing it for? Why is it worth it? What do you want to accomplish? Ensure that you read the conclusion in this book, as we will clearly tie power, happiness and success together, so that we know what must be done in order to live an extraordinary life. Let us begin now.

Chapter 1 – Thoughts, Emotions and Actions

The Conscious and Subconscious

"The conscious mind may be compared to a fountain playing in the sun and falling back into the great subterranean pool of subconscious from which it rises." - Sigmund Freud

The door-to-door salesman, on probation at work, needed to sell his double-glazing service. This extremely eager and motivated individual consciously wanted to sell, and thought he could, but he had an underlying belief that would redirect his positive intentions: his subconscious was not conditioned to help him get the result he sought. His conscious thinking was saying, "You can do this. You can do this!" However, his subconscious had the overpowering belief that said: "You've never sold, and you don't know how to get strangers to believe in you." Incessantly, the salesman knocked on every door. He had a forced smile on his face that said, "Sorry to bother you," and his eyes communicated total uncertainty. He opened his mouth, and out came his sales pitch: "You wouldn't be interested in having double glazing, would you?" Even though the salesman wanted to sell, he had an underlying belief that he could not, and so almost all customers will reject him as his demeanour lacked confidence and congruency. He will need to change the roots, and not even consider picking the fruit yet!

Firstly, our subconscious is where our deeply held beliefs are. It dictates the majority of our actions without us even knowing. The subconscious is where the foundations of our belief systems exist. If our subconscious and conscious are not singing from the same hymn sheet, then things will not work out the way we would like. Our conscious consists of what we actively think to ourselves. Anything that we repeat enough (in our conscious minds), with enough strong emotion, will permeate into our subconscious over time. If your conscious is saying "I am confident," but your overriding subconscious says, "I am fearful," then this will become apparent to all and yourself. These two dimensions must coincide to spur the success we truly want.

Over time our conscious thoughts can infiltrate into our subconscious, but the subconscious can easily overpower our conscious whether it is through our words or body language. Think of it as the river trickling water (consciousness) down into the ocean (subconscious). Affirmations and incantations can help to drive supportive, uplifting notions into the subconscious through repetition. Incantations, in particular (putting your body into what you say to yourself, and thus creating intense emotion), embed positive notions more powerfully. Think about it, whenever you attach a strong emotion to newly learned material, you are able to store it strongly into long-term memory. In particular, whenever I made a mistake when doing something, especially in front of others, then I certainly remembered this new information from that point onward: I had the strong emotion (of embarrassment in this example) to help remember the material. However, we want to remember information due to strong, positive associations rather than negative ones ideally.

Our subconscious directs the show. It can be seen as the people behind the scenes who make the big decisions. Our conscious is just the face of the organisation; the conscious is what we see and hear, and with great work, we can actually contact the boss: the subconscious. Whenever we are in a trance, our subconscious is present, and our conscious takes a back seat. For instance, when we are fully immersed in driving and daydreaming, our subconscious is often at the forefront, and we go into autopilot. We can influence our conditioned belief systems and meta-states through internal representations in the form of visualisation and positive self-talk, which will be explored shortly.

"Intuition is unconscious accumulated experience informing judgement in real time." - Alain de Botton

When we use our intuition we are reacting based on our deep knowing. We are not over-thinking and listening to the conscious thoughts within our prefrontal cortex. We should always follow our intuition as it encompasses so many past experiences, decision-making and information that our conscious mind (only capable of absorbing $3 - 7$ processes at a time) can utilise. Always go with what feels right rather than what pleases our thinking at that moment. Many things can attract our attention in the present moment, and so it can prove difficult to think straight. However, our intuition holds access to a range of material that will guide us better.

Could it be that our subconscious minds interact with one another? Whilst we may think that only one person's conscious thoughts interact with another person's conscious thoughts (in the form of communication), perhaps there is something deeper taking place. If we know that our subconscious dictates much of what we unknowingly do and communicate, then we can comprehend that our subconscious minds (deep underlying beliefs) are always communicating with others. This is where intuition takes over. Have you ever told a lie, and had the other person simply know that you had just lied? Of course there are telltale signs, but something deeper is taking place. This is where people can see through false behaviour.

"The subconscious is ceaselessly murmuring, and it is by listening to these murmurs that one hears the truth." - Gaston Bachelard

Our subconscious holds all of the power. The conscious is simply an intermediary, a tunnel that transports information. The conscious is simply the pathway to the subconscious, and the thoughts that carry more emotion with it, are the thoughts that become engrained in the subconscious. Similar thoughts (and emotions) congregate to form a bigger paradigm. For example, if you fail at a physical sport that you like, you may say to yourself, "I guess I'm not as good as I thought." Subsequently, if you take part in another physical activity that you like, such as weightlifting, and your results are disappointing, then you might say to yourself, "I guess I'm not so psychically strong either." And there you have it: two similar activities have incurred failure, and, consequentially, a larger belief has been consolidated: "I fail and underperform when I take part in physical activities." Our reactions to perceived shortcomings monumentally shape how we approach future activities. We must therefore change our automatic responses before we even encounter another physical activity otherwise we are setting ourselves up for unending affliction.

Thought and Emotion

"Human behavior flows from three main sources: desire, emotion, and knowledge." - Plato

Not all thoughts turn into actions. Only thoughts that have enough emotion attached to them turn into physical actions. So what are thoughts? Thoughts are very direct and clear statements. What are emotions then? Emotions can be seen as thoughts that are unclear, ambiguous, indiscernible, and thus are more gripping. The more you break an emotion down in terms of what has caused it, the looser its grip becomes. These emotions (unclear thoughts) are either negative or positive. So, for example, if you have a thought that says, "I could become rich if I applied myself more," and if you have a strong emotion (say excitement or intrigue) that attaches itself to this thought, then you will take some kind of action and press forward (say write a plan of action for yourself, or talk to someone who can support you and so on). Unfortunately, there are two sides to the coin. Another thought could be, "I'm just not smart," and if this thought creates a strong emotion within you (such as anger or bitterness), which you entertain, then you will act in a way that conforms to this judgement: you may start an argument, or blame someone when the topic is brought up, or you may commit a crime as a result of your anger, or you may just become despondent and inert. We want to remain indifferent to unsupportive thoughts. Let them pass by.

Being analytical and evaluative are great skills, but over-thinking can be perilous. Why? Because when we over-think, the negative voice (which exists within us all) tends to show up more as over-thinking frequently creates uncertainty. Subsequently, our imagination takes over, and we begin to play out all of the different possibilities in our minds, which further complicates matters, often resulting in disempowering outcomes. Thoughts and emotions have different energy; emotions clearly contain much more energy than pure thoughts. This is why incantations add power and substance to our thoughts (as motion creates emotion and vice versa).

What makes a thought spring to mind? Past conditioning, associations, primitive desires (id), our understanding of right from wrong, our values (superego) and so on. A thought consists of the language we have accrued being formed syntactically to make sense and to direct understanding. The words we learn and know are so significant. If you want to happier, then predominantly explore and speak of quality, positive things with rich vocabulary. How would you describe your life for instance? If you want to be richer and wealthier, then study the terms and vocabulary that the rich and wealth learn and use. Conversely, understand the words that the poor and depressed use, and stay clear of their lexis. In a way, we must exaggerate things to ourselves in order to motivate and influence ourselves. For instance, if you wake up, and you think, "Today is just going to be another monotonous, average day," then how badly do you want to jump out of bed and get on with it? Alternatively, if you wake up, and think, "I am going to kill it today. It is going to be a massively important day, and I am going to give it my all," then I am sure you will get out of bed with more zest!

Thoughts and emotions are accessed differently. In the brilliant book, *Emotional Intelligence*, Daniel Goleman explores LeDeoux's research, which expresses the human brain's evolutionary process. Our brains have developed tremendously, and they are becoming even more acute and responsive. Sensory indicators, from the eye or ear, journey first from the brain to the thalamus, and then to the amygdala. Another signal is then transported to the neocortex (the thinking part of the brain). The initial reaction enables the amygdala (emotive/reactive part of the brain) to react sooner than the thinking brain as the amygdala was implanted for survival purposes. The neocortex takes longer as it is more logical, rational and comprehends information until it is completely refined and tailored to fit our values and beliefs. Emotions are quicker to gather and more effective when an instantaneous and immediate response is necessary (especially when reacting in a fight or flight mode) whereas the neocortex comes to the forefront (no pun intended) when deep thought, detail and consideration are required. Emotions are pure sensations whereas thoughts require detail, specifics and formation.

In order to comprehend our emotions, we must explore the art of motivation. Motivation is the desire to take action. People are either motivated by fear (feeling that they may not be enough, or feeling like they may lose something), or by the prospect of greater gain. So, for instance, the thought, "What will my financial future be like?" can actually spark two reactions: you will either feel motivated by the fear of losing the money you already have now (fearful motivation), or you will become motivated by the potential to monetize (gainful motivation). Most people operate out of fear, and yes the best business people always protect the downside, but to be truly happy in life, we must have more pleasure to really succeeding financially than the pain we have by having to do something differently with our money.

We cannot prevent all poor quality thinking, as it is simply part of being human. However, we can choose to remain indifferent to these thoughts. We will want to detach any emotion from our negative notions, and pump energy (emotion) into our more empowering ideas. So, for instance, if you think of something that cannot support you, then purposefully make the effort to shift your attention; do not attach physical movement to this thought (hitting a desk, covering your face, holding yourself tightly, biting your nails etc.) as this can strengthen your emotional response to the negative thought, and thus engrain them more deeply within you.

Become indifferent to this thought. For example, if the thought comes to your mind that you will never meet the love of your life, then simply sit still indifferently, and instead appease this negativity by being grateful for what you have, focusing on things that you can do to change the situation, and attach stronger physical movements to these thoughts. You can then purposely choose to think, "I am enough as I am, and I can put myself in different situations to attract the kind of person I want," and then you can add some form of intense physical movement (fist pump, nodding fervently etc.), so that this idea is more emotionally triggered.

If you ask questions with enough passion and enthusiasm, then the answers will soon appear. Weakly phrased questions delivered tediously will induce frail, fragile responses whereas open, positively phrased questions will cultivate potent, empowering solutions.

The Insecure Partner

A jealous husband would always argue with his stunning, talented wife about how much attention she gets. His insecurity led to his mistrust. His desire for control and certainty sparked fear into his partner. He was afraid that she would leave him. In his mind, he had the thought, "I am not enough for her." The thought of losing the woman he loved was too powerful. His insufficient masculinity and low self-esteem manifested in frequent confrontations with his wife. The argument took different forms, but the reasoning behind them was always the same: "I do not deserve you." The thought, "I am not enough" became stronger became stronger and stronger within him. His feelings gave life to what would just be a simple thought. His fearful emotions spurred these countless arguments. His bemused wife, growing weaker and emotionally distant with every hurtful encounter, lost trust, and what was once a fun, exciting relationship became entrenched in turmoil, manipulation and abuse. She eventually left him for another partner. She did not choose to leave him; he chose to leave himself.

The husband's pattern:
Thoughts: "I am not enough for her. She will leave me."
Emotions: Abhorrence and indignation (fear)
Actions: Conflict and argumentation

The wife's pattern:
Thoughts: "He does not deserve me."
Emotions: Dissatisfaction and pain
Actions: Abandonment

The Drive

Imagine that the cars on the road are our thoughts. There are so many cars (thoughts) going in different directions with their own journeys or sometimes driving around randomly. The traffic lights are the emotions and signals we give to these thoughts: green represents go; amber represents being indecisive; red represents stop. We should give the green light to the thoughts that enable and empower us. We want to encourage these thoughts by accepting them and strengthening them. Choose to show red to the thoughts we wish to deter and disempower. What we emote, we promote.

The Sequential Trio

"Your beliefs become your thoughts, Your thoughts become your words, Your words become your actions, Your actions become your habits, Your habits become your values, Your values become your destiny." - Mahatma Gandhi

Setting up a successful pattern (thought, emotion, action) starts with the smallest of things. We can then work our way up. The smaller things we accomplish can sometimes foreshadow the larger things to come. Our thoughts trigger other thoughts; our emotions trigger other emotions; our behaviours trigger other behaviours. Many, if not all, of our actions are linked to one another. Everything within us flows from one thing to another seamlessly. If we want to change one behaviour, we must first analyse the surrounding behaviours both beforehand and thereafter. If we want to stop smoking, what actions usually take place leading up to the act of smoking? What happens after we smoke that makes it so strongly engrained in our action-based repertoire? For example, do you bite your nails (because you emotionally thought about something), and then go for a smoke, which is then followed by a more relaxed conversation over the phone? These physical actions are sequentially habitual. They must all be changed if you really want one to change in particular.

"We are what we repeatedly do. Excellence, then, is not an act, but a habit." - Aristotle

How can we begin to transform a negative habit into one that is more supportive? We must, firstly, be aware of something if we are to change a negative trio pattern. This is known as conscious incompetence. Catch yourself making the error. This initially breaks the pattern even if we continue to make the mistake in future. By just making it explicit to us, it sets the change in motion. Subsequently, we can literally act out this same negative pattern on purpose when a similar event occurs, as it will serve to emphasise the folly of its enactments. Once we play with the emotions associated with the actions, then we can take control of our feelings and detach from these actions. In addition, we can also practise improving our own reactions and patterns by changing how we react when another person makes an error. For example, if we get angry with ourselves when we accidentally smash a glass, then we can start to correct this harsh perception by changing our response when another person accidentally smashes a glass. It conditions us to react more favourably, so that we choose more uplifting ways of treating ourselves. This shift will improve our thoughts, emotions and behaviours in other areas also.

Furthermore, internal representations are also important. Part of successfully changing a pattern, or your perception, is to detach ourselves from the actual experience. This enables us to comprehend how our brain usually works (automatic response) when in the moment. We begin to play with the relationship between our thoughts and sensations. So, for example, if you have a fear of public speaking, and you are about to speak in front of an audience, the following pattern might occur.

Thought: "Don't begin to sweat now. I must impress. Oh no, now you are blushing and embarrassed. You cannot make a mistake! See you are trembling and murmuring your words now; I bet they all think I am an idiot."

Emotion: Embarrassment and disappointment.

Action: Sweating, blushing, closed body language, lack of eye contact and so on.

A strong emotion is tied to this: fear. This fear then overwhelms the immediate experience; you become exceedingly focused on the inside (ourselves), and what you are thinking. Your internal dialogue shifts from being about the audience's experience (external) to being totally focused on you and what you are doing. This sequence of events become so engrained that it is exactly the process that takes over when in the same or similar situations. However, we can become aware and interrupt this pattern: "Actually, so what if I make a mistake? No one is perfect. Why am I expecting myself to be perfect? Actually they may like me more if I am just natural." Your new emotion might be one of peacefulness or acceptance. Our new actions might take the form of speaking more loudly, making more eye contact, showing relaxed and confident body language, and most importantly, staying focused on what we are saying.

The sequencing of particular thoughts, emotions, and actions solidifies and intensifies every time it takes place. It has a domino effect. Positively, good things can occur, and positive language can be reinforced, which perpetuates our mental fortitude. We may say that we are successful at this or that. Then our beliefs in this aptitude transcends into an ability to learn and grow in another subject or discipline. The meta-belief then becomes, "I can succeed wherever I put my attention." Our paradigms shift, and our belief systems alter. Small things accumulate and transform into larger structures. These larger structures, now programmed into our subconscious, determine our core beliefs. We begin to move toward and attract affluence. Like takes place in the conscious; love develops in the subconscious. Sadness takes place in the conscious; depression pervades the subconscious. A subconscious pattern is shaped through the repetition of conscious thoughts, feelings and actions. The cycle continues. Generally, our subconscious dictates our actions and behaviour.

When the subconscious works toward our goals, incredible things can happen. The conscious is at the water's surface; the subconscious lies deep in the sea. The conscious is the tree; the subconscious is the roots. Water the roots, and the tree shall grow, but if you neglect the roots, the tree will wither and die or fail to grow at all. I am reminded of the Chinese Bamboo tree. This spectacular tree is wonderfully unique. If you were to water this tree's seeds, it would not even grow an inch within one year, nor would it grow at all the second or third… It is in the fourth year, after constant watering, that the tree begins to grow substantially and monumentally. Not only does this tree begin to grow, but within just a few short weeks it can grow up to ninety feet tall! Astonishing. Think of your life in this way. The roots and seeds need constant care, support and attention. If you suddenly achieve something fantastic, trust me, more often than not, it happened because of changes you began to make a while ago. Once you have laid the foundations, marvelous and incredulous things can develop. We always need to get to the root of the problem!

Our Senses

"Love is of all passions the strongest, for it attacks simultaneously the head, the heart and the senses." - Lao Tzu

Yes, love influences what we think, feel as well as our physical sensations, but it works the other way around as well: our senses can project an experience, which in turn ascertains our thoughts and feelings, ultimately resulting in the strongest of all emotions: love. The immediate experience, and all of the senses immersed within this moment, can have a vastly profound influence on how we perceive things.

The more we affect the senses, the more powerful our connections and associations shall be. For example, there is a certain sentimental and nostalgic smell I encounter every now and then, and it invokes the beautifully visceral memories I have with my grandfather. All it takes is a smell, and wonderful images of my grandfather and his house appear in my mind. Our senses (sight, hearing, smell, taste and touch) have such profound implications on our actions because, automatically, they trigger thoughts and feelings (some of which we are unaware).

This understanding can be used in many settings for many outcomes. I once dated a woman; I thought I was using the most sensual aftershave until midway into our date… She said, "That aftershave you have on… it's the same as my father's." I later learned that she disliked her father. Needless to say, I never used that aftershave with her again. We make all kinds of associations and connections with things that we can use in our favour. The more we can manipulate our senses, or the senses of others for that matter, the more we can adjust perceptions and reactions.

If you want to make an experience more meaningful, simply change the senses you experience. Our senses can massively affect what we think and feel, and thus, the actions we take. If we look in the mirror, and see what we like, then we will feel positive emotions about ourselves, and this will encourage beneficial actions. Success builds upon success. If we smell something desirable, we naturally want to be closer to this person or thing. If you are tired or apathetic for whatever reason, all can be changed through the senses: change your surroundings; change the smell in the room; change what you hear; change what you can see and so on. A woman may splash an intoxicatingly sweet smell over herself to further entice a man for example. This smell finds its way onto the man's own clothing, and when he later wears this clothing, the woman's smell brings back the encounter he had with her. We can use this same strategy in terms of how we react to things, so that we can trigger empowering states. If you associate success with a certain smell (which you can create by choice), then use this spray whenever you want to be at your best. If there is a sentimental piece of jewellery you believe brings you luck or support, then you can wear this to trigger feelings of success and comfort. If there is a certain movement you perform that enables you to access feelings of fortitude, then you can do this before a challenging activity.

We should definitely be more fixated on what we cannot see, but we live in a physical world and communicate physically through our words and body language etc. Maybe when we die, we communicate in ways that are far less tangible, and maybe we become beings that communicate omnipresently, but for now, we must be astute when communicating with others. Interestingly, generally, it appears that men fall in love more quickly than women because men can be more easily swayed by aesthetics and visuals. Women, on the other hand, may be influenced more based upon what they hear. Women are often better at being observant, and analyse what people say more deeply. On average, women speak about eight thousand words a day whereas men speak around only around two thousand words per day. Women love to share thoughts and feelings. Perhaps understanding these distinctions will assist us with better understanding others and ourselves.

Mind and Body

*"To keep the body in good health is a duty...
otherwise we shall not be able to keep our mind
strong and clear." - Buddha*

Our emotions are the intermediaries between mind and body. Our mind thinks of something, our emotions are stimulated by these thoughts, and our body acts and reacts accordingly. The body, our form, is a physical expression of how our minds function. If we want to remain calm, and have fewer physical illnesses, then partake in yoga and meditation. If we want to be mentally open and flexible, then stretch frequently, and keep the body agile. If we want to be mentally strong and assertive, then lift weights and train intensely. The mind can dictate how the body operates, and the body can dictate how the mind operates. Sharpen both mind and body, so they continue to support one another.

An emotion can be seen as an energetic thought that has not yet been mentally processed accurately enough to become a complete meticulous, distilled thought. The unknown (an emotion) is then the intermediary between a thought and an action. Uncertainty then becomes the driving force that powers us to go from a thought to taking action. A thought is precise and definable. An action is a reaction to strong emotion. An action can be seen as trying to find a result of one kind or another. Perhaps actions want to make sense of something. Actions can therefore be seen as movements that derive from unspecific thoughts; it is the desire for clarity that we take action.

When people are highly sensitive and emotional, they lack clarity, and so often seek solidarity in a strong, authority figure (someone more certain and logical). Interestingly, we experience more sensations per minute than thoughts. Perhaps this is because emotions are easier to feel than thoughts are to think. Why? Thoughts require accuracy, meticulousness and clarity whereas emotions require a plethora of information that has not been ruminated or granularly broken down. This is because an emotion can be anything, and its indefinable nature keeps it intriguing and influential. If you want to become less emotional, become more thoughtful.

Purely feeling and reacting takes away our control. Emotions are not in any sense futile or less valuable as they drive us to do things. This is why a healthy balance between thoughts and emotions are necessary. The purely emotional person does a lot, but does not get anywhere whereas the extreme thinker does not get anywhere either because they just think. There is a time to think, and there is a time to feel. However, once you take the time to think an emotion through thoroughly, you take back control and it becomes a thought. You now have control of your actions. This is why, in many ways, it can be beneficial to really break down the steps of any negative emotions you experience. This may not be as necessary for your positive emotions as we conspicuously want to keep our energy in these areas!

In order to change a negative emotion, we must be able to trace it back to its most fundamental origination. All negative thinking can be traced back to an element of fear. Let us revisit the example of the insecure husband who feared that his wife would leave him. These are some of the questions he would have wanted to ask himself. What does she like about me? What doesn't she like about me? What can I change? What can't I change? He could also trace his fear to a larger fear. Why am I afraid that she will leave me? Because I am afraid that I will not have a partner. Why am I afraid of not having a partner? Because I am afraid of what others will think of my broken marriage. Why am I afraid of what others think? Because I want to be perceived as successful and happy. Why? Because my reputation is important to me. Why? Because I have a big ego. Why? Because I have a lack of balance and perspective in life. Why? Because I have not taken the time to develop my own self-worth and self-esteem. We have broken down the emotions we experience in this situation into only thought processes, which takes away a lot of the emotional connection we might have with this experience. This will make us feel more in control.

If we break negative emotions down like this, then we realise what we must do. We learn more about ourselves, and how we function, which provides greater control. We can easily identify when and why we experience negative emotions, and trace them down to our deep underlying beliefs. However, we must be totally honest with ourselves if this is to work powerfully. Emotions are only useful if they incentivise us to go for what we want in life. The person who knows why they feel the way they do has control of it, but pure thought, without emotion, will not allow us to use this feeling to drive an action.

An action is never random. An action is never separate. Even actions that we think are random and impulsive have emotions attached to them. A random action is a reaction to the desire for something different for instance. Thoughts, feelings, actions and circumstances continuously flow from one to the next. They go around and around, always changing, our moods ceaselessly shifting, building upon one another or changing completely due to a particular incident. Our emotion is the catalyst: it is the fuel that turns our thoughts into actions. The way we live our lives is a reflection of how the brain works. If bad things happen to us frequently, then dreadful things operate in our brains. As the old saying goes, "Everything happens for a reason." Everything is synchronised as shared by the brilliant psychologist: Carl Jung. If we are accumulating success in several avenues of our lives, then it is a reflection of our successful thinking.

Could it be that the body inevitably grows older, which forces the mind to slowly deteriorate? Could it be that diseases stem from a dissipation of cells that spread as a result of mental entropy? Damaged cells spread deleterious reactions in the body that gradually pervade organs. Oftentimes we operate genetically, so if we were to contrive a disease, it is likely to be the genetically predisposed disease formulated by our ancestors. Peacefulness will keep these at bay. The mind's clarity and purity will enable us to make the right decisions and, thus, remain impervious to any disease we were predisposed to possibly acquire. We must defend the mind from entropy and the detrimental patterns that subjugate hope and health. What leads to the creation of metal impairment before it becomes a physical disease? Stress. Stress is the biggest culprit. What is stress? Stress is often what happens when we become excessively drawn into our lives, and we fail to step back in order to view our lives from afar. It is the detrimental disharmony and discord within us. Stress is what happens when we take on too much mentally or physically at a certain time. Stress occurs when we feel overwhelmed. Stress is a form of anxiety; stress is therefore a form of fear. Fear is therefore our biggest enemy; it is the biggest killer in life. We must address the different types of fear we experience, and link these to how they affect our health and physical bodies.

Mirror Madness

Every time Susan went to look in the mirror, she was always instantly drawn to the parts of her body she did not like: her belly and love handles. Not only did she focus on these areas, but also she would always say to herself something along the lines of, "Why can't I lose weight here?" This question can only drive negative and hurtful responses: "Because I am lazy. Because I eat too many cakes. Because I never exercise. Because I'm weak." The mind tells your eyes to look at your problems (your belly and love handles), and your emotions are disempowering. No wonder why Susan never takes the necessary actions that can actually change her physical appearance. Next time you look in the mirror, focus only on the things that you like about yourself (or could like). Interestingly, the more you focus on what you like about yourself (your eyes, lips, arms etc.), the more your weaknesses will tend to improve because you naturally begin to make better choices as it relates to food choices, exercise, sleep etc. The same applies to our habits. Focus on the brilliant or beneficial things you do every single day, and you will miraculously begin to implement even better habits in other areas. Some beneficial habits can be as simple as brushing our teeth, writing out our goals, showing someone how much we care about him or her or making an important phone call. What we focus on expands.

Chapter 2 – Fear and Failure

"We can easily forgive a child who is afraid of the dark; the real tragedy of life is when men are afraid of the light." - Plato

It is mandatory to uncover all matters relating to fear and failure as they are by far the biggest barriers preventing people from being emancipated, joyful and self-actualised. Until we understand what constitutes fear and failure, then we will fail to understand what we must change in order to maximise our happiness and feelings of success.

We are even more docile, vulnerable and changeable when weak. This is why corporations and the media inundate us with ideas to make us feel that we lack something in order to sell their products or services. We allow externals to dictate how we feel about ourselves. Our ego gets caught in a net, and our souls have to suffer. The key is to not get caught. We are more with less. You are great enough just the way you are, and anything else simply enhances you rather than defines you.

Fear is the biggest time waster and limitation in life that we all experience or have experienced. Anxiety, guilt and over-thinking are different forms of fear. If we reduced the feelings we attach to these inevitable thoughts, then we would live far more prosperously. However, experiencing fear briefly at times is inexorable, and in many ways useful in preparing us for an eventuality.

Our Ultimate Fear

"There are things known and things unknown and in between are the doors." - Jim Morrison

We are about to explore where our fears originate, and the importance of dealing with this governing fear as a means of reducing all forms of fear that stem from this meta-fear. While some level of fear (anxiety, stress or anger) is inevitable and, at times, necessary in life, being able to control its constant impending manifestation is paramount if we are to utilise our potential and live the life we deserve.

We have all experienced that moment in our childhood where we first learned that we would eventually die and so will those with whom we love. I remember an eye-opening conversation with my father where we discussed passing, and that it is a natural part of life. Understandably, I was so overwhelmed and bemused by the realisation. As we grow older, wiser and more knowledgeable, we develop coping mechanisms for this inevitable ending. We may distract ourselves; we may construct fantastical beliefs that we will live a fairy-tale story; we may avoid silence and moments of deep contemplation. Obviously, there is nowhere we can run or hide, and how we choose to cope with death's looming presence will determine our automatic responses to the unknown aspects of life.

All stress, one way or another, trickles down and emanates from our fear of death and/or the unknown. Death is the unknown. This is why many people fear the unknown or new situations because our brains are wired to be wary of anything that can be associated with death: an unknown thing. This is why people become so fixated with having control because they fear change (death). If we change what passing away means to us, by dealing with this overriding fear healthily and appropriately, then we can respond to life's comparatively minute issues more befittingly and effectively.

Firstly, we must confront and come to terms with death. Accept that whenever it is time to pass on, then it is the right time for us. This knowing will not allow you to be fearful if you incur any physical ailments or illnesses. If your heart irregularly palpitates, just relax and allow whatever happens to happen (more than likely it is just a normal bodily reaction). The more you try to force yourself to be a certain way, the more you inadvertently add fuel to the problem.

Secondly, whatever you fear, apart from death, you must move toward. You will realise that things are never as bad as your mind projects. The wait and build up to the unknown are always worse than the actual experience. Fear shows what must be surmounted. Whenever you experience fear in any and all of its forms (anxiety, anger, stress), then put yourself in those experiences more often, but not necessarily at the highest degree straight away. For example, if you fear getting into a physical fight with someone, then start by partaking in boxing or wrestling classes. If you fear public speaking, then start by talking more often in small groups. If you fear losing your job, then talk to your employer about how things are going, and what he or she thinks of your current effort and results.

If we take life seriously, then we tend to take death gravely also. Consequentially, all matters under life's umbrella of experiences will, therefore, be approached with similar severity. We become immobilised and incapable of facing our fears with the wrong mindset. Those who are highly religious use their principles and practices as a powerful coping mechanism for death. Some people feel like they need to control death (by having a clear understanding of what death will bring them), and this need for control (certainty) continues into their daily lives. Others choose to see life's folly, and choose to view death more entertainingly and less severely. Whilst having firm rigid structures has its positives and negatives in life, so does living in uncertainty by accepting that it will always be an unknown outcome. This more carefree fundamental belief may result in a more open and flexible existence, but you may never feel grounded, and, therefore, never truly feel stable throughout many of life's experiences. I honestly believe that whatever you choose to believe is what will become your eventuality. As long as you are happy and secure with what you believe, then I am happy for you.

How we approach the small things in life reflects how we approach the more immense, encapsulating things in life. Once we eradicate the biggest fear we all have, the fear of death and the unknown, then frivolous matters can no longer immobilise and suppress us. We no longer get severely stressed or fearful of things like intimacy, public speaking, and conversations with authoritative figures and so on. Why? We have made peace with the biggest challenge that we must accept: our demise in this physical form. Once we truly believe that there is madness in worrying or overly planning things, because it is trivial regardless, then we can live freely. We can then take action towards our true desires without our unconscious having to carry this burden of the unknown. We must learn to function without giving power to death's looming and impending cloud that encapsulates all our other, smaller fears and apprehensions.

The more we purely live in the physical form, the more psychic entropy, pain and confusion we will face. People actually feel guilty if they do not worry! However, you do not need to experience fear in a way that immobilises you. Displace the self-sabotaging thoughts and feelings that return time and time again to keep us stagnated. Clear the windows of your brain, so that you can see clearly.

Anxiety, guilt and over-thinking are just different forms of fear. If we reduced these thoughts and feelings, or at least mitigated them, then we would live far more prosperously. Experiencing these feelings briefly are unstoppable, and in many ways useful, as they can prepare us for any eventuality. Living without experiencing any fearful moments is impossible as balance within the emotional spectrum is necessary: you do not know what peace is without noise. However, you can choose to experience far more positive and empowering thoughts than negative ones by developing your emotional intelligence, and being able to quickly change your state. If we are the ones who create stress in our minds, then we can also appease ourselves. We must have positive, strong thought patterns that show up at will, without conscious thought, whenever these negative emotions show up, so that we can ride the wave of fear.

People fear what they do not know; they fear the other; they fear what they cannot control, even though what we cannot control fascinates us, but isn't that what we should embrace and appreciate most? Flexible people are able to adapt to many situations. They do not allow themselves to be immobilised, and to not always *need* to stick to the 'plan' and 'rules.' If we are inflexible, we become rigid and unable to flow with life. Instead be open to whatever cultivates itself. Move toward your desires and passions, and do not ponder on the losses; instead concentrate on the gains! People are more afraid of losing something than having the excitement of something new and rewarding. This is very much an indicator of whether they believe life will last forever (in their disillusioned minds), and so they are attached to things and hoard whatever they have, fearing that they will lose it all. Others appreciate the life they have, and live life knowing that it is all going to be gone very soon! They take calculated risks. They refuse to care about being judged and making mistakes because they know that if they do not take action, they will die having lived a life not worth living.

Whenever we attempt to force something, we consume so much more energy. It is much more efficient to calmly allow movements to unfold. How can the smaller person defeat the much larger person in jujitsu? They are able to use leverage, and the opponent's force to generate the movement for them. The same applies to our internal world: we cannot fight against our negative thoughts, fears and anxieties; instead, we should know how to calm ourselves and use our own 'mental' leverage. Trying to force things to happen will ironically ruin its chances of materialising. It is like trying to keep hold of water by gripping it. Instead, hold your hands open, and calmly allow your hands to be filled. This approach is necessary in life.

The fear of making mistakes can immobilise us. We are so afraid of being viewed as imperfect that we flood our brains and nervous systems within toxic thoughts and emotions, which invariably result in our incompetent actions. Confidence is actually more important than ability in many situations. Would you rather your favourite sport's team had incredible talent, yet played with the lowest confidence, or a team with average players playing with the highest confidence? But why do many competent and adept individuals have such low confidence? One reason might be that, because they are so intelligent themselves, they assume that others around them are of the same level or even better, and they do not want to appear weaker.

What is the worst thing that could happen by being yourself? One strategy to help break this fear of imperfection is to actually make some mistakes on purpose. Obviously, it is unwise to make mistakes in the most important and urgent of matters, but purposely misspelling a word in an email or neglecting a very small aspect of a project or giving a very basic response in a meeting can be a way to lessen the tension and stress you feel in high stake situations. Once you allow yourself to make mistakes, and accept yourself when making mistakes, you can now take control of your future, and ironically, make fewer life mistakes by putting yourself out there more often. We become fixated on external forces, caring so much about what others think that we do not follow our life's purpose.

The way in which we handle or do small-scale things is a reflection of how we handle or do larger-scale things. Here are several vastly random examples, so that you can begin to think about the different ways you foreshadow larger events to come: if someone lies about what they did over the weekend, then they are more capable of lying about their loyalties. If someone cut scorners to meet their project deadline, then they are more capable of cutting corners when getting promoted. If someone borrowed fifty pounds from you, and never gave it back, then they are more capable of stealing larger sums of money from any provider. If someone was angry with a waiter because their food took a little bit longer to be brought over, then they are more capable of getting angry with someone closer to them whenever they do not get things when they want them... This is how you can learn so much about someone by seeing how he or she behaves with small-stake things. Always watch what people do (their true selves) rather than what they say (people trying to mask their ego and claim false reputation). Consider how you handle different situations. If you want to change a massive, crucial thing in your life, then trickle your way downwards to see this thing on much lower scales. For instance, if you want to save large sums of money for investments, then consider where you spend a little bit of money frequently, and change these smaller scale habits first. Start from the top, and work your way down.

People react to their fears in one of two ways: they either avoid them like the plague, or they face their fear and eventually conquer these mental demons. If you face your fears often enough, then they will turn into strengths. This is the law of the universe: if you become obsessed with what was once your weakness, then it will eventually become one of your biggest strengths. Lionel Messi, possibly the greatest footballer of all time, was once told he was too small; he had a growth hormone disorder, and he needed treatment just to get sufficient male hormones. Les Brown was labelled mentally retarded in school, and he struggled to talk at all by the age of four; he is widely regarded as one of the very best motivational speakers of all time. We need to be resilient and believe in ourselves. A wise teacher once told Les Brown, "someone's opinion of you does not have to become your reality." This is why you must value your own opinion, firstly and fore mostly, and only take on others' opinions if they support your beliefs. We all have different strengths, and where there is strength, the opposite will be your weakness. This is just natural. Instead of hating what we are not as good at, all we need to do is build a team of people with other strengths than us, so that we can maintain a healthy and solid life whether that be with family, friends or business partners etc. There is no such thing as a perfect person, but you can build a perfect team with different perceptions and skills coming together.

Fear and the Ego

"The ego is the false self-born out of fear and defensiveness." - John O'Donohue

Let us consider the many ways in which we hold ourselves back, and begin to analyse our own decisions, actions and current situation. One of the main struggles people have is their inability to realistically reflect on their current strengths and areas for improvement. What is it that holds us back? Fear. Fear holds us back. Fear can save your life. Unfortunately, fear can also create a life unworthy of being saved.

People lie to themselves as a way of protecting their egos. They may make themselves appear to not need something, when really it is the thing they need most. It is akin to this fitness analogy: the exercise you least enjoy doing at the gym is the one your mind and body needs to do most. So why do people find it so hard to be honest with themselves about their circumstance? They are simply too immersed in their own lives. Like a rat in the rat race, they are too narrow-minded and fixated on purely what they see in front of them. They never take the time to step back and view the consequences of their limiting thoughts, negative feelings and ineffective actions. They convince themselves that things happen to them, and it is not their fault. They convince themselves that they do not need to improve, and that improving is for people who lack something. They have brainwashed themselves into believing that their way is the right and only way.

Conversely, these blinded individuals may just be extremely apathetic. Change and reflection requires objectivity, energy and focus. It is easy to look at others and focus on their faults, but when people do this, it is often a form of procrastination, as they do not wish to work on themselves. Unfortunately, self-reflection requires a humble, honest approach. It requires the ability to think, "I am not amazing at this or that, and I want to improve, so I will be seeking help from others one way or another." The following example of inner dialogue is negatively phrased to truly illustrate how a person's mind might work, and how habits can be changed through persistent questioning:

> *"Why don't you exercise more?"*
> *"Because I do not value being pretentious and focusing on looking good."*
> *"Why don't you value looking good?"*
> *"Because I value the mind more."*
> *"Why do you value the mind more?"*
> *"Because the mind is the most important thing."*
> *"Why is the mind the most important thing?"*
> *"Because it does all your thinking and determines your future."*
> *"How does it determine your future?"*

"Because you can think things through and plan things out."

"Why do you want to plan things out?"

"Because I don't want to make mistakes."

"Why don't you want to make mistakes?"

"Because I don't want negative things in my life, and I don't want people to judge me because of my mistakes."

"Why don't you want negative things in your life?"

"Because I wouldn't know how to react."

"Why wouldn't you know how to react?"

"Because I'm not that mentally flexible and positive."

"How can you be more flexible and positive?"

"By reducing stress, and being able to relax."

"How can you reduce stress and be more relaxed?"

"By exercising more."

This example foregrounds the importance of questioning everything we do. The honest answer to the above dilemma is as follows: "I'm lazy when it comes to exercise because, deep down, I know I will never be able to compete with others in this field, so I reject its importance. It's easier for me to stay as I am, and refute the truth even though it would make me a better, happier person. I guess it's just my ego getting in the way, preventing me from progressing." The things we find the hardest to do are the things we need to do the most. The ability to think and self-reflect is of monumental significance. Our ego, left unattended, is our biggest enemy. We all have, or have had, false paradigms and perceptions that veneer the truth. Self-reflecting, and being brutally honest with ourselves, will prevent us from experiencing copious affliction again and again. We all have challenging things happen to us, and we possibly felt that they were undeserved. We felt we could not make sense of why it had to happen to us. If we still cannot conjure a positive spin on why a bad thing occurred, then we must at least understand that there is a message currently indiscernible to us. We must be careful with what we expose our eyes and ears to, as it dictates our focus, and therefore our thoughts. We find what we seek.

"I'm not afraid of dying. I'm afraid not to have lived." - Wim Hof

In order to live the life we want, we must stretch ourselves and conquer these dragons (more often than not they are not fierce dragons, but puppies masquerading as dragons). If people fear many things (they experience stress, anxiety, worry and are quite rigid), then they must learn to love and give more to themselves and others: when we love, we cannot fear. Why fear when we can love? When we experience love in the present moment, then it is impossible to fear anything. Therefore, love as much and as often as we can. Love our families; appreciate our friends; give to charities; share our skills with strangers. Our existence on earth in this form is limited, so we must go for what we want. Dream big and live abundantly. It is never too late to change and thrive.

The Perfectionist's Perfect Downfall

"But I am learning that perfection isn't what matters. In fact, it's the very thing that can destroy you if you let it." - Emily Giffin

Perfectionists are some of the most talented and intelligent people in the world. However, most perfectionists tend to underachieve. Let us clarify the traits and consequences of being a perfectionist. We must firstly appreciate the value and beauty of making 'mistakes,' and we must accept that no one is, or is expected to be, perfect. Therefore, we should never be preoccupied with always doing things perfectly as this can crate an insurmountable amount of pressure, and so no positive things can ensue. Now, this does not presume that we should never do an amazing job, especially in things that take precedence, but the most salient point to take from this section is the following: if we always have to do things perfectly, then, more often than not, we will avoid taking action. In writing terms, this is referred to as the writer's block. It therefore seems appropriate to call it: the perfectionist's block. These people will infrequently enter a state of flow because of the immense pressure they place on themselves. Perfectionists fear being judged. They fear appearing weak to themselves, but even more prevailingly and damagingly, appearing inadequate in front of others. The perfectionist is often the person who fears the most. They certainly fear failure, and it does not need to be this way.

We all take pride in doing something brilliantly, but these individuals take their performances so seriously that they judge and demoralise themselves in the face of failure and rejection. Where did this perfectionist mindset originate? It stems from a fear of being unloved. Parents, teachers, siblings and peers have wittingly or unwittingly infused this need to do things perfectly within us. Perhaps these individuals only received great attention from parents and elders, or perceived it this way at least, whenever they did something extraordinarily. At a young age, we do something well, and subsequently get rewarded; we are shown acceptance and affection. We get a good grade, our teachers tell us how good we are; we clean our room, and our parents display their love; we win a competition, and our friends want to spend more time with us. However, when we do not stand out, when we do not win, or when we do not do something impeccably, we fail to receive adulation, encouragement and the love we all crave in life. The perfectionist learns to seek approval, and they have linked in their minds that it will only be given if they do things perfectly. This fear comes from never, or rarely, receiving unconditional love. Unconditional love comes from being shown love and care whether you win or lose, whether you succeed or fail, and whether you do right or wrong (to an extent). This is why it is so important to teach children that they are great people because of who they are generally, and not because of their achievements. Unfortunately, the perfectionist wants to please everyone, and thus he or she never pleases himself or herself.

"Healthy striving is self-focused: "How can I improve?" Perfectionism is other-focused: "What will they think?"- Brené Brown

Critics are often perfectionists. However, the extreme perfectionist will never be truly successful at what they love. Perfectionists analyse and evaluate the work of others, yet they are too afraid to put themselves on the line. They like to think things through, sometimes religiously and meticulously, but this usually results in putting others down, and they never really try to shine themselves. Everyone wants to always do things to their best abilities, but this pressure, if taken out of context, must be surmounted.

The perfectionist is almost always immobilised. They cannot take action because of the fear of making a mistake. There is always more we can do, but this way of thinking will prevent us from attempting, completing tasks and eventually succeeding. Most perfectionists end up living a life of mediocrity and lost potential. We must learn that the only way to be loved by others is to love ourselves. If we approve of ourselves, and appreciate ourselves for who we are, and how we are, then no one will ever have power or dominion over us. We are at this point currently because that is all that we know so far. We can never fully know something unless we are living it. You may know that exercise is good for you, but if you do not exercise then you, essentially, do not understand. Knowledge in and of itself is not power; it is potential power. Knowledge and execution induce success.

It is not Failure!

"It's fine to celebrate success but it is more important to heed the lessons of failure." - Bill Gates

Failure is an opinion, a perspective, and so never a fact. Every negative thing that has happened to you happened for a reason. They are all blessings even if you cannot see them now. The minor car accident was necessary to prevent the fatal accident you would have later incurred if you had not gone through that previous event. That separation you had with your husband or wife prevented you from living painfully permanently. That failure you had at school saved you from following the traditional path into mediocrity and complacency. A failure is a blessing in disguise if you choose it to be.

Our 'failures' often lead to our biggest triumphs. We can learn an unlimited amount of things and lessons from our failures, but we rarely ever learn much from our victories (unless we had to battle adversity to win). Why? Once we win, we move on right away to our next challenge without evaluating all aspects of the victory vigorously. This is why people with natural aptitudes will only go so far in their fields whereas the person without inherent skills, but who has a relentless work ethic, will soon surpass the natural talent. The grafter knows it is not about the outcome, but it is the process that they must learn to love. Whenever we truly go for what we want in life, we inevitably face criticism, judgement and potential public embarrassment. Again, we must see the foolhardiness of these innocuous and futile perceptions.

The more we live for what others want for us, the more we suppress our love and passion. Ironically, we actually lose more respect when we seek it. However, if we believe in ourselves, and follow our dreams, then others will eventually approve, and become beautifully infected by our energy and clarity. We must see, but continue; we must hear, but persevere; we must know, and live the life we want. People will pass on, people will leave you, people will go from liking you to hating you, but the person you will always have is yourself.

A belief is created when you communicate something to yourself consistently. Beliefs are created through the repetition of thoughts until they are embedded into your subconscious. A belief is simply having certainty as it relates to a certain thing. For instance, if you do not like change, which is akin to saying, "I am fearful of not having control," then you will avoid any novel experiences and challenges. This is devastating because you are declining in terms of happiness, success and growth if you are not pushing your limits. And if you do the same things over and over, and keep it this way, then there is no room left for anything new (growth). Nothing flows when there is no room. Life, and nature, itself is all constant change and flow. Nothing in nature stays the same: the seasons come and go for instance. Nothing in life stays the same: new cells are constantly being formed in our physical bodies for instance. This is why staying the same mentally is unnatural.

The quality of your life depends on the quality of the questions you ask yourself. Your belief-systems are then shaped and fixed based on these frequent questions and answers. You associate yourself to an, 'I am,' in which you label yourself as something that defines your identity. So let us have a look at some examples. Imagine the following scenario: you approach, and interact, with someone you find attractive. For one reason or another, this person expresses that they are uninterested in getting to know you any further. Two options exist in terms of how you frame this to yourself. Firstly, you may think to yourself, "Why doesn't this person want to get to know me? I must not be attractive enough; I must not be funny enough, or I must have a weird approach. I AM NOT GOOD AT CHATTING SOMEONE UP." And there you have it. The first question you asked yourself gave you no positive or useful answers: "Why doesn't this person want to get to know me?" Can any positive answer derive from this question? No. Subsequently, you answer this question with a negative response. In fact, you answer this question with several reasons why you 'failed.' You view several different possibilities, adding layers of uncertainty, which culminate and compound into a powerful and all-encompassing 'I am' statement: "I AM NOT GOOD AT CHATTING SOMEONE UP." What you think about, and emotionally invest in, will determine your reality. You are always consistent in applying what you believe, so you will now either create actions that coincide with this lousy belief that leads to feelings of unsuccessfulness, or you totally give up interacting in flirtatious ways with new people because of this pain and hopelessness.

Secondly, you can reframe the question in a way that is more promising: "Well it didn't work that time; she must be distracted by something that is out of her control at the moment," or "What can I do to make myself come across even better next time?" The first question totally empowers you as you shift focus from any thought of your own ineptitude; you deem it to be someone else's error or issue. In this case you did nothing wrong, incorrect and you did not fail (even though failure is success in disguise). The second possible response keeps the focus on you; this time your self-questioning is empowering as the answers are only going to be beneficial and motivating. "What can I do to make myself come across even better?" Even though similar answers can derive from the negatively phrased question, the word 'even' presupposes that you did some things successfully, and you also established a growth mindset: there is room for improvement. The use of successful syntax determines your current and future results.

What is frightening, or pleasing, is that these strong belief systems attach themselves to other belief systems to create a meta-belief. So, for instance, imagine that you have now told yourself that you are no good at attracting people upon first meeting them. What might happen when you approach a client at work to get that all-important commission? They may say no. So what could happen if they do? "Why doesn't this person want to do business with me?" Whoops! Here we go again. Numerous self-repudiating answers gush forth to support your misery. Where is the 'I am' that usually follows? "I GUESS I AM NOT GOOD AT SELLING." Now that you have made it explicit to yourself that you cannot attract or sell, it is time to cultivate that meta-belief: "I GUESS I AM NOT GOOD AT CONNECTING WITH PEOPLE: I AM NOT LIKEABLE." This meta-belief is now embedded into your subconscious, sabotaging any potentially successful interaction with another human being one way or another unless it is changed. Your identity is malleable, depending on how you use the words 'I am.' What we attach to the words 'I am' is important; it claims part of your identity, and we always act consistently with who we think we are. Be very vigilant with what you say after the simple personal pronoun and modal verb: I am.

A quote from Thomas Edison resonates with me in relation to how he conceived his supposed 'failures.' When the renowned innovator was questioned about his failures, he delivered a fabulous response: "I have not failed 10,000 times—I've successfully found 10,000 ways that will not work." The next time you 'fail' at something, congratulate yourself for your effort, and for knowing that you are one step closer to getting it right. This mindset keeps you on the right path. It enables you to be resilient, and to keep pushing forward. Only beautiful things come out of struggle: character, love and appreciation.

We have all experienced pain from a conceived failure. We all felt the embarrassment, humility and self-questioning that inevitably arrives from taking a risk, and not seeing it work out the way we would have liked. Incidentally, I have always been fascinated with how people speak about the past, present or future. There is much to learn from how people refer to time. For example, listen to the way people think about artists and athletes. Some people think that the best musicians were Elvis, Michael Jackson, Madonna and they believe that the best football players of all time were Pele, Maradona or Zidane. Whilst it is hard to refute this, it is conceivable that these people think that the past will never be beaten or better. The problem with this is that we do not look forward to the future by living nostalgically. Others think that today's musicians and football stars are better than ever before, or that the future will produce even more talented stars. Whether they are right or wrong is irrelevant. I am more interested in their beliefs that things will always get better, and there is hope for more success ahead. We have all stumbled when we least wanted or expected. Accept the past; there is no need to dwell on what could have been or once was. Forgive your mistakes, and vow to never allow the repercussions of a perceived failure stop you from taking action and eventually breaking through. Where there is struggle, there is resistance. Interestingly, the resistance is oftentimes either yourself or something not as powerful as once imagined. Failure is not the outcome; your reaction to the result is what matters.

Stress

"It's not stress that kills us, it is our reaction to it." - Hans Selye

What is stress? Firstly, it is intangible. Stress is an internal representation. To experience stress is to create disharmony within. Therefore, we create stress. We choose to experience stress based on the things we think we should do or what we might have to do. Stress is pressure. It is a build-up of all the things that we supposedly need to get done that do not appear pleasurable. So why do we choose to experience stress, and to release such toxic and radical reactions in our minds and bodies? Stress can be seen as responsible for all illnesses and diseases. It is the ultimate killer of lives. We must be able to notice when we are stressed on a daily or weekly basis, and have habits in place to best reduce this stress. Consider the things you do to reduce stress, and whether this actually creates stress in other ways. Do your utmost to utilise positive, supporting stress-reducing activities to support your health, joy and self-esteem.

Is stress at all good for us? Hormesis is when we have to deal with a little bit of stress as a way of strengthening our will. Exercise is a form of hormesis. Therefore, we can never totally eliminate stress, but only engaging in minor stress will be beneficial. If stress levels rise too high, then that is when less desirable effects arise. When you truly experience nature you cannot be stressed. Living in an urban, busy city can make it harder, but we must enjoy nature where possible. Seeing, hearing and smelling the sea, trees, grass and so on can really put things into perspective. I am aware that this is a very romantic ideal, but enjoying the most basic, natural things in life will always alleviate stress.

We all struggle with stress to varying degrees. Everyone in life has their own coping mechanisms: exercising, driving, talking, socialising, sex, over-eating, under-eating, arguing, OCD and so forth. Choose more productive methods of releasing stress. Many people choose to self-harm: smoking, alcohol, illicit, or even licit, drugs and so forth. All forms of emotional eating and physical self-harming exist here too. Positive stress relievers are far more beneficial: exercise, martial arts, sex, meditation and yoga. These experiences can increase the state of flow whilst simultaneously keeping mind and body robust. Even things like conversations, going for walks etc. are better choices. It is a choice that we all have, and one we are all accountable. Even though we all encounter moments of stress, we must embed positive stress-mitigating practices that will serve to relieve stress. We must enhance the general quality of our lives by doing what we enjoy, such as playing golf or tennis, which do not have any repercussions, and which do not exacerbate stress, depression and illness.

We must take care of ourselves first. Only when we are happy are we truly in the right position to give to others freely and openly. We can only successfully take care of others in the long term if we take care of ourselves first. Admittedly, we may be able to do nice things for others even if we are unhappy. However, we will become resentful or worse, and we will end up taking our frustrations out on people even closer to us, or people who will put up with our tempers. Some people sacrifice their own enjoyment in order to give to someone else. This altruistically loving, yet potentially self-righteous behaviour, will manifest itself in some other form of conflict and negative act in the future unless we are happy and content with ourselves. If we have short-tempers, then we should reflect upon this cycle of stress and whether we, in a way, add stress (anxiety and pressure) on top of stress in a kind of self-destructive cycle. What do we think about before we lash out? How can we better control our emotions? Our habits create our character. Do our habits induce affliction for others and ourselves, or do they inspire, motivate and catapult us, and others, to another level?

Ideally, we want to release stress in the healthiest ways. There is no need to take our stress out on others in the form of passive aggression or arguing or starting a fight or looking for someone to make a mistake so that we can embarrass him or her. Others will appreciate our emotional intelligence if we remove our stress more appropriately. Firstly, we must consider what happens when we get stressed. What can we do to reduce stress? Can we be more proactive and plan better? Can we train our minds to expect stress on certain days or in certain situations? Can we seek support from others to reduce stress? Secondly, consider the ways in which we release stress, and assess how this empowers or disempowers us. Stress is not necessarily a bad thing. However, too much stress can be overwhelming, and it makes us lose all sense of control. Therefore, it might prove useful to evaluate what we could control, and what things will work out just fine if we are unable to control them. After all, stress is a loss of control. The more controlling we are, the more inclined we are to experience high levels of stress: we are dealing with others in life who also want a sense of control.

"The greatest weapon against stress is our ability to choose one thought over another." – William James

The Roundabout

When there is traffic build up leading to one exit at a roundabout, then the other exits will also become detrimentally affected. This is a great analogy for how your mind works: you may be struggling with one area, or 'exit' in your life, and this can have a profoundly negative effect on other areas within your life. This is why we must constantly seek to improve in all areas of our lives in order to be balanced, and to sustain positive momentum and flow. Write down your goals and objectives. You may think that these different goals etc. are all separate, but they are more congruent than you may believe. They all coincide in bringing you happiness whether they are to lose fat, get promoted, find a partner, travel the world and so forth. When one of these are achieved, you will notice a shift; you will notice that you become, or at least feel, even closer to achieving other desires and aspirations. Unfortunately, life works the other way too. When one aspect is decelerating/declining, a person's will to progress weakens, and he or she will notice errors creeping in. If there is something that means a lot to you, and it is falling apart, you will also find a drop, one way or another, in other things that take precedence also. Focus on your successes, and keep moving forward in all key aspects of your life.

Worry

"If a problem is fixable, if a situation is such that you can do something about it, then there is no need to worry. If it's not fixable, then there is no help in worrying. There is no benefit in worrying whatsoever." - Dalai Lama

Worrying about something is incredibly futile. If we can control something, then why worry about it? If we cannot control something, then why worry about it either because there is nothing you can do about it? Worrying weakens us. It is biologically part of our brain to look for things to worry about (a survival tactic), but if we know that this is natural, then we can just address it as something that is there but should not be known as really us: it is a biological construct, and not an identity construct. It is not ME who is worrying; it is the human condition itself. This is why we should never disparage ourselves for worrying or being apprehensive.

What happens when we worry? Worrying about something is a form of anxiety; anxiety is a form of fear, and so when you worry, you are afraid of something. Usually this is a fear of not being in control of a situation: "I am worried about what will happen to my children." "I am worried about what will happen to the economy." "I am worried about whether the business will downsize, and if I will be made redundant." You can only worry about something that will happen some time in the future, and so worrying in and of itself is unnecessary as it is not within your control. What we should ensure, however, is that we are prepared for any eventuality. Preparation alleviates fear.

Why should you fear something that you do not know would happen for sure? The things I worried about most are the things that never actually ended up happening. Excessive or constant worrying can make us take less action. The more action we take in our lives, the more we learn, and, therefore, the more opportunities we create for success to follow. Worrying is not the problem (apart from stressing us out unnecessarily); the problem is when we take less action as a result. If we worry, but do, then we can still thrive. However, if we worry, and hold back, then we limit life's more beautiful opportunities. What you think about expands. Your worries can detrimentally affect your actions, thereby fulfilling your ominous foretelling. Why invest mentally and emotionally into things that you cannot control? Why give power to things that do not contribute to your well-being? Could worrying itself just be a form of self-sabotage?

Why use your present moments worrying about something that has not even arrived yet? It all relates back to how we conceive death. It is akin to the martial artist who is afraid of getting knocked out by a ferocious opponent. The fearful fighter somehow manages to walk into the opponent's deadly strike. Why? The fearful fighter constantly worried about getting hit, and so that is exactly what happened. Make sure you focus on your strengths, and just allow everything else to naturally unfold however they were intended to unfold. Surely it is healthier to live moment by moment, consumed with your life's purpose, and not limiting your thoughts and experiences by concerns that detract your potential.

Either come up with a solution to the thing concerning you, or just accept that whatever happens was meant to happen. It can be useful to come up with affirmations that your mind uses automatically whenever something worries you. Some people have programmed themselves to worry so often that it has become their core emotion. I call it their subconscious emotion. This is a person's emotional home. They have programmed themselves to worry about things so much that they find new things to worry about – even things that are clearly innocuous! They need to fill in this gap because it is part of their identity. Unusually, they have control and certainty when experiencing this negative emotion. Worrying can actually become an addiction. How? People know that they will be worried about something, which provides stability and control. They do not know to which degree they will worry, which creates uncertainty, and thus an emotional pull, and they gain attention from others because they are worried and upset, which enables them to feel loved and a sense of connection. These powerful human needs result in an addiction. No amount of worrying or feeling guilty (the equivalent but regarding a past event) will create a more favourable result. So what is the point?

Worrying reveals negative emotion and thus uncertainty. In fact, worrying is a form of procrastination. When you are worrying about something, you cannot be dealing effectively with the problem facing you or another problem that you should be addressing. You allow yourself to ruminate deeply, which drains you, leaving you feeling overwhelmed. Nothing productive comes from worrying. If you know you need to focus on something, then simply attack this with your aptitudes and strengths.

For instance, we have all worried about being late to work when things did not go as planned that day. What use was it ruminating about being late, and about the consequences of letting people down and showing poor punctuality? You would need to do the same actions anyway, right? You still needed to get the kids ready for school, clean the unexpected spillage in the house, lose your car keys (or didn't you?), drive to work, avoid traffic and so on. Go through these steps in the moment, and decide to just accept your current situation rather than unnecessarily repeating derogative things in your mind psychotically (about being late) as you go about doing the exact same activities.

From Worrier to Warrior

We all have obligations, and we all have problems. Some problems are short-term, and others require resilience to surmount. Whilst everyone worries about certain things, people react in one of two ways: they either worry themselves into inaction and hopelessness, or they face their concerns full on, and they give whatever they have. It is not the worrying that is the worst part: it is the subsequent inactivity and learned helplessness. Everyone has problems, but the degree of these problems differs. One person's worry may be another person's strength and vice versa. Worrying is really just about perception, and the types of questions you ask yourself. For example, say two people have to partake in a difficult activity such as deciding upon the right investment: one might think, "what about if it is the wrong time to invest, and I end up losing all my money?" Whereas the other person may think, "This is so exciting. What a great opportunity to further my wealth and learn!" It is the same problem, but different perspectives. It comes down to what you focus on. Some become defensive and crumble when worry sets in whereas others acknowledge this feeling, but go for it regardless. They know what needs to be done, and they do it!

I was clearing out the attic one day, and there were various bags filled with various things: childhood toys, cloth, ornaments etc. As I was rummaging through these things, I was thinking, "that's no good anymore; it better go," and after doing this consecutively with a few futile things, I went into auto-mode, and began to just agree that everything I saw in the bag was rubbish. This was not always the case! When you are accustomed to seeing rubbish, you see it more and more. Unless you take a step back and assess, then you fail to change your reactions to anything. You end up simply repeating the same mistakes over and over again, and we all know the definition of insanity…

The Setback

Two women, Suzette and Michelle, were made redundant in the same workplace as the company was downsizing. They both felt the same pressures and worries as they sought their next job. Suzette tried a few times, and with each rejection, she became more and more anxious that she wouldn't find work: she soon gave in, succumbed to her anxiety, and lived a life without much meaning or finances. The other woman, Michelle, the warrior, ate up all of the rejections. She heard what the employers had to say, and she just kept moving forward. Yes, her ego took a battering, and she knew that those around her could see her failures, but she did not stop. She refused to quit. From heartache to heartache, her trepidation grew, but she kept the end goal in mind: she wanted a better existence for her family. Yes, she had many worries, but one thing was different. She understood her worries, but she rejected its seemingly never-ending pressure. She took action after action until she made it. She found work in an even more successful company, and her resilience made her appreciate her new role, and self, that much more. Choose to become the warrior. The warrior will always find a way. The battle scars are worth it.

Problems

"We cannot solve our problems with the same thinking we used when we created them." - Albert Einstein

All our troubles stem from larger psychological structures many of which we have unwittingly been conditioned to believe. If you do not have money, what is the root cause of the problem? If you do not have high self-esteem, what is the root cause of the problem? If you are single, and would love to meet the person whom you will spend the rest of your life with, what is the root cause of the problem? These meta-questions must be addressed if we are to limit the cracks in the ceiling, so that the entire construct does not collapse.

Every single person has problems in life. Some attract, and choose, unnecessary negative and self-inflicted problems while others recruit better quality problems. No one ever eradicates every problem. However, we can create, and choose, good or bad problems for ourselves. One way to become happier is to supplant your bad problems with problems that are more 'impressive.' A bad problem is, "I do not have enough money, and I do not know how to get it." A good problem is, "I have too much money, and I do not know where to put it." Good problems are the following: creating time for loved ones; studying for your degree; choosing better investments; socialising with better quality people. Bad problems are problems that individuals either consciously or subconsciously create for themselves for any of several reasons: drama, procrastination, low self-esteem, poor emotional patterns and so on. Some examples of negative problems are as follows: habitual arguments with strangers or loved ones; spending more money than that which is earned (liabilities above assets); frequently finding yourself injured or unwell and so on. Do you know people who frequently have bad things happen to them? Why? They received the attention and sympathy from others when bad things happened, and so they consciously or subconsciously create these perilous predicaments for themselves.

People get into arguments to distract themselves from what they should do in life. They painfully pile the pressure on one on top of the other, and instead of being honest with themselves, tackling their more painful issues and moving forward, they remain stagnant and justify their hopelessness with nonsense. When people have spare time, and they do not have anything productive to do, then only bad things can happen. Psychic entropy and sinful activity are usually some of the consequences. Unfortunately, one problem often triggers another. People distract themselves from one pain or problem by creating another less painful issue. They cannot face the misery of one issue, and so concoct a smaller problem that is more urgent (immediate distraction) or even a bigger problem. They then use these problems to complain, to evoke sympathy from others and to have something to talk about. They feel significant because of their perceived problems. The troubled seek distractions from their troubles. Unfortunately, people often look into the drama existing within others' lives as an attempt to feel better about themselves. People focus on others to avoid focusing on themselves. Your pain shows where your energy must go. It is something we must address, and not cowardly run away from.

When someone is in a mood, it is often a result of not effectively dealing with a problem. They tend to make decisions that coincide with their pessimistic state. Have you ever started the day undesirably by accidentally kicking and tripping over a table chair, or by rushing and arriving late for work? Suddenly, all kinds of unfortunate events occur whether mild or severe. This is when a pattern interrupt is necessary. Your state depends upon what you focus on and your internal representations (what you are saying and imagining in your mind). A dramatic shift is required. Your state can be altered by utilising affirmations, incantations, modifying your breathing and shocking your nervous system by changing your physiology (your body language and posture).

The importance of frequent change, and the desire to continuously learn are indispensable because if you are not getting better, then you are getting worse. As Wayne Dyer once stated, "You will never reach an ultimate goal. Life is transition and growth." Yes, attaining certain things will bring more moments of happiness, but you must find ways of experiencing happiness and serenity on a daily basis. This comes down to your psychology: appreciate where you are now, and become excited by where you are going.

What steps can you take now to mitigate negative feelings regarding your problems? Firstly, the most perilous thing you can do is to fuel your problems by attaching strongly charged energy to them (in the form of emotions). It is unnecessary to get stressed, fearful and angry about your problems. You give your problems life when you converse to others or in your mind about such issues. What you repeat with energy, you recreate and perpetuate. Secondly, avoid or minimise watching the news and other negatively exaggerated forms of media that give a less than accurate portrayal of how things really are. If you always hear negativity, then you subconsciously look for it in your own life. Practice focusing on what is going well, devise an action plan to surmount your problems, and appreciate that you are doing your best.

The grass always appears greener on the other side. You never know what you have until it is gone. Appreciate, and be grateful for, the blessings you have as this always puts things into perspective, grounding us when our egos run amuck. We know when we need to experience more peace and appreciation when we exaggerate the importance of things that are not really that devastating. Take a step back when we find ourselves exaggerating things. An attack is a great form of defence. Look to resolve any problems you have by being assertive and proactive. Anticipate when certain problems might show up, and plan your schedule in a way that provides the necessary room to deal with these issues whether they are work related, financially related or family related. Move in the direction you desire rather than being focused on getting out of the mess. Follow the light ahead, and the light will broaden; look back at the darkness behind you, and find yourself lost in the abyss.

Mistakes

"You build on failure. You use it as a stepping stone. Close the door on the past. You don't try to forget the mistakes, but you don't dwell on it. You don't let it have any of your energy, or any of your time, or any of your space." - Johnny Cash

Mistakes often happen when overwhelmed (stressed), psychologically beaten or when the mind becomes sloppy. Our mistakes should reveal the need to bring order to the mind's chaos in order to provide the clarity needed to perform at one's best. Moreover, mistakes derive from ineffectively dealing with our problems. People tend to be more forgetful when there is a lack of mental clarity. It is fundamental to understand what mistakes show us, and where our attention must go if we are to eradicate any future unnecessary struggles. Interestingly, once we make a mistake, it is easier to make mistakes either within that same field or within another. Why? Uncertainty and self-doubt pervade the subconscious. Because we are being harsh on ourselves for making mistakes, we then trip ourselves up more often as pondering over the mistake attracts additional errors. Once we allow something to own our thoughts and feelings, it becomes easier to be owned in other areas. This rippling and crippling effect occurs because of negative perceptions.

Mistakes often occur as a result of being lopsided. When we always follow our strengths and avoid our weaknesses, we become more inflexible in our approach to things. If we have a business or are managers, then we can always delegate tasks that fall into our weaknesses. However, significant personal weaknesses must be addressed if we want to be happy in all key areas of life: health, relationships and wealth. We become susceptible and weaker because our foundations are not robust enough. There is a time to be assertive and aggressive; there is a time to be spontaneous and outgoing; there is a time to sit in silence and ponder; there is a time to show love and affection; there is a time for experiencing pain. One of our greatest assets can easily become a major weakness; our greatest weakness may in fact become our biggest strength. Sometimes the greatest thing to ever happen to us is the thing that brings us the greatest pain. We must not immerse ourselves in its experience, but learn the lessons that are always there. Contemplate how and why it brought us pain. Our pain shows where our energy must go (but not stay in!).

We are constantly changing physically, never to be the same again. However, we often struggle to accept change mentally. Yes, a certain level of mental change is inevitable in a world where experiences and situations are never exactly replicable, and so slight adjustments can be made. The body changes drastically from childhood to adulthood to an elderly age, but one thing remains: most people are still afraid to change their perceptions, paradigms and belief systems due to fear. However, it is the act of pushing through our comfort level that fulfils our deep desire for progression. People usually create negative experiences and emotions in order to stay where they are. They choose to experience anger, sadness or guilt to ensure that they do not have to do more fundamental work that is necessary to progress as a person. They think, "I'm angry right now," so the last thing they want to do is that house chore, or work project or have a portentous conversation that has been long overdue. Ignorance and stubbornness can keep us stagnant and thus depressed. Our mistakes demonstrate the need for greater flexibility. If we are making mistakes in any avenue, then we must become more flexible.

Every situation can be interpreted positively, even though it appears negative or destructive at the surface level. Getting fired from a job could be the event that provides the impetus to start that long-awaited business. Infidelity taught you that you needed a better quality partner, or to escape when you did as it perhaps saved you a lifetime of limitations and conflict. Seek to find the positive in everything that happens. It allows us to take on more, and thus grow more. If small problems are perceived as big problems, then we will never have the wherewithal to attack the bigger things in life. The more stress we can handle or mitigate, the more we can take on and thus accomplish. Our inner energy, that which is intangible, dictates our circumstance and happenings. There are energy sources indiscernible to us. The mistakes we make were supposed to happen. They are small signs for us to change what we are doing. The real pain is not in the mistakes we make, but in our inability to learn from these mistakes. We learn a lot about people's characters by how they deal with smaller things. How a person resolves their problems reflects how they conduct their lives, how they filter things mentally, and present things to themselves mentally to mitigate the damage. Unfortunately, it is all too easy for people to fail in life, and point the finger. The harder thing is to develop the resilience needed to stay in the fight, and refusing to lose until we eventually win.

"It is not over until I win." – Les Brown

Refuse to stop because of consternation. Depression develops as a result of learned helplessness, and labelling oneself as a victim. Unfortunately, many people choose to be the victim because it is the easy way out. We must take responsibility for our circumstances. People are ignorant because they choose to be. People are ignorant because they are afraid of the truth; they are afraid of the other. Our ignorance allows us to keep making mistakes. Ignorance is oftentimes the ego at play. In order to progress, we must distance ourselves from the familiar. Familiarity is a trap, even if it is a good habit. Whatever omniscient power exists, know that it is interminably testing us. We cannot control every single experience in our lives, but we can always control how we perceive things. Our perceptions are vital for establishing how we view ourselves, and what our standards are.

We must spot our mistakes earlier rather than later to avoid any significant damage physically or emotionally. We can spot the simple signs of faltering attention or ineffectual thinking by even the most minutia of instances. Again, it may seem like over-thinking and hyperbole, but small things always creep up on us until something major happens. Maybe burning that dinner highlighted just how busy and overly mentally occupied we had been. These smaller-scale issues and irrational actions illustrate the need for either something to be enhanced or something to be lessened. Take the time to reflect, learn and come back with greater fortitude.

Very early in life we develop powerful belief systems often involuntarily based on what we saw all around us especially through the actions of those who raised us. "Jake, don't run!" "Jake be careful because you know what will happen." "Jake you cannot do that." "Be careful" or "Don't drop that!" or "This is serious, so do it right." Inadvertently, the parent is setting their child up for uncertainty and limitations. Be vigilant, yet assertive. Be calculated, yet practical. Our risk-taking ability and confidence become diminished over time because of what we choose to hear and accept as truth. We must question our deepest paradigms and indoctrinations, but that does not necessarily mean we must always change them. Simply become inquisitive.

William Blake interestingly taught in his poetry that eternity loves the creations of time. By this we can infer that we love things that contrast our very nature because they make us think and grow. They challenge our ways. They challenge our notions and belief systems. They either strengthen our notions, or force us to consider anew. Either way, our biggest adversaries are oftentimes our closest allies. Our mistakes are our warnings. Our failures are our saviours as we learn most during the process of the recovery. Our necessary failures and mistakes often hold life's biggest and best teachings. We just need to be ready to listen to nature's lessons. Mistakes can be signs of lacking clarity and direction in life.

How we react to our mistakes and failures determine the amount of mental and emotional success we will have in life. The person in the middle of an important presentation who becomes flustered and muddled in words can do one of a few things: break down, admit defeat and vow to never present again, which builds an entire web of fear, a bubble that limits growth, experience and learning, or they can laugh it off and/or vow to do better next time. Maybe you were distracted, less prepared or took the process too seriously, and you got in your own way by thinking too much. You learn most about someone when they supposedly fail than when he or she wins. We should not be evaluated by our successes, but by our reactions to perceived failures. It is in adversity where we are truly challenged, not when we win or achieve the goal.

Procrastination

"Only put off until tomorrow what you are willing to die having left undone." – Pablo Picasso

Distractions impede our concentration and clarity. Procrastination, problems, and mistakes are all related. Some people procrastinate by opting to choose negative feelings; they make excuses as to why they never make it to the next step: "I feel bad, so I do not have to work harder." "I feel awful right now, so I don't need to exercise." "I feel lethargic and hurt now, so why should I bother making that important phone call?" These are often excuses made to protect the ego. No one wants to admit that they cannot achieve (hurting one's ego), and so they manifest negative feelings, which almost always include external factors. They excuse themselves from not having to improve, and it prevents them from doing what they should do. Some find excuses to do things or not do things: "I have a meeting today that I am not looking forward to, so I am entitled to eat poorly and unhealthily." "My wife does not treat me the way she used to, so I can have an affair." If we look for excuses and reasons, then we will find them. These forms of justification have the same purpose in that they stop us from taking responsibility for our actions, and thus empower our weaknesses.

Having the ability to do what we want to do is incredible. Firstly, we must be aware of how we procrastinate. Secondly, we must be able to overpower these detrimental habits by taking pressure off ourselves. If you know you need to write for ten hours straight, then you will do anything and everything to delay the process. If you know you have a daunting project that requires you to be at your best for hours on end, then you will come up with excuses to do other things. This is why we must alleviate the pressure by saying, "I am just going to relax and do what I can." Interestingly, you will consistently end up doing so much better simply because you lessened the pressure, which enabled your creativity to flourish whilst also increasing your energy levels. You will have an extra spring in your step. You will want to give more. Why? Because you are defeating what is meant to be defeated. You take one step closer to achieving your purpose. Starting the work every day is the hardest part. Show up consistently, and things will begin to work for you. However, you always need to know why you want to accomplish these things. Ensure that your why is bigger than your own needs. For example, are you doing it for your family's future? Are you doing it to end some kind of suffering in the world? Are you doing it to improve humanity?

Know that you are always being tested. Once we take action and stop procrastinating, we will set a chain of events in motion. If we continue to grind daily, we will defeat procrastination, and develop the resolve needed to accelerate the quality of our work. Perhaps we all exert the same amount of energy: some use it to win; others use it to fail. Trouncing procrastination, and avoiding drama, will assist in bringing your dreams and desires into fruition. How do you procrastinate? Procrastination takes many forms. We may be conscious of some while others are insidiously running our lives. Why did we have that argument yesterday when we knew we had a deadline on Monday that required our absolute attention? OCD in itself can actually be a form of procrastination: why do we inundate the mind with incessant and compulsive cleaning when we have far more demanding and worthwhile endeavours to pursue? It does not matter how or where we were bitten, what matters is that we were poisoned.

Fighting the Familiar

"Success breeds complacency. Complacency breeds failure." - Andy Grove

How we react after a successful accomplishment determines our future happiness. If we become stagnant after achieving something, then we will soon become content. Being content means to be complacent. Complacency is being comfortable with where you are. It means remaining certain and in control. Unfortunately, certainty on its own will kill our drive to experience uncertainty (in the form of risk-taking and challenge), and this is where we grow as human beings. Life is about moving toward new areas (experiencing uncertainty), which creates emotion. Once we experience this emotion (and succeed), we have conquered this particular emotion (in the form of an action), and so we look to find a new one and so forth. It is in our biology to continue to conquer, succeed and explore. It is where we test our skills, and it is when we are tested most. It is how we experience anew. Therefore, uncertainty is life's very nature. If we regularly experience boredom, inertia, or lethargy, then it can be attributable to not challenging ourselves.

"The more you seek the uncomfortable, the more you will become comfortable." - Conor McGregor

Paraphrasing from Lau Tzu, once you label something, then it is lost. Once you think you understand something, you lose the drive to find out more about it. When something becomes automatic and familiar, it becomes easy, and so you lose the intense focus to achieve even more. Stay uncomfortable. Once you label something, you limit it. For example, if I postulate, "Sport is the only thing I'm good at," then I presuppose that I will fail miserably at all other things. You are in fact restricting your successes by presuming things. Become fascinated by your own use of language, and the deep meanings behind the things you say or think.

Let us look at an example. Think about someone who has a characteristic 'problem.' Say, for instance, that a friend is sternly stubborn. Whenever this friend says or does something, your brain will search for what your friend has previously done, and you will make it somehow relate to your perception of his or her stubbornness. For example, if my friend tells me that she has been invited to a party (but I know that she abhors atmospheres where people are under the influence of alcohol), then I could assume that she will not want to attend the party. We limit other people's potential and also our own, due to our perceptions of them. If we categorise people, and ourselves, it can be extremely unjust and inappropriate as people are complex individuals capable of change and growth. Whenever you think you know something for sure, then the picture changes.

Continual progression and stretching one's abilities develops our self-esteem. However, in order to progress, we must embrace at least some change in our lifestyles. Those who succeed at something, and simply try to hold onto what they have accomplished, will soon descend (what stops rising, must soon fall), which is oftentimes followed by regression and depression (they live in the past successes that seem so long ago). People do not usually question the familiar. The familiar is everything that we do habitually. We live in our own little box, and, due to fear, we infrequently step out of this box, thereby becoming self-absorbed, and stuck in the rut of our repetitive, learned behaviours. We experience fewer emotions in this box, and therefore we take less action. What problems arise from living in this metaphorical box? There are things in this universe that we cannot, or struggle to, conceive. Why? We are so concentrated on our physical form (our daily activities, occupational duties, driving here and there, living by the watch and so on) that we fail to self-reflect and guide our ship.

Self-reflection is about being thoughtful regarding what we do and why we do them. It provides opportunities to consider differently, and to choose the best course of action moving forward. Choice creates power. Self-reflection requires effort; it requires you to put your ego aside, which many people prefer not to do. It can be daunting to focus solely on yourself in such detail because it requires a certain detachment from the ego. Many individuals simply understand how they feel, but do not ardently focus on changing their circumstance.

Moreover, many people cannot sustain such effort and standards because of the pleasure and pain principle. Everything we do depends on this principle. Whenever we are about to do something, we weigh up whether an action will bring us more pain or pleasure. In many ways, this is about whether people are short-term or long-term thinkers. Sometimes people can have a mixture of both, but more often than not, if you really look into things then you will see whether they prioritise the now or their future. Unfortunately, many people seek immediate gratification, and so cannot do the necessary things to incite long-term success. They can only see so far ahead. It is like a cap, a force field, preventing others from delaying immediate contentment, which seems to be worsening in an ever growing impatient world.

The short-term thinker will only do something if it is easy and/or if it will bring immediate rewards, but this is rarely plausible. The short-term thinker will never get started: "Why go through the torture of lifting weights if there might not be a drastic change for this coming summer?" "Why bother working hard on my career now if I won't get that specific job promotion any time soon?" "Why should I start this business venture if I know I will not make substantial profit instantaneously?" The ability to enjoy our internal struggle will ensure longevity in our self-confidence, inner peace and long-term happiness. So how can we train our minds to put off short-term gratification to manifest long-term happiness? Whenever you delay gratification and achieve something, regardless of how small, reward yourself by doing whatever makes you feel good. This rewarding system is essential if we are to diligently continue with a positive activity that contains onerous or painful moments ahead.

Our Emotional Home

"That's the thing about depression: A human being can survive almost anything, as long as she sees the end in sight. But depression is so insidious, and it compounds daily, that it's impossible to ever see the end." - Elizabeth Wurtzel

We all have an emotional home. It is the preponderant emotion we experience. We can improve our relationships with others, as well as ourselves, if we understand the core emotion people choose to experience: some people tend to get angry in order to take action. Some people do everything they can to be relaxed. Some people tend to worry more than anything else in order to keep active. This is the main emotion you tend to experience when on autopilot. Whenever we are not consciously thinking, this is where our subconscious leads us.

Experiencing a positive or negative emotion frequently enough will inevitably lead to a longer-term emotional state. Depression derives from experiencing moments of sadness so often that it takes its subconscious place as being the default experience. This is how a person can be around or with so many people, yet feel miserable and lonely inside. They might fleetingly experience a positive emotion, but their predominant emotion, dictated by their subconscious, is one of hopelessness. Depression exists when a person's present moments are impossible to be fully lived with joy and pleasure. If we are depressed, then even when we are doing something deemed enjoyable, we simply cannot enjoy it because depression is the long-term, embedded emotion.

Happiness is of course the opposite, and it is also an overruling state. Any activity that comes our way can be approached positively. We can be washing the dishes, in a hostile environment, having had an altercation with someone, yet recognise that this moment will only bring discomfort or pain for a very short moment if at all! Happiness stems from experiencing joy and laughter recurrently meaning that it takes its subconscious role as being our default experience. This is how people often focus on good things when something seemingly upsetting has happened. The good news is we can program our minds until it falls into a certain automatic response. We want to love how we think, imagine and perceive things. While it may not appear so, we choose how we think and feel about any matter. We choose the grand state we wish to dominate our daily lives. Our habits and rituals determine the quality of our lives. Overcoming depression, and the ailments that come with it, cannot simply be achieved by taking part in fun and joyous activities alone. Instead of adding things, we may need to deduct other things. We can relinquish ourselves from the webs that entangle us, and from the depression that pervades our unconscious.

Fortunately, we can change our emotional centre by conditioning ourselves. Firstly, we must become aware of our emotional home. What emotions do you experience daily? We must be completely honest with ourselves if we are to make a profound difference. See if you can group certain emotions together if they are similar. Anxiety and worry are very similar. Joy and excitement are quite similar. Anger and frustration are quite similar. I am not talking about the way you portray yourself to strangers or the public because these are often inaccurate depictions of how we really feel. The way you interact with your friends, family and yourself are much more accurate. We can work toward embedding a positive preponderant emotion subconsciously by being honest with ourselves, and by admitting what it is that depresses us. This is how we take control of our issues and underlying pain. If we cannot pinpoint why we feel a certain way, then we cannot resolve the issue. This takes being incredibly honest with ourselves, which many people either cannot or do not want to do because it messes with our 'story.' Secondly, we must let go of the immobilising, reigning and overriding emotion that pervasively hinders the quality of our lives. We must forgive ourselves, and any others involved in what has deeply hurt us. We must learn to love ourselves, and feel empowered enough to transcend this debilitating feeling.

Secondly, it is beneficial to understand where this core emotion originated. What pain or pleasure may have influenced us to create this predominant emotion? Did something traumatic happen in our childhood? Is it the way a relationship ended? Is it from the teachings of a mentor? Is it what we experienced at school? Once we know the main things that shaped this core emotion, we can then make peace with these events. We can choose to let these past moments, or thoughts of the future, pass us, by changing what these events mean to us.

Thirdly, we can explicitly choose which core emotion we want to experience daily and often. We can then condition our past experiences, or perceptions of the future, to match this new emotion. For example, if we are angry because a family member or friend betrayed us, then we can choose to forgive them (internally) because we wish to live a peaceful life. If we do not trust people, because a previous business partner stole money from us, then we can be happy that this malevolent person is no longer part of your life as he or she could have done even worse. If we are always worrying about what is going to happen to us or people close to us, then we can choose to be grateful for all the things we, or they, have. Our past experiences and thoughts of the future have shaped our core emotion, yet we have the personal power to reframe these experiences and develop an uplifting portrayal of the future, so that we can experience more beautiful emotions frequently.

The following hyperbolic metaphor enables us to comprehend how the mind works. There is both a divine force and a devilish force that operates in the mind. Whichever we give power to and accentuate, or reduce, will dictate our life's course. It influences not only ourselves, but also how we affect others. The more we follow our purpose, the more action we will take, and the more energy we will have. When we do something for something much larger than ourselves, then there is a divine force that mysteriously supports us. Conversely, the more we perpetuate and encourage disempowering thoughts, drama and negativity, the more dissatisfaction and pain we will inflict upon ourselves and others. We will take less action, feel more lethargic, and, thus be unable to give to ourselves and others fruitfully.

This symbolic devil (encompassing all our negative thoughts and fears), takes many forms (self-sabotage, feelings of unworthiness, anger etc.) while our divine presence (our logical, accepting and optimistic selves) can override and trump any form of decadence. It is the water that can extinguish the fire. Love trumps hatred or anger every single time. Gratefulness suppresses fear every single time. Appreciation stifles anxiety every single time. Love yourself. Love others. Our biggest challenge is subduing the challenges within ourselves. Once we learn to control our inner demons, then we can focus on supporting others. We must be flexible in our thought; we must resist rigidity in our beliefs and abilities. Be open to new experiences and ways of perceiving events.

Oftentimes, when we first hear something, we initially experience a negative thought (our devilish side), and then we usually (I hope) correct this disturbing thought by choosing to think something more positively and lovingly. Knowing that this primitive reaction is not really us (but part of our biological makeup), then we can understand that we are all good people really. Perhaps every person is a good person, but because we do not understand how the mind works, we think that our biological, devilish thoughts are really who we are, and so people unfortunately act upon these. We may just get confused with what thoughts are ours, and what thoughts we should, or should not, empower. The only difference between a good and bad person is the thoughts they choose to follow. The more we decipher the thoughts that are biologically installed (more primitive and negative), then the more we can readily notice them and cast them aside. We then have the power to give light to our positive true selves. We think sixty thousand to seventy thousand thoughts every single day, and yet we only attach emotion to a certain amount. The more emotion we give to a thought, the more we are likely to take action in that specific direction. We must condition ourselves to dismiss our unsupportive thoughts, and champion the thoughts that we know to be our true selves.

Whatever we believe becomes our truth. We are right no matter what we think because these are our overruling beliefs that dictate our journeys. Whatever we believe, we move toward. Whatever we move toward, we manifest in the physical form. Our natural gifts can be our biggest failures if left unconditioned. If we simply rely on our natural, inherent gifts, which we all have, then we can achieve life's purpose: striving to get better, to give more and to design our journeys most meaningfully. The beauty is in the process not in the accomplishment. Building your character is what brings true happiness. The results are what our egos gravitate toward, but it is not about that. It is about who we become. It is about how far we have travelled both literally and metaphorically.

Why do some people enjoy their own pain or that of others? Let us look at the brilliant ideas regarding meta-states as taught by Michael Hall. There are often many emotions that are linked together, which makes it so much harder to decipher and change. The entire process becomes harder to entangle. One emotion is linked to a bigger emotion, which is then wrapped again in an even bigger emotion. Think of it as passing the baton in a relay race. For example, a person might experience fear or revulsion, which then triggers the need to rebel. They rebel when they see or do the things that they fear. The feeling of rebellion is then wrapped within a larger emotion: excitement. They become excited when they rebel due to initially experiencing fear. A perilous pattern has been constructed. This pattern becomes engrained within his or her 'emotional system.' They then search for the familiar, and so seek opportunities that trigger this sequential emotional response and connection.

Let us consider another example. Have you ever felt embarrassed by something you said, or by the way in which you reacted to something? The feeling of embarrassment may become entangled with another emotion: anger. So you become angry because you felt embarrassed. This feeling of indignation can then get wrapped in another emotion. You may then become sad because of the anger you felt from being embarrassed. And there you have it. You have created a deeply embedded emotional pattern. We cannot simply look to change one emotion. We must understand the pattern we have created, and rewire it. We must break the emotions down, and change them one by one if the entire trio is to collapse. Ideally, it is better to start by changing the very first emotion we tend to experience. We must supplant one emotion with another. We must choose a counteractive emotion that can succumb and encapsulate the preceding emotions in order to break this sequence of emotion (energy transference). We can break this pattern by disrupting it when we notice one of the emotions coming on. This can take the form of doing something outrageous as a way of stifling the emotional triggers. It can be helpful to become interested, fascinated or by simply being able to laugh at this unhelpful emotional response. For example, whenever you become embarrassed, then angry, and then sad, become fascinated by your sadness, or laugh at how you have become angry at such a silly incident that is meaningless in the grand scheme of things.

Everything in our internal and external world is analogous with water: they flow together seamlessly and ceaselessly. Everything in our lives is connected. Our thoughts are connected to our emotions, and our emotions are connected to our actions. Our actions trigger other sequences. Our subconscious is our long-term memory, which has unlimited storage and capacity whereas out conscious mind can only process between 3-7 different pieces of information. When we see life's fluidity (within our interactions with others and nature itself), then we can appreciate the beauty in its complexity. We do not have to tell ourselves that we must breathe in order to stay alive. It happens naturally. However, we can choose *how* we want to breathe to create different states. The brain works similarly. Our thoughts, feelings and actions work congruently, but you can decide *how*. Accept your thoughts; channel your emotions; act on your purpose.

Chapter 3 – Negativity

"When someone tells me "no," it doesn't mean I can't do it, it simply means I can't do it with them." – Karen E. Quinones Miller

As taught by Steve Peters in The Mind Management model, we all have a human, logical part of our brain, and a primitive, often negative side. Both are constantly engaged in discourse, a debate if you will, until one wins within a certain context. Sometimes we feel that the way we think is necessary, but what you emote and act upon is pure choice. Every single one of us has negatively framed an event due to a whole range of aspects: our mood, upbringing, dissipating hormones, stress levels, and so on. These factors all contribute to how we explain things to ourselves: our own biased outlook. We have all had internal dialogue hinder our decision-making: "I should definitely ask him to join me for a drink this evening… BUT what if he already has plans? What if he tells others that I am desperate? He could even just look at me in disgust… I'll just wait and see if he ever asks me out." We allow negativity to infiltrate our desires. How foolish is that? We influence and convince ourselves in order to protect ourselves, but is this best for us? Instead of wanting to protect ourselves (and our egos), look to stretch your potential by going outside of your comfort zone. Sometimes we choose to negatively conceive an idea, thereby preventing us from going for what we really want. Even worse, we restrict the potential for bettering the lives of others. Imagine how happy you could have made that person if you just approached him or her? The workings of the primitive, rudimentary brain wins again.

It is part of your biological make-up, but it is not you. It is a biological reaction that genetically derives from our fight or flight response. When we lived primitively and had to fear constant threats from beasts, this survival instinct (protective, paranoid impulse) was obligatory for our rudimentary and physiological needs: eat, sleep, shelter, breed and survive. It has lost most of its uses today as it primarily functions to further our pessimistic thoughts and hold us back. Train yourself to speak predominantly positive things. This can sound a tad unrealistic and impractical in a world where we are bombarded with negative news, drama and disappointments. However, we can always phrase and interpret things differently. We can always choose to limit the negative things that we will inevitably encounter every now and then.

Context reframing is a beautiful tool to utilise. Is the glass half empty or half full? Is it a bad thing if your spouse is opinionated and loud? Well not if your spouse used these strong opinions and expressivity to do their job well, or to raise your children to have strong viewpoints. Is it a bad thing that your sibling was always curious about what you got up to? Well not if this same possessive skill was responsible for you feeling nurtured and protected during your childhood and adolescence. Is it bad that your child wants to be an artist instead of following the family's legacy of being firemen or teachers? Is it not beautiful that they feel confident enough to follow their own dreams and passions? Isn't it more important to live a happy and vivacious life? People appreciate you more if they know that you support them on their journey. Isn't it amazing that they will grow up to be even more giving and loving due to following their own ambitions? We can use context reframing in any situation. Anytime we feel like we made an error or failed at something, we can choose to perceive this experience positively. Maybe we were supposed to follow a different path. Maybe that failed long-term relationship was not a waste of time as you experienced the highs and lows of a relationship, and you can now steer your future relationship in a more acute and adept manner. Being overly late for that date or meeting may have held a promising result: maybe you were destined to avoid that interaction. Maybe that meeting or date would have held you captive and suppressed you.

Why do people find it hard to resist negative talk? Negative talk can enhance drama, and drama is a great distraction. Emotions, especially ones that conjure pain of some sort, can captivate people. They allow people to take the role of the victim, which makes them feel sorry for themselves. It allows them to focus on others, perceiving others as the issue. People also feel more connected to others and more significant when they express how they feel to others. Some people enjoy talking about their problems; others enjoy listening to their problems because it makes them feel happier about their own situation. We blow things out of proportion, so that we have interesting things to talk and moan about with friends. We inundate our minds with copious problems that hold us back. We are not what we think about, but we are what we act upon. Unfortunately, people often reduce their own exuberance and vivaciousness in order to fit in and make others feel comfortable. It is all about setting high standards for yourself, and hopefully those we interact with can also become more positive and optimistic.

The Battle

Think of every decision you make as being a fight between your highest self and your most self-sabotaging, grotesque self. The brilliant boxing movie, Rocky III, truly encompasses the battle of the mind as exemplified by the main contest. At first, the bullish Clubber Lang was victorious in dismantling the courageous stallion: Rocky. However, with support, experience and will power, Rocky dethroned the seemingly impregnable villain, and he retained his title in an epic war in the ring. The mind goes back and forth, sometimes the protagonist loses, and sometimes your inner good defeats the antagonist. It comes from learned conditions and experiences. The more you are accustomed to negating the negative voice, the better momentum and energy you will have, which will serve you greatly when it comes to taking future action and making massive decisions. The same dilemma exists in all of us mentally: do we get intimidated by the relentless, devilish 'Clubber Lang', or do we persist and laugh at its attempts to discourage us?

You may not always win the battle, but ensure you win the war.

The Negative Voice

"Learn to forgive others so that you can release yourself from being held captive by the very negative thoughts around you." – Stephen Richards

The quotation above also relates to how we forgive and accept ourselves as a way of releasing the shackles of negativity that prevent us from truly living abundantly. We can never demolish our negative voice, but we can learn to calm it down, and to question its cogency. The more we question something, the weaker it becomes, and the more it loses its validity. We must question this diminishing puppet whenever we experience a negative or limiting thought. We must question all of our negative thoughts and feelings, but we must learn not to question our positive thoughts and certainties regarding our aptitudes. Perceive a positive action as being a brick that we must add one on top of the other to create our mansion of joy.

Our intrinsic negative voices are not really us. It is often the part of our brains that attempts to compromise our success. It can take many forms. It is our self-doubt. It is our feelings of inadequacy. It is the masochist within that relishes in our misfortune, or the sadist that enjoys the difficulties that others face. The negative voice questions our actions; it is the voice that forces us to remain inert.

Have you ever convinced yourself to give something up, or to do something that you knew was deleterious? Think of a goal you had, or still have, that you have not achieved yet. How did it fall apart? How long did it take to dissipate? What did you say to yourself? What obstacles intervened? How did you present this failure to yourself?

There is a reason why those who take the illicit drug ecstasy experience an immense surge of the happy, love chemicals. Unfortunately, what comes up must come down. The chemical is then depleted, and the ability to conjure serotonin becomes unreachable. The person then goes through the withdrawal process, feeling even more down and demoralised than usual. The same can be said of how steroids affect athletes or bodybuilders: you have this intense surge of testosterone, recovery and feelings of confidence, and then once you are off the steroid cycle, you naturally produce less than the average man's testosterone levels. This is just the mind and body's way of remaining balanced. You can view it in the brilliant movie Limitless where the protagonist, Bradley Cooper, demonstrates how a magical pill has incredible benefits, but it induces terrifying side effects. There is a yin and yang to this world and, thus, there cannot be a good without a bad. We cannot always be, and do, the ideal thing because we are not infinite, perfect human beings. Therefore, the 'devil' within will always need to be appeased or expressed in one way or another. This can be seen, albeit in an extreme example, in the movie, Purge. It is impossible to live only with positive energy, thoughts, emotions and actions. However, we can control when we wish to allow our darker side expression, or calm this primitive brain by having a loving, supportive logical voice to keep it in check.

Here are some prevalent, common things we would expect to hear from the negative voice: "Why are you even going to bother trying to write a book when you can just accept that you'll never be a writer?" "You will never be with a partner like that; he or she is too good for you." "You can't learn a new language; you haven't even mastered the English language!" The negative voice knows your weaknesses, and it zooms in on them. It is like a professional, personal bully that we have to deal with for the rest of our lives. We have to learn to calm the bully down by making it less insecure, giving it metaphorical hugs and showing it affection whilst rarely listening to it of course.

Accept that this voice, to some extent, is impossible to eradicate. The divinity within must flourish and overwhelm in order for you to live abundantly and with clarity. What type of things can we say to appease our built-in negativity? "I deserve to be happy." "I am going to forgive my enemy because they do not know any better." "I am so grateful for everything that I have. Any more is just a bonus that I will make the most of." "I am going to randomly kiss my wife." "Why? She hasn't done anything to deserve it?" Whoops! That last one was the negative voice, not me! The problem people may have with accepting this notion is that they confuse their logical human mind with arrogance, and so suppress the light that should be allowed to spread. Some people think that loving themselves is narcissistic and repulsive, but if we do not love ourselves, then how can we ever attract the quality things that we all deserve? In writing this book, I had so many internal battles, at different stages, regarding a whole host of different aspects. This book, in itself, exemplifies how our human, loving side can, and should, influence the negative side.

Giving up is easy, but resilience takes effort and energy. Whatever is hard to achieve is always more valuable. We need to get used to seeing things through to the end. It is crucial to persist when facing negativity or self-repudiation. We might have an idea (say to start up a business) and then, over time, if not initially, we begin to allow negative suggestions to intrude and impede our dreams: "Oh don't be daft, you will not be able to start up a business at this age." This limiting belief will soon seep its way into our reality unless we have strong affirmations and incantations in place to keep us moving forward. Life works like a seesaw. Think of your brain as the stable part in the middle of the seesaw. You now have two sides that swing back and forth: the positive voice and the negative voice. The side that wins will be the side that has more weight: more affirmations, energy and momentum (a stronger emotional charge). It is your seesaw after all, so why not choose its constituents? If it is your playground, then play it by your rules.

Limiting Beliefs

"Whatever you hold in your mind on a consistent basis is exactly what you will experience in your life." - Tony Robbins

Until we work on our beliefs, especially our limiting beliefs, then we will massively struggle to attract what we want in our lives. We must work on eliminating our limiting beliefs. Firstly, what is a belief? A belief occurs when we feel absolutely certain about something. What is a limiting belief? It is a way of thinking that prohibits us from developing in an area. We therefore feel absolutely certain that we cannot overcome certain things. Here are some general limiting beliefs to help us to identify our own underlying limiting beliefs: "I can't get a degree because no one in my family has ever got one." "I can't learn about stocks because I am no good with charts and numbers." "Hats do not suit me." These are signs of having a fixed mindset: we do not believe we can make progress, as we believe skills are purely natural. This then becomes a self-fulfilling prophecy. Carol Dweck teaches the importance of having a growth mindset: being open minded, and believing that we can improve regardless of our current aptitudes.

We all have negative beliefs, some of which we are aware of and others we are completely oblivious. These assumptions do not help at all, and in many ways, the more we question these things, the less certainty and confidence we have in our capacities. It is detrimental and immobilising to ever say that we cannot achieve something. Considering that something can be attained creates the possibility for creativity, and the drive necessary to take action. However, saying something will never happen, for whatever reason, drives this affirmation into a stable belief system, a negative paradigm, that can even have a knock-on-effect on other things that we 'cannot' do. For example, we must believe that we can dictate our physical appearance by being able to control our thoughts, feelings and actions. For example, people whose finances fluctuate randomly are usually those who have things dictated to them in their lives. They are moulded the way others have chosen indirectly financially whether it is in the form of taxes, bills, expenses, loans and so on. If you consistently have ever increasing income and savings, then it is a sign that you are in control of your life and your destiny.

"The only differences between people who think they are creative and people who think they are not are their beliefs about their creativity. Start telling yourself that you are a creative person." - Sanaya Roman

We must always question the negative thoughts that we have, but never question when we are confident and certain. Examples for how to question negative thoughts are as follows: "Should I always be so harsh on myself?" "Is it healthy to oppress my true feelings?" Only question these things IF we have positive answers to respond with! For example, "How come I get completely stressed?" A negative answer would be: "I get stressed because I am not enough, and I am setting myself up for failure." A positive answer would be: "I get stressed because I want to present myself in the best possible light, which I can do if I just relax." Questioning our confidence and ability can have an adverse effect. "Am I really as good as I think?" "Will I be able to perform like that again?" "Is my personality enough to keep her happy?" The more we question positive thoughts, the less certain and confident we become. Instead, we want to question our negative thoughts, so that these debilitating thoughts become less and less impervious.

How can we change our limiting beliefs? Have you ever thought you could not achieve something (a job promotion, getting a six pack, being in a relationship with a great person), and then one day you did? You now know this it is possible. We all encounter negative, limiting beliefs, but we must understand that this fearful side is a primitive part of our brain, and that it is not actually our own thoughts! Furthermore, we have a 'human' part within our brain, and this puts things into perspective. It is loving and logical. Unfortunately, according to Steve Peters, the primitive part of our brain is five times more powerful than our human side! Therefore, it is down to us to condition our brains to ensure that we know when the primitive brain is hijacking us, and to know when, and how, to emphasise the human whenever the 'chimp' comes out. This takes practice, so be patient. Here is an example: You are in your office contemplating whether or not you should start a business. Below is your inner dialogue (your human brain (HB), and your primitive brain (PB)):

HB: "I should just go for it, and start this business."

PB: "Don't even bother."

HB: "But you never know. Maybe I should just begin the process."

PB: "What is the point? You never finish things anyway."

HB: "But maybe I can develop my current skills, and go on courses to help me set up the business."

PB: "You will just embarrass yourself."

HB: "There is nothing wrong with doing your best, and learning from the experience."

PB: "But if you do the wrong thing you can lose a lot of money!"

HB: "I will really respect myself for going for what I want in life."

In this instance, the HB does a great job with calming the 'chimp.' We can never eliminate our primitive thoughts, but we can learn to dance with it and appease the PB. The most important thing is to cut this conflicting inner dialogue short to prevent ourselves from overthinking: paralysis by analysis. Take action.

Our minds often work on autopilot. This is when the subconscious takes over. This is where learned thoughts, feelings and routines circulate, and continue our underlying belief systems. The mind is left to wander, and it reverts to what it knows (our default mode), where it is comfortable, and that is where our deep desires and fears live. These can definitely be changed if we are self-reflective, persistent and catch ourselves when the mind falls into the same trap.

People believe that for one thing to get better in life, something else has to fall back. This is untrue. Yes, to reach a high level of achievement in any endeavour requires great focus, dedication and sacrifice, but this does not mean something else has to cave in. That in itself is a limiting belief. Instead, perceive things as working synergistically: it is about improving our self-esteem. Confidence means feeling competent at a given activity. However, self-esteem refers to how we respect and love ourselves, and thus partake in challenging activities with more self-appreciation. The stronger our self-esteem, the more we are likely to put ourselves out there, and really go for what we want.

The Penalty Taker

"You attract your dominant thoughts." - The Secret

Why is taking a penalty in football a challenge? There is time to think, and when thought intervenes anything can happen if you let it. There are so many variables and psychological factors: the goalkeeper will try to delay or distract; the crowd may boo, jeer and affront, thus tumbling focus; the grass may not be perfectly aligned; the players try to make you emotionally charged; your ego may intervene: "If I miss this everyone will think I lack ability." But the concentrated mind allows form to follow through. A clear mind can enable flow – it is just the goal, the moving person in the goal, the ball, and you.

If the person taking a penalty kick in football misses the shot due to nerves, overthinking and so on, then the penalty taker can react in differing ways: "I will never deal with pressure effectively." "I am a failure." "It was just a bad moment." "This miss was supposed to happen." "I will practice penalty-spot kicking more often." "I will never practice penalty kicks again." Never let this negative voice immobilise you. Instead, listen to it, and either make a positive action toward improving it, change the internal representation to feel better about the moment, or talk back to his negative voice letting it know that you hear it, but you know what is best for you. We must filter through the possibilities that our mind generates, and ask ourselves a simple question: "Which one of these potentialities holds the greatest benefits to me and my future?" Why light the fire if you know it will soon fade?

Be selective when deciding what to give power and energy. What you talk about dictates the direction of your focus. Remove the nonsense. No one can perform well if they have lingering, troublesome issues infiltrating their mind. If an individual performs with uncertainty in one topic, it can easily transfer into another. It is about channelling your focus, the muse, which only appears once we detract negative thinking. Refuse to give power to others with whom you do not like as this weakens your resolve. It diminishes your clarity. It mitigates your fortitude and focus. Happiness depends upon progressing in an area that holds significance to us. Therefore, stagnation and complacency breeds helplessness, hopelessness and hurt. Sometimes the best thing we can do for ourselves is not to listen to ourselves.

Attracting Negativity

"People think about what they don't want and attract more of the same." - The Secret

The more we win, the less we learn. The more we chase, the less we capture. The more our ego soars, the more our soul drowns. What you focus on magnifies. Whatever you do, do not think of a rainbow. I knew you would. Choose to focus on what you want in your life, and ask open, positively phrased questions until the answers show up.

As taught, by Rhonda Byrne in *The Secret*, if you incessantly say to yourself, "I do not want to bump into my colleague at work today," then guess what is going to happen? Yes. You will bump into them, and at the least opportune time. However, this negatively energised affirmation works the other way too! On a positive note, I believe that if both people want to see each other, then that will also work because their thoughts, emotions and actions (being in the right place at the right time) are working congruently. I understand what you may be thinking: if I keep saying I own a Lamborghini, I will never cultivate this thought into reality, and this is true because you are working on thought alone (that is just the first hurdle!). Instead we must drill this positive affirmation into our subconscious, so that it rouses your emotions intensely. We then need to take quality, consistent action to ensure its attainment. If you take the necessary actions and procedures, step-by-step, then you will be pleasantly astonished with what you will manifest.

The most perilous thing you can do is give energy (emotion) to your problems. You give life to what you passionately talk about and imagine. Repeating the following statements consistently can influence your future actions whether knowingly or unknowingly: "I think I am coming down with something." "I don't feel all that right recently." "My soreness could be a sign that I'm developing a cold." Negatively phrased statements project the notion that you are acquiring something misfortunate, and your mind will seek ways to bring it closer to reality: you may leave the house without that much needed coat; you may forget to drink that green tea with lemon and honey; you may suddenly find yourself seated next to someone with a cold! You move toward what you project in your mind whether wittingly or unwittingly. What happens when you have an itch? You give it attention, you think about it, and you tell yourself what not to do: "Don't scratch it!" "Do not even think about touching it!" The same applies to headaches: your headache exacerbates the more you think about the pain. Interestingly, this pain subsides if your brain is forced to focus on other things. The same applies across a spectrum of experiences.

Trepidation and Repudiation

"The true measure of success is how many times you can bounce back from failure." – Stephen Richards

Your mind is your most powerful asset. So be peaceful, giving and fall in love with learning and growing. Follow your path, whatever it may be, and everything else will work itself out. What do you love to do? How could you make this a reality? What steps do you have to take? When can you realistically achieve them? We only ever really have the present moment. We can ruminate the past; we can contemplate the future, but it is the now that we can change. My grandfather taught me to never leave today's tasks for tomorrow. What you decide to do in your present moments holds the key to your overall direction. Your past is irrelevant, unless you are using positive past experiences to empower you of course. It does not matter who betrayed you, or what traumas and tensions you experienced. As Mark Twain brilliantly elaborates, "I have been through some terrible things in my life, some of which actually happened." The mind will concoct all kinds of terrible stories, but things are never as bad, or good, as you imagine. This is often why the hardest moment leading up to a challenge is the wait itself. Use your vivid, potent imagination to your advantage. Be careful where you place your attention, and how you present things to yourself. We must pay attention, and listen when nature/the universe speaks to us.

Obsessions and Addictions

"Every form of addiction is bad, no matter whether the narcotic be alcohol, morphine or idealism." – Carl Jung

There is a thin line between magnificence and madness. An obsession can be both incredibly beneficial yet incredibly destructive. We all have obsessions and addictions. It is down to us to choose those that are positive and beneficial rather than self-destructive. Negative addictions can provide instant relief, but they increase stress levels in the long run. Negative addictions might be pleasurable in the moment, but they can set us back when we stop doing them. Our addictions, even beneficial ones, will ultimately lead to our downfall. However, it is better to choose a downfall that had many amazing, pleasurable moments rather than a downfall consisting of pain and struggle throughout. An obsession can take many different forms. An obsession occurs when we cannot take our minds off something even if we wanted to change our focus. An obsession is a mental compulsion whereas an addiction is when you are physically compelled to do things (this often incurs withdrawal symptoms when abstaining from them). If we do not change our behaviours when we know we should, then, quite simply, we have not suffered enough. It relates to the pleasure and pain principle. If there is more pain than pleasure when doing something, then we will not want to do it and vice versa. It all comes down to our perceptions of what is pleasurable and what is painful.

All obsessions and addictions, in one way or another, stem from our fears. If we fear not being attractive enough, then we become obsessed with our appearance, and so addicted to improving our looks. If we fear being lonely, then we become obsessed with being around other people, and so addicted to manifesting bad things just so we can gain sympathy from others. If we fear losing control in life, then we become obsessed with monitoring everything around us, and addicted to telling people what to do. What we fear most comes true, so why not work to change our fears? Everyone will encounter moments of struggle when improving and becoming more adept at something, so consider what you say to yourself to keep you going in moments of uncertainty. We have been programmed to always be fearful of something. This fear shifts throughout our lives depending on what we have learned to conquer. At one stage in our life we might fear losing our spouse, at another we might fear developing an illness, at another we might fear losing our looks, at another we might fear going to sleep, at another we might fear our financial futures and so on. Once we conquer one fear, then another one will appear. It is very important to understand this because when the fear changes, it is a sign that we have conquered the previous one.

There is a difference between being driven, and being unable to stop ourselves from doing something. Motivation and inspiration are pleasant whereas obsessions uncontrollably weaken our very sense of self. An addiction controls us; it has leverage over us. An obsession originates from a set of patterns. We become so engrossed with the emotions experienced that we allow the emotions to override any rational thought. Most people know when they are obsessed, yet they cannot withdraw from thinking, feeling and acting upon it still. This is because the entire process has not been fully thought through and the root of the obsession has not been fully explored. However, the more we activate our rational brains, the more we think things through, and break down the emotions attached to this action. Once we break an obsession down into the steps that we take mentally and emotionally until we complete the action, then it is much easier to intervene. An obsession also becomes less powerful once we break it down because we have taken some of the variety and excitement away: we know the process that we are going through, which takes away some of the impulsivity, therefore making the process more mundane and less gripping. Extract all of the reasons why we do whatever it is that we do. Then we can naturally dissipate the emotions involved, and it is precisely the emotion that drives us to act upon our compulsions. These emotions strengthen over time, and the more we take part in the activity, the more we naturally want to push the boundaries more and more. Doing too much of anything is dangerous. Our obsession will lead to our downfall if not managed properly. Our obsessions and addictions create mental chaos. These addictions make us lose trust in ourselves. This mistrust pervasively affects how we think about our competence in other areas too such as our discipline, focus and beliefs.

Chapter 4 – The Ego

"You can either be a host to God, or a hostage to your ego." – Wayne Dyer

We all get humbled in life. We all have an ego, and to be fair, to an extent, it is necessary to have an ego otherwise we will not be bothered about improving the quality of our lives. However, we must either check our own egos (know that even though we are fantastic, quality human beings, we are not that special in the grand scheme of things), or life will humble our egos for us (we might get into an accident; we might be cheated on; we might lose all our wealth etc.). Change the internal, and the external shall change. We must not want something too badly as it can make us choke (metaphorically at least). As Wayne Dyer elicits, we can want something, but we must not be attached to it. Enjoy the process leading up to success. Happiness is a journey; it is not a destination. If we only feel happy once we have accomplished something, then we will only experience true happiness for very short glimpses in our lives, if any at all.

We must be brutally honest with ourselves. Some people cannot be true to themselves usually because their ego is in the way. The ego can sometimes protect us. However, it is far more perilous if we fail to dig deep enough to uncover the latent and pervasive thoughts that truly exist. Every time we get angry, it is our egos controlling us.

This requires us to understand that we are imperfect, and we must know that we will never be perfect. Having the attitude that we are continuous learners who will never be complete will ensure that we maintain high standards and that we are ever improving. Happiness can be defined as feeling and knowing that we are progressing in something that is a priority to us. This priority can be anything: being gregarious, creative, giving, affluent, intellectual, and so forth. If it is important to us, then we must be developing that side of our lives in order to thrive.

Everything that has happened to us thus far has been the right thing to happen on our particular journeys. Though this may not be apparent and conspicuous now, or ever for that matter, we should know that everything has happened to make us who we are today. Choose love rather than fear. When we experience love in the present moment, then we cannot be fearful, stressed or anxious because love is the most impregnable and impervious experience that it overwhelms all other insufficiencies. Love is therefore the main way to overcome the ego. It is the best way to alleviate the pressure that results in unhealthy living.

A balance must be made between giving energy to our egos (feeling unique, special and significant) and our superegos (being humble, virtuous, respectful, giving). Once we go one way or the other between these two conceivably distinct stratums, then we either become too serene and passive or overtly narcissistic, greedy and cynical. The ability to float between these intrinsic perspectives enables abundance, awareness and excellence. Obviously, there are times in life when we will need to market and sell ourselves (the ego): when getting a job, attracting investors, persuading our children, attracting a partner etc. However, we also need to understand that our lives in this world will soon be over, and we are practically nothing in the context of this world and nature. Approach everything with an open and growth mindset. It is important to truly believe that we can accomplish anything in life. All it takes is great discipline, energy, a drive to continuously learn, and a healthy attitude to supposed 'failure.' The moment we say something cannot be attained, then we are correct. We limit our experiences and aptitudes by initially stating that we are not good at something or that we could never be good at it.

Our egos are responsible for being judgemental and for stereotyping. When we label or judge someone or something, we limit the potential to notice other things about them. We will literally look for things that support our initial judgements, and our ability to perceive alternatively will be blocked. There is nothing wrong with stereotyping instantly (because this is a way to condense knowledge or perceived knowledge quite rapidly). However, it is very important to be open minded, and to be willing to change your assumptions if presented with new information. In many ways, this relates to the ego, as people do not like to see many talents within the same person as it makes them feel inadequate. We must break the limiting belief that tells us that we must compromise something if we are to have a successful career or family for example. This is wrong, as we can be successful in *all* key areas in life.

The ego is necessary in that it is our driving force as it relates to the 'survival of the fittest.' It is the part within us that thinks we are special, unique and powerful. It is a necessary component of life, but must be kept in check like all things. We must feel as though we are special whilst also believing that every other person is just as worthy in his or her own way. Everyone has a gift to give the world. Maybe their errors serve to show how we must give more. Maybe the poor person on the street teaches that we must give more. Maybe the murderer on the news teaches us what can go wrong when people have hatred within their hearts. Every person has different priorities, relationships, coping mechanisms, interests, experiences and so forth. How could we possibly expect or look down upon someone for being different? Unfortunately, the ego can backfire on us. Our egos trick us into believing that we are greater than we really are, and we all, in our own ways, are humbled one way or another. The ego breaks on many occasions. The more egotistical and materialistic we are, the higher our ego shall climb, and so the fall shall be far more devastating and immobilising. Everything will work out for us in life if we simply get out of the way. Having to always be right immediately makes us wrong.

The stronger our egos are, the harder it is to self-reflect.

Perhaps the ego was a biological creation in order to keep us alive: a survival instinct and adaptation. The obsession with the ego is what keeps us moving forward and immersed in our own experience, which is both worthy and wicked. The ego can therefore be seen as the ultimate creation due to our fear of death. Death and ego are always in conflict. In order to be self-reflective, we must therefore detach ourselves from the ego, and this is unnatural, as the ego was created to combat death. If we are changing our personality (which we all must do by changing our thoughts, emotions and behaviours – the entire point of reading this book), then we will inevitably face resistance by our ego as it associates change (the unknown) with death: our ultimate fear.

Dangerous Dynasty

A father raised his son to be the best, and to claim superiority over all his peers. He built his son's ego, and taught him that in life, you must take because the world is a selfish place. The father taught his son that he could do whatever he wanted, and that there were no repercussions. Needless to say, his son grew up to have a huge ego, and to be a selfish human being. His son did what he wanted, when he wanted. The young man developed into an egotistical individual who looked to use others, and cast them aside when people lost their uses. Expectantly, his son soon discarded of his father as well later in life. The father showed him the way, and the son did exactly as h was taught: take from all, and do not give back. Now the father needed his son, and his son was nowhere to be found. We create our own downfall. If you do not parent well, then your children will make you suffer the consequences. Great parenting will result in your children doing their best for you when you are too old and weak to take care of yourself.

"A true man hates no one." – Napoleon

People's Opinions

"Do not go where the path may lead, go instead where there is no path and leave a trail." - Carl Jung

We can listen to other people's opinions, but we can choose whether or not to accept what they say. Most people listen when someone gives them compliments, and when people notice what they are good at. The issue is that if we listen to people when they say good things about us, then we will also listen to people when they say bad things about us. I listen to everyone's opinions because I feel that we can learn something valuable from anyone. However, I choose to only accept the ideas of a few individuals and on certain matters where they are more proficient and experienced. Purposely, we should choose to not attach any emotion to what people say about us whether they are positive or negative because it is a form of indirect and usually unintentional manipulation. This is primarily because it is important to keep tabs on our egos whilst detaching ourselves from people's beliefs. Instead, write out your goals, remain focused on your path, and avoid what others say about what you are doing. We are not what others think of us; we are what we think of ourselves.

It takes courage to do what no one else around us is doing. It takes total certainty and belief in ourselves to step away from what the others do. If we listened to what others say, then we will be the same as everybody else:

most people live unhappily and without exceptional lives. Why would you want to do the same as them? It takes great self-esteem to create your own path. This is true independence. People want to fit in so much that they actually jeopardise great mental and physical success in order to be the same, or similar, as those around them. We must set higher standards for ourselves, and hopefully those around us will follow their dreams, or we must simply allow others to continue on their own path. Never try to change someone. Simply model and allow.

Having the mentality that we must put ourselves first may appear egocentric and conceited, but it is the least selfish thing we can do. Many people restrict what they do and experience in order to put someone else first, yet this altruistic act is later demolished at a different time one way or another. For example, say if we wanted to go out for dinner, and we both wanted a completely different cuisine. Let us say that I gave in to what you wanted, and I was the more giving person. One of two things could happen in the future. Either I would not want to go out for dinner with you again, because I know I truly will not be able to look after my own needs, or I will find a way, consciously or unconsciously, directly or indirectly, of getting my way another time. For example, I might let you decide where we go that night, even though I really want to go elsewhere, but how will I act that night? I may not create the energy and fun I might have; I may not have supported you when you wanted to talk with new people and so on. We do this all the time! Every single one of us does this in our own way in every relationship. We have to otherwise the relationship would not work. Now, if I did restrict my actions, am I really being a great friend in the long run? No because I would want to keep my distance, or do things to get my way in other psychological ways.

Judgement

"The ability to observe without evaluating is the highest form of intelligence." - Jiddu Krishnamurti

In this section, we will be conditioning ourselves to release, or gradually release, the fear of being judged. The more drama we encourage in our lives, the more we become fixated with judging others and therefore being, or feeling, judged ourselves in other interactions. We must remove the urge to judge others, and thus become indifferent to the possible judgements others will make of us. The more we put ourselves out there, the more we will be judged. It is natural, and it is a good thing. You will never make everyone happy. Not wanting to be judged, results in not putting ourselves out of our comfort zones. Judgement goes back to being consumed by our reputation, and our reputation is linked to our ego. There is nothing wrong with projecting ourselves favourably, but the problem exacerbates exponentially when we stop taking action because we fear how we will be perceived. The more we suppress our desires and purpose, the more petulant, aggravated and depressed we become. We learn to put other people's opinions of ourselves above how we think and feel about ourselves. People with high self-esteem primarily care about what they think of themselves; people with low self-esteem are fixated on what others will think and feel about them. In order to fix these issues, we must start by changing our thoughts and emotions during smaller issues. If we care too much about how others perceive us when we are food shopping for instance, then these emotions proliferate and are strengthened when doing something more challenging such as approaching someone we really like or releasing artwork into the public domain. When we begin to change our focus when little things take place, we can indoctrinate ourselves helpfully and correct past conditioning. These notions will eventually seep into how we handle situations where the stakes are higher. We will have laid the foundations in our subconscious minds because of the many small incidents that we have worked on.

Constantly feeling as though we are being observed, scrutinised and judged makes many people remain inert. As children, we neither noticed, nor cared about, what strangers or our peers thought about us. We did what we wanted, when we wanted and that was that. During adolescence and puberty, we noticed more and more confinements and judgements being made about us, and we became more uncertain about what to do and how we would be perceived. As adults, in many ways, we would benefit by going backwards: we must keep our inner child (to a certain degree) as it mitigates many faulty fears. The older we become, we seem to want acceptance from more and more people (in our jobs, personal lives, dating and socialising), and we begin to limit our experiences, and what we can share or do in front of others. We lose our childlike and carefree attitude for fear of offending, or being seen as weak in another's eyes. Does this constricted mentality reduce our confidence? Of course it does. The more we feel like we can be ourselves, the more confident and outgoing we become and vice versa. If we ever get shy or embarrassed in front of others, it is because we feel like we have to put on a certain register, or that we cannot say and do the sort of things we would if with close friends and family.

During our daily interactions, we may have a tendency to think doubtfully: "I can't believe I said that," or "How did he or she interpret what I said?" Instead, learn to simply accept whatever happened, and remain fully focused on what you think and feel about yourself. A powerful affirmation I like to use in these instances is to remind myself that neither I, nor they, will live forever, so why should I let something really get to me? This allows us to detach ourselves from the experience, and stay in the state we wish. We must learn to let go of our judgements, and what we expect others to be like. There is no need to judge or label, and do not expect that others will judge either as this can influence how we engage with others or choose not to engage with them. A general perception I have found to work is to double your positive beliefs in every situation. For example, if you are in a meeting, and you feel as though you want to say something, but you are unsure, then simply double your positivity, and how you perceive the quality of your potential response. If you are thinking, "I have quite an obvious answer, so I doubt anyone will want to hear it," then at that moment, simply think to yourself, "It is a relevant, beneficial and valid answer that they deserve to hear." The primitive brain will often belittle our notions in an attempt to keep us safe, but this is counterproductive because we will need to be expressive and opinionated in order to thrive in our careers or businesses etc. See if you can cultivate this belief in all interactions.

We all have our purpose in life. We all have our own path. We all have our own obstacles and challenges. Some inherit copious money; others live in impoverished areas; many grow up taught to be dependent; others learn that you can only count on yourself; some people lose their parents at a young age; some grow up in a hostile environment while others' parents divorce and separate the family; some *choose* to live happily while others *choose* to be a victim; some children are brought up religiously; other children are abused; many travel and experience vast cultures while others have never left their city; some grow up with disabilities while others are angry and have no ailments. Every single person is different. Every single criminal and murderer was once an innocent child. We learn to judge others. We are quick to blame, and become defensive when we are blamed, but if we were to just accept and forgive people for their problems (again to an extent of course), then maybe, just maybe, we would be able to accept ourselves more.

The Cake

There was a boy who did the unthinkable: he ate the last slice of cake! Those who witnessed the atrocity, made it clear that the boy needs better social etiquette. He was judged. As many cake-like instances occurred over time, the boy reached adolescence continually feeling judged and labelled as a brat, so one day he lived up to the role he was assigned: he stole money from his mother's purse. Ignorantly, he felt that if he was a brat, then this is what brats do. Subsequently, he was judged again. His thieving mentality did not stop there, and so he began to steal in shops until one day he was caught and imprisoned. He was judged and labelled even more: a criminal; the scum of the earth. Unfortunately, he believed them. Subsequently, he killed a prison mate during his imprisoned service for calling him selfish. Damagingly, he served a longer sentence. He was judged as inhumane and a disgrace. Regretfully, he listened to them. Foolishly, he took drugs until his conscious completely disintegrated. He was judged: a selfish, drug addicted murderer who does not deserve to live. He listened. He committed suicide. That cake certainly cost a lot…

All labels have limitations, even ones that appear positive. We can be labelled everywhere we go, and we act learn to act accordingly to these labels. This is how we begin to form our identity and intrinsic beliefs about who we are, and what we are capable or incapable of doing. Whenever someone says or infers that you cannot do something, continue to be respectful, but make a point to either lose contact with this person or simply do not express anything meaningful with them as they must clearly not be part of your 'troop.' We are told what we are by everyone in many different ways whether directly or indirectly. An example of a direct attack could be, "You are not very social are you?" whereas an indirect example would be, "You'll love it there because it will just be us there." Indirect presuppositions or assumptions are more likely to be accepted subconsciously by us, so be perceptive with what people may infer about you, and be wise about what you wish to accept.

When we begin to simply listen to others, then we become sheep. We become followers. We give control and power to others to dictate our beliefs about our identities and thus ourselves. We lose control of our own lives, and we give others the power to shape and determine who they want us to be. Know your strengths, know what you like, know your potential, and detach from anyone else's perceptions of you especially if they are restrictive. The most important thing to take away here is that to accept that judgements will be made, but keep these judgements from affecting how we think, feel and act. When we judge someone, we claim superiority. Once we understand that we all have different strengths and skills, and that we all lead different lives, then we learn not to judge or at least hold onto initial judgements. Judgements mean there is an absence of love and acceptance; displaying insufficient love means that we are fearful: to judge means to fear.

Self-Sabotage

"Resistance by definition is self-sabotage." - Steven Pressfield

Many people obtrusively entertain self-sabotaging behaviours more than they may think. Self-sabotage can be as mild as quitting a healthy-eating plan just when you are about to notice significant physical and mental advances, or when you know you need to impress at work leading up to an interview, and yet you do something that makes you appear less favourably. What are your underlying beliefs? "Am I really worthy of that job?" "I'm not spiritual or intelligent enough to make it." "I am too busy raising my children to even think about my passion." These negative connotations can swirl around our subconscious, making all our decisions without us even knowing.

As we have way too much on our plates (hopefully only metaphorically speaking), we often function on autopilot, and this is when the subconscious runs amuck, unless it has been conditioned to think positively and optimistically. Our deepest fears and self-sabotaging beliefs manifest. We question things continuously: "Why do I always feel this way when this happens?" "Why do I always question myself in these situations?" These thoughts are inevitable, and to an extent, necessary. People often fail to push forward in life because they fear that they will not make it. If we feel unworthy of something, then we will wittingly or unwittingly create ways to ruin the opportunity. We will say or do something out of character, and inevitably destroy the chance we had to break through. Unfortunately, like quicksand, once we are in, and we try to force ourselves out, it is easier to get sucked in deeper and deeper until we are engulfed in debilitating actions.

> *"The ego mind both professes its desire for love and does everything possible to repel it, or if it gets here anyway, to sabotage it. That is why dealing with issues like control, anger and neediness is the most important work in preparing ourselves for love." – Marianne Williamson*

Interestingly, the more important and challenging moments in the day are not when we are most active, but during moments of rest and silence. We are truly tested during moments of boredom. Why? Firstly, moments of boredom should be very brief; our lives should be so inundated with challenge, personal development and quality time with friends and family that we should rarely ever be bored! Frequent bouts of boredom are signs that we must change our lifestyles. We must embed better quality routines. Secondly, moments of boredom or silence are great opportunities to be appreciative, to self-reflect and to explore our goals.

Renowned scientist, Blaise Pascal explained that, "All man's miseries derive from not being able to sit quietly in a room alone." Sitting in silence mitigates all obstructions, distractions and, thus, detractions. We slow down our movements, thoughts and feelings to better access our inner workings and discover solutions. The more we move, the more we feel; the less we move, the more we think. The mind never at rest is the mind that stays in the rat race, unable to find more efficient and productive ways of living. Fascinatingly, French musician, Claude Debussy, claims that, "Music is the space between the notes." Therefore, the beauty within the music is not in the sounds, but in the silence. Our more prodigious actions are not when growing most and succeeding; it is in our inaction where we can work on the invisible, and, thus, influence the visible much more vigorously. In many ways, if we want to do more, we need to physically do less. If we want to change more, then we must give ourselves the space to mentally manoeuvre. Unfortunately, many people sabotage themselves without knowing. They inundate their lives with chaos and distractions, and fall into unnecessary traps when all they needed to do is reflect and ponder over their circumstance. If they do mentally learn something beneficial, they do not provide the mental and physical space to put it into practice. Knowledge itself is not power; knowledge comes from learning something, and then living it!

If we are to grow and become self-actualised, we must test our character. We must test the beliefs we have, whether these beliefs are positive or negative, so that we can find the truth. Think of a skill that you possess. Whenever you need to exhibit this proficiency, how do you test yourself? Do you play against as easier, less skilful opponent, or do you choose to face someone equally or better equipped than you? People often choose the first option because it provides them with greater certainty as they are more likely to succeed, but they will not grow if they do so. We must struggle if we are to take our aptitudes to the next level.

"The ultimate measure of a man is not where he stands in moments of comfort and convenience, but where he stands at times of challenge and controversy." - Martin Luther King Jr.

How do you react in times of adversity? Adversity builds character and resolve. Many people look for the easy way out. They go through life looking to win only if it is easy. This creates weak, short-term thinking. It creates a weak defence, and so this person breaks when they encounter struggle and challenge. They will find a way to lose, and they will mentally capitulate. Everyone can be the hammer, but not many can be the nail. They have not practiced at the highest level; they have not conditioned their minds to function supportively when things are not going according to plan. Their egos will not allow them to fully be tested and risk being wrong. Instead, they will say things like, "It is all right if it doesn't work out." "My team let me down, not me." "No one helps me, so I might as well leave it." Until we take responsibility, and see what we are made of, then we cannot even begin to make the necessary changes to generate abundance in our lives. We are truly tested in moments of mental and/or physical exhaustion. Winners always find a way to win, even if they are not at their best…

What do you say to yourself in moments of adversity and struggle? If you are losing in a sport, what goes through your mind? "It is too late now, we have fallen behind," or do you say, "this is fine, I am going to build momentum and come back?" These are key moments when you really learn who you are. When you play a team sport, ensure that the opposition has the better team. When you create teams at work to accomplish certain projects, ensure that you have the weakest team. It is fine to 'fail.' In fact, I will use the analogy of failure in weight lifting: if you do not reach a point where you 'fail,' (cannot lift another inch) then your muscle will not grow. You need to lift until another rep cannot be completed. That is when you know you have given your all. This is how you know that you are progressing because you are going to reach the very end of your boundaries, and you are still pushing. The same works in other scenarios. How do you react after you have had an argument? Do you keep calm, and think about how you can improve things for the next step, or do you burst out of the door, get drunk and most likely commit another wrong-doing? What happens when someone you are totally infatuated with rejects you? Do you wallow in self-pity, and accept that you can never get the person you desire? Do you lower your standards? Do you feel that you are to blame, and that there is something wrong with you? Do you think of positive ways forward, and that there are other options available next time? Do you feel proud of yourself for attempting to get what you want? Do you wish the other person well still? If chosen carefully, these responses will lead to success in every avenue because it is not the mechanics that lead to success, but your psychology.

Jealousy

"Always dream and shoot higher than you know you can do. Do not bother just to be better than your contemporaries or predecessors. Try to be better than yourself." – William Faulkner

Jealousy is massively futile and injurious. Do other people's successes inspire you or debilitate you? What do you think about yourself and your future? Jealousy occurs when we attach emotion to negative beliefs about what we cannot or will not accomplish. We all experience jealous thoughts at times, but what is important is our ability to remain detached from these thoughts. Subsequently, we must think positively about the other person's successes, consider our own potential, and attach emotion (energy) to these more beneficial thoughts. We must steer clear from jealous people. Their negativity can only detract from our successes whether they mean it or not. If someone is jealous, then they are unhelpful. Therefore, surround yourself with people who belong in your troop. The rope never runs out for some people: some want to just take and take, pull and pull, and unfortunately these people will never actually be happy. The more they take, without effort (actually doing something about their situation), the less they have. Where there is power, there is a struggle. We do not need others to influence our goals and desires.

"Loneliness does not come from having no people around you, but from being unable to communicate the things that seem most important to you." - Carl Jung

It is always beneficial to express our ideas and feelings. We must never bottle them up – it will manifest itself somehow in one form or another. Possibly, many serious illnesses derive from rigidity, and from being unable to express our inner thoughts and emotions appropriately with ourselves as well as others. This disharmony within induces illnesses. Ensuring that there is congruency amongst our thoughts, emotions and actions primarily attains mental and physical health. No one will be able to live happily and healthily if they have certain thoughts which give rise to certain emotions, but which is often suppressed for one reason or another. We must know ourselves, how we operate and provide opportunities to express our personalities appropriately. Disharmony within creates additional stress, which appears in one way or another in unhelpful ways, thereby compromising our success and happiness.

Moreover, some people innately find themselves jealous. It is the state that they have become accustomed with, and it is where they return (their emotional home). Money will only make you more of what you already are. Alcohol will only make you behave how you really are or want to behave. The truth always rises to the surface. We can fake things for a moment, but no one can ever fake it for their entire lives. This is how people suppress their desires until they eventually do something awful. Acquiring more will not make us less jealous; it will just make us more jealous of people who are at the next level. Jealous people must attack it from the source: the roots of their emotional tree (what experiences have made them feel inadequate, and have ruined their self-esteem).

We can still get quite far in life if we have powerful, yet harmful emotional homes:

anger, jealousy, anxiety etc. These people use these deleterious emotional homes to perform at their best. For them it induces such emotional intensity that it gives them the energy to take action. Unfortunately for them, these painful emotional homes will never lead them to the top: true happiness. Having an emotional home of joy, peace or gratefulness will enable us to access our utmost best, and live a life of fewer afflictions. It will allow us to reach the fruit of our trees. The aim is to not have any enemies. If we are bitter or angry with someone, then these emotional connections will create chains and restrictions in other avenues. Instead, we must free our souls, and unlock our true potential.

The Driver's Enemy

"As if on a conveyer belt, there will be a never ending supply of idiots and jerks that come and go in your life. Whether you stop the belt to dance with any one of them is up to you." – Dan Pearce

The actual act of driving can reveal many things about a person. It is a truer reflection of how people are when social etiquette is less meaningful: we can get away with more when driving than when standing in front of others. Drivers fall into their emotional homes when driving. Be perceptive of others when they drive: you are interacting with their core being. We should pity the angry, reckless driver.

Consider how you operate on the roads. How do you respond to impertinent and disrespectful drivers? How does this experience affect your day? What might this reveal about you? Is the driver fearful that others are getting ahead of them, and so they lash out? Do they feel that others must fail for him to succeed? Are they anxious that they will never get where they want? Well if that is the case, then they clearly will not. Your reactions to these thoughtless drivers are also significant. Do you feel the need to get them back? Do you take this out on a fellow driver, or do you not let this conspicuously negative and selfish behaviour influence your mood and how you interpret the world? Do you continue to moan and inappropriately release your indignation in other interactions, or do you immediately decide to let it go, and not allow something external to determine your mood?

How you are as a driver is indicative of how you are in life: do you let others affect you? How do you react when things do not go your way? It is crucial to be self-sufficient in life. It is important to be able to function at a high level on your own. The key to self-sufficiency is to be happy on your own, and to love and be with another only if he or she enhances us, not if they make us who we want to be. Being reliant on another person is damaging to the self. One must never need another person or thing to feel satisfied and content (unless a child or adolescent). Shakespeare masterfully illustrates how jealousy and indignation result in fatality and self-destruction in the tragic plays *Macbeth* and *Othello*. Rather than being the jealous villain of your own play, why not be the narrator who remains detached and can see it all?

Moving away from Fear

If we 'fail' at something, then it does not mean we are failures. If we lose at something, then we are not losers, and vice versa. A winner in life manages to sustain happiness for long periods of time whilst creating time for all types of flow-inducing activities: family time and subjective interests etc. Someone who spreads joy and knowledge creates an energy field that is impregnable, virtuous and, ultimately, undeniable. What does failure really mean? We have all 'failed' at something. Does this mean that we are all unworthy? Then what is success? If success applied everywhere, then would success even mean success as we define it? There is a yin and yang to this world: we all need to experience something painful in order to know peace. In order to have a winner, there must be a loser. In order for death to exist, there must be life. In order to have light, there must be darkness. Without discomfort, we cannot appreciate laughter. However, we must be careful not to create unnecessary pain in our lives. Instead of pain, we want to experience challenge. The more challenging our lives are, the richer our lives will become. The richer our lives become, the more energy we have, and the more we want to share and accomplish.

Discomfort teaches us that we must attack that source of discomfort one way or another. We must do the things we least want to do. We must overcome the fears that hold us back because they are never as bad as we think. Comfort teaches us the need to change our situations. When we are uncomfortable, we must seek comfort (by improving upon our weakness), and when we are comfortable, we must seek discomfort (push ourselves and continually grow). This continuous cycle results in successful accomplishments. It is all about pushing our boundaries even if we currently feel successful and happy. There is always more we can learn. There is always more we can give. There is always more we can create. We must seek discomfort. This is why many of our daily routines must be uncomfortable: we want to remain disciplined, and to build our mental and emotional stamina.

Life incessantly tests us. It throws challenges upon us to see how we react: not getting the grade we wanted, arguments with friends, losing a loved one and so on. Be like water: be flexible; flow naturally; be yourself; give life (energy). Unfortunately, many people design their own misfortune, wittingly or unwittingly, and they can be created for different purposes (often procrastination, avoiding boredom perilously, having something to talk about and becoming the victim as a way of blaming others for our dire state). If we lived forever, we all know that life would become lacklustre. Phrases like carpe diem and live for the moment would not exist because we can always live another moment infinitely. This is why we must maximise our potential, and live this way for as long as we can. Make the necessary changes now. Failing can be highly beneficial or devastating depending on our conditioning: if we value what others think about us above our quest for inner and outer success. If we do not fail, then we are true failures in life itself. We therefore failed on the largest scale of all: we failed ourselves.

"You might never fail on the scale I did, but some failure in life is inevitable. It is impossible to live without failing at something, unless you live so cautiously that you might as well not have lived at all – in which case, you fail by default." – J.K. Rowling

Signs

"The past speaks to us in a thousand voices, warning and comforting, animating and stirring to action." – Felix Adler

Our egos are our biggest enemy as they can blind us from seeing what we need to see. Everything happens for a reason. Life's nudges are always asking if we are ready to learn, change and grow. Let us look at an example where something horrible had a beneficial lesson: I once had an awful chest infection. One of the symptoms and consequences of chest infections is that your appetite is significantly suppressed (this will be important shortly). Obviously, I was bedridden, and so I had no option but to watch the television (something I am not a proponent of generally). Over time, I had accumulated many unseen movies that I intended on watching. One was a movie about Mahatma Ghandi. While I was watching the movie, there was a scene where Ghandi would fast as part of his philosophy regarding non-violence. Whilst watching, I thought to myself, "I wonder if fasting would benefit my current situation since my body is naturally telling me not to eat." I would usually force myself to eat during colds because I believed that it would increase energy and recovery. However, I learned that when eating solid foods, our digestive systems work hard to digest and assimilate these foods, and so I became intrigued.

After researching the usefulness of fasting, I somehow found my way onto YouTube videos that elicited the benefits of intermittent fasting. My curiosity propelled me to read various books and listen to various audio books alike that exclaimed the usefulness of intermittent and full-day fasting. After incorporating these strategies into my health regime, I felt lighter, more energetic and sharper, and my body has never looked or felt so good. The moral of the story is simple: all things guide us down the path that we truly want or need. Our unconscious desires create circumstances and events that manifest our reality. Unfortunately, many people do not recognise the signs in their lives where they can change their thoughts and feelings about something. This is mostly due to being unchangeable due to fear, stubbornness/ignorance and losing control. Sometimes 'bad' things must happen for better things to come.

There are signs and signals all around us. The universe is constantly communicating with us. A physical injury tried to teach someone something: maybe it is to slow down, or maybe it is a physical manifestation of negative thinking, an accumulation of fearful and anxious thoughts that imploded indirectly. Maybe it is that we must focus more on our minds rather than perpetually living purely in the physical and active world. Alternatively, that minor car accident could be the most important thing to ever happen to a person: it may have prevented them from experiencing a far more fatal car accident later in life. It may have foreshadowed an ominous danger that someone fortunately and hopefully learned from. That missed job opportunity could be a godsend; a person may have found his or her way into a totally different and far more rewarding profession as a result. That breakup that felt so devastating may be a wonderful separation: a person may have realised that his or her partner held them back in many ways, and now this individual has the time and energy to pursue something far more worthwhile (emotionally and/or financially). These are life's signs that we must change. If we do not observe them, and do something about them, then greater afflictions are forthcoming. We get so immersed and absorbed in our own lives that we cannot notice the holes we will soon fall into. These are signs and opportunities for us to reflect on our lives up until now, and evaluate how we can move forward. Every event has its purpose. If we cannot see it, we are not stepping back enough. Take a step back, check our egos, slow down our processes, and objectively make the changes needed.

It is immensely significant to address and tackle issues sooner than later. When we notice a subtle issue in something we think, feel, do or see in others, then we attack the issue then and there. Whether it is by subtly and empathetically letting someone know that a behaviour was wrong, or directly doing whatever we want to resolve the issue, we must kill it while it is small. Leaving things because they are 'small' is precarious and unwise. Never underestimate the opponent due to its current size. Think long term and imagine the kind of monster that it can turn into if we arrogantly allow it to do so. All things start small. We want to prevent its escalation by improving communication with others and ourselves.

What makes people change their lifestyles? Unfortunately, many people have to experience life threatening or devastating consequences for them to make a change. Life will throw many incrementally and progressively painful signs our way until we learn from our mistakes and sometimes not even then! For instance, if a person is always very frantic in the morning, doing many things hurriedly, and then leaves a tap running by accident, then that is a small sign that they must have a calmer start to the day. On another occasion, if the same person is excessively rushing through things, and then on the way out of the house, leaves the front door open by accident, then that is another sign. One day, this person will forgetfully leave the cooker on, and accidentally burn the house down. Why? They never listened to and reacted to the smaller signs! Others, fortunately, do not wait. Instead, they always want to push forward obstinately, always improving and appreciating that they will never become happy, as they *are* happiness itself. Happiness is incessant progression in any avenue that holds significance.

"While it may seem small, the ripple effects of small things is extraordinary." – Matt Bevin

Chapter 5 – Happiness and Success

"He who is not contented with what he has, would not be contented with what he would like to have." - Socrates

People get what they accept.

We all have different, subjective definitions for success and happiness. We will also have different priorities, and we will rank different components in order of significance. For instance, the main way to achieve happiness for some is to have close, trusting relationships whereas the main method for achieving happiness to another might involve acquiring great wealth. Develop a mindset that is open to all, but attached to nothing. True happiness is possible when our priorities are on the right path. Personally, my health, relationships and wealth take precedence. If these three are going well, then I will feel powerful, happy and successful.

Success is determined by how we perceive inevitable failures. Enjoy the process because that is all we ever really have. We will achieve goals over time, but this feeling does not last because we will soon want to accomplish something else. We must learn to love the process of working towards the attainment of our goals. We will never arrive at happiness. There are no signs on the road to guide us to this 'destination.' Happiness needs to exude through us no matter what we are doing. We must seek self-sovereignty. Self-esteem partly refers to being who we really want to be. It is about being true to oneself. People who are more optimistic are more likely to follow through with their endeavours because they envision success. Alternatively, those who are more realistic can be overly critical, and thus sabotage or squander future opportunities because of inaction.

Are you a thinker or a doer? Unfortunately, many people fall into one of these extremes. Some predominantly think about things, continuously over-thinking, and therefore not taking action at all. An extreme thinker critically finds faults in others' actions, but they never take a risk, not even calculated risks, because they are too fearful: fearful of making a mistake; fearful of being judged and fearful that their ego will be obliterated. Alternatively, the other extreme consists of those who simply do because they hate to think. These people tend to be quite good in the moment (because they have to spend most of their lives being reactive to things). However, being active and reactive does not necessarily equate to success in terms of a career or business or relationships. We should be selective with what we do. If you are a doer, then you may be capricious, which can result in great lucrative opportunities, but this is sparse. Extreme doers find themselves in a great deal of mental and/or physical pain, and they may find themselves bankrupt, in debt, and living a life of disorder and disharmony. In many ways, the ultimate thinker is an introvert at heart whereas the ultimate doer is an extrovert. Being an extreme version of one of these two is perilous. Balance is key. Successful, independent and confident people tend to be great thinkers who take action consistently.

"The fight is won or lost far away from witnesses – behind the lines, in the gym, and out there on the road, long before I dance under those lights." – Muhammad Ali

Those who are great at exercising, but awful with healthy eating, are generally brilliant offensively but weaker defensively. They are adept at pushing forward and being the aggressor, being at the forefront and being on top of things, but when it is time to put in the work when nobody else is watching, they cannot display the same level of proficiency. Some people can do the 'sexier' things well (training). However, they cannot maintain the same sort of discipline or proficiency when facing the more monotonous and laborious side to things. They can be the hammer, but they can never be the nail. These are the same people who never stay on track to complete projects. They may portray other talents such as being creative, developing ideas, starting projects, but they do not have the endurance to follow something through to the very end. We must condition ourselves to complete what we start. As with most things, this begins on a much smaller scale, and insidiously pervades and escalates to some of the most important areas in our lives. In order to get better, we can start by working backwards. Practice the completion of small projects such as completing your daily to do list. Become familiar with getting small wins, and develop the confidence you need to step up when no one else is watching. Conversely, if you cannot complete monotonous or laborious tasks, then complete the 'sexier' things yourself, and delegate to those who can do the things you do not wish to do. Either way find a way to strengthen your weaknesses.

"The ultimate measure of a man is not where he stands in moments of comfort and convenience, but where he stands at times of challenge and controversy." – Martin Luther King, Jr.

True success is determined by what you choose to do in moments of boredom. Boredom kills your energy. What do you do when you are bored? Some people get into trouble; other people start unnecessary drama; some people overeat; others distract through illicit means. What we choose to do in moments of boredom will determine our levels of success. This is when the winners rise, and the losers cower. Feeling successful means being productive with your time, but feeling happy means doing things that create the state of flow. Sometimes they correlate and sometimes they do not. The best lifestyle is one that alternatives with feelings of success (getting things done, and achieving our goals), and feelings of happiness by doing the things that we love to do (our interests and hobbies).

What is the difference between someone who is successful or depressed? The depressed succumb to the voice that says, 'why go to the gym? I won't eat well anyways,' or 'I need to eat this cake, so that I have energy for work.' The successful also have this self-deprecating voice, but they *choose* not to listen to it. Instead, the successful individual presses forward. This can partially be achieved by repeating positive statements in your mind whenever you think a negative thought, and by making this positive voice sound louder and more powerful internally. This is how our will strengthens and momentum accelerates. This is how successful routines are inbuilt, and our minds change what it thinks about.

Context Reframing

We must be able to change what things mean to us if we are to choose the answers that will serve us best. Everything in life has a positive outcome available. It all depends on how we experience it. We abide by the norms and rules within so many different contexts, which reduces the size of our inner and outer 'box' of possibilities. This, in turn, reduces our ability to think and behave outside of this 'box,' hence why people say things like, "I'm not creative." These people care too much about how others perceive them. If you feel as though you cannot make a mistake in front of someone, then it is clear that they do not have unconditional love for you. Anyone who does not have unconditional love for you is therefore untrustworthy, as you know they will not always be there for you as it is all about how you are within the rules of his or her own "box." How can they if they will leave, abandon, fire or boycott you if and when you make a mistake, or if they deem that you are not good enough? Knowing whom to spend time with, and where to devote your energy is massively important for our health and goals. For example, the biggest reason why people cannot lose more fat or gain more muscle is predominantly because of their psychology, and our psychology is largely affected by our surroundings and lifestyles.

Reject negativity, and encourage positivity. Make your smaller achievements larger in your mind. It means you are one step closer to achieving your goals. It is all about building momentum every single day! This is how we maintain our inner energy and drive. Those who feel like they never achieve enough or do enough will have low energy because their daily thoughts and emotions are often unnecessarily harsh. Be proud and content with yourself if you know that you had a productive day. Forgive yourself when you are not at your best. Know that you may need to take a small step back and gather yourself. Surround yourself with positivity and optimism. If you do not know many positive, inspirational people, then listen to podcasts, interviews and so on from people who inspire and motivate you. Negativity is contagious, and so is positivity. Avoid jealousy and envy because they are really thoughts and feelings that support the notion that you are not successful enough or will never be where you want to be. Be happy for others because, firstly, that is the right thing to do, and, secondly, because you want others to send positive energy back to you when you also achieve that level of success and happiness. We attract what we put out, as taught in *The Secret*.

Be able to take something, anything, and present it to yourself more favourably and pleasantly. Ask yourself some of the following questions when something challenging occurs: "How can I grow from this?" "What can I learn from this?" "How can this benefit me?" "Why will this support me?" Only positive answers can derive from these encouragingly phrased questions. These questions ensure that we focus on possibility and remain centred. Simply choose positive emotions rather than disempowering ones. Understandably, it is impossible to not experience the full spectrum of emotions available to human beings. No one has that innate ability. There will be moments when we feel stressed, angry, sad, fearful, anxious and so on. The key is to only experience these emotions for brief moments. One of the main aspects of emotional intelligence is being able to quickly change our states. There is a difference between momentarily experiencing something negative and expanding the experience. The key to becoming enlightened is to make this negative experience last as minimally as possible. For instance, how long are you angry for when a driver disrespectfully drifts into your lane? For me, the displeasure lasts for literally a second, and then I detach myself from the situation, and remind myself that I cannot affect another person's actions, and I will not allow it to affect my experience, as they would win if I did. It is perilous to let another human being dictate our feelings especially for a sustained period of time. Instead, anticipate that we will encounter lunatics and awful drivers on our journeys; envision the best scenario, but be prepared for the worst. This is how we avoid disappointment, yet remain focused and driven to achieve the very best outcomes: arriving safely at our destinations! We have control of it, and no one has the right to influence our thoughts and feelings.

How can we use our energy in more empowering and productive ways? Daily, weekly and monthly planning will keep us on track and centred. Make time for the things you love in order to increase your energy, so that you can deliver in all avenues passionately. I used to think I needed at least eight hours of sleep to functions well. Sometimes I would sleep for eight hours and still be tired! Now this may not be the case for some as a result of their poor eating and drinking habits, but I was still healthy, and yet unable to have that strong drive upon waking. That all changed when I had more exciting things to do! We know that we live captivating lives when we do not want to go to sleep (because we are excited about doing and creating things). The same applies for waking up. If we know that we have a lot of important and exciting things to do, then we really want to kick start our day. If we do not have this feeling, then we are not being as creative, driven and excited as we should and could be. What was once a weakness can become a strength. I have observed this in my own life within many different contexts: I once hated to exercise, and I use to avoid it at all costs; now I love to train, and do so daily with great pleasure and eagerness. Moreover, I once disliked reading, and was resistant when my mother encouraged me to read when I was a child; I now teach, read and learn for a living. I have never been happier. Do not fear what you initially do not like. It may one day turn out to be your greatest joy. These changes were only possible due to my desire to improve, and to not accept that I was incompetent at something.

What is your endgame? How do you know if you have lived a fulfilling life? Isn't that the real definition of success? Success, and being a winner in life, is about living a long, healthy and exciting life. These three constituents encapsulate the meaning of success and happiness. Self-esteem refers to your ability to think what you choose to think without letting anybody dictate your inner processes. There is no endgame; it is an ongoing process. There is no line that you pass that ascertains whether you are happy. The process of life, and the entire journey, provides happiness. Happiness never arrives. This is one of life's biggest illusions. Life is a game; we must create our own stipulations for this game. In many ways, to remain focused on what is important in life, it is always beneficial to start from the end, and work your way down: imagine yourself as an old man or woman. What kind of lifestyle do you wish to create for those who are close to you? What would you have wanted to achieve as an elderly person? What did you want to see? How do you want your friends, children and grandchildren to think of you? How can you make this a reality now? What will you need to accomplish? How can this be done?

Real Success

We lose what we do not use. Muscles, skills, knowledge etc. are all lost over time unless we constantly reuse these influential assets. The same applies to our thoughts and emotions. If we do not show love, affection, intimacy, then we lose the ability to experience it fully and often. I like to use the muscle metaphor. If we gain a large amount of muscle, and then lose it, it is actually very easy to accumulate the same sized muscle again. It is called muscle memory. The same exists for what we feel. If we do not eat or train well, then we lose the ability to keep and build muscle. If we lose the ability to kiss, cuddle, laugh and so on, then we lose the ability to express and feel. We must constantly condition ourselves because we are creatures of habit. We must have the energy to sustain our habits. Every time we break a habit, we can become a little weaker with another habit. This continuously goes up and down depending on our discipline. The more we keep our habits daily, the more often we deliver. Not doing seemingly innocuous things such as doing your bed in the morning, or brushing your teeth, or meditating, actually begins a cascade of broken promises to oneself. The next thing you know, you laid in bed instead of getting up to go gym. Subsequently, you fail to prioritise and complete the most important action of the day. Stick to your promises. If you consistently let yourself down, then you lose trust within yourself. Can you imagine what this does to your self-esteem?

Success is an accumulation of small wins. The small things add up, which help you to accomplish the bigger things. If you ask a professional or master within a certain field, "what makes you outstanding?" do not expect an incredible mind-blowing response, as you are likely to be disappointed. Their response will leave you thinking, "Well, I can do those things as well, or most of them at least." The answer is yes you can, but most people do not because they are driven by a more fantastical dream: that outstanding achievers can do things that normal people cannot. Yes, people have varying degrees of talent and energy etc., but real success is not sexy at all. It is about grinding consistently. It is about showing up, and doing the small things ceaselessly regardless of how we feel. Achievements create fleeting moments of happiness, but continual progression, in an area that you deem important to you, builds long-lasting happiness and strong self-esteem.

Honesty

"Love your Enemies, for they tell you your Faults." - Benjamin Franklin

Honesty is not only imperative when communicating with people, but even more of a necessity when communicating with ourselves. Happiness is about the brutally honest communication between the different areas within our brains: our ids need to be fulfilled (the need for immediate protection and pleasure), and our superegos (strong, core beliefs and true identity) need expression also. Our egos are where these two areas meet, and a decision must be made. The more honest these three areas are with each other, the more smoothly they will exchange, which will enable mental and emotional balance. If the id always wins, then we suffer long term; if the superego always wins, then we always feel like things are too strict and rigid. If you know yourself well enough (your beliefs, how you react, your mood, what is on your mind etc.), then you will be in a place to make better decisions.

In many ways, the people who have hurt us the most are the people we owe the most. Regardless of how much pain or displeasure they may have caused, they have revealed the weaknesses within us. We all have weaknesses. Fortunately, the more we self-reflect, and make necessary changes, the less likely others will need to say and do to humble us into making the necessary changes. Maybe the man did not need to go through that divorce, if he simply took the time to understand his partner better and was attentive to his partner's needs. Maybe the woman did not need to have that car accident if she just listened to her friends who told her that she drives recklessly and impatiently. Maybe if the man listened more to others, then he would not attract so many painful and troublesome occurrences. It is very important to spot the small things that foreshow the more ominous things that will loom in the future unless we make the changes required. Be vigilant, reflective and therefore proactive. Make the appropriate changes now rather than simply denying or justifying its inevitability.

Inner Workings

"Control of consciousness determines the quality of life." - Mihaly Csikszentmihalyi

Whenever our inner voice says something disconcerting or disparaging, ask it a question: "How does this help me?" And if it does not, which is usually the case, then simply acknowledge the thought, but appease it by providing evidence of times when things went well in similar situations, or remind it that you have certain skills to help in these situations. Strong, concrete evidence and affirmations will calm this fearful voice. For instance, if you are making a sale at work, and something in your mind says, "You don't know everything about this service, why are they going to buy from you?" What is this purpose of this derogative statement? It may serve to remind you to do some extra research about the service, but how is this beneficial to you right now when selling the service? Not at all! Tell the voice, "I know enough to make the sale," or "I am doing the best with what I know at this moment in time." "This is true, but I still believe I can help this person by selling the service." Proactively prepare for any negative thoughts to occur before beginning an activity especially one that is significant.

A quick learner does not mean that the person is necessarily brighter and more adept. It is how they approach a new activity. Quick learners know that a negative voice will appear at some point during the learning process, and so they prepare themselves to deal with this. Quick learners have strong meta-cognition: they know how they learn best; they know what procedures to follow. They look to find similarities between activities, so that they can transfer existing skills and knowledge to new situations. Unfortunately, many people are fearful when first learning something or doing something new because they are uncomfortable with change. They may fear what others will say and think, or feel inadequate and out of their depth due to past conditioning or experiences. They may think things like, "This will take me a long time to develop," "I don't know about this," "What if I fail?" "What's hard about this?" and so forth. These punitive declarative and interrogative statements already implant the notion that this person is excessively challenged and incapable of achieving in this activity now or later. In contrast, the successful, natural person will approach new experiences and challenges more positively, knowing they will not do brilliantly first time around, and so they are less tense during unfamiliar situations. They may think things like, "How can I do this really well?" "I have all these strengths in other areas, which is why I will be great at this also," "I am intelligent, so will automatically be able to surmount this," or "I always manage to find a way, so I will be fine," and so on. Positivity and optimism are the only way forward.

"Let us always meet each other with smile, for the smile is the beginning of love." – Mother Teresa

Give, love, appreciate and observe the many sensational things that begin to happen to you. Why? We get what we give. Serotonin is a chemical that has copious functions within the human body. Robust levels of serotonin have been linked to improving our feelings of happiness and wellbeing. If serotonin drops, so does your brain's ability to function at a strong level. A vicious cycle ensues. So how can we boost serotonin levels naturally? Get enough sunlight, exercise often, eat quality, high-nutrient foods and meditate whilst thinking about the positive things to come and any prominent positive memories. Serotonin is seen to help regulate our mood, and thus what state we experience. If we are in a powerful, energetic and productive state, then we are more likely to follow through, and not just complete things, but also complete them at a high level. Conversely, if we have low energy, are bored and inert, then completing things seem like a fight, and we rely on pure willpower in order to get through. Willpower is not enough in the long-term. We must live peacefully if we are to maximise our true potential.

"Forgiveness is the fragrance that the violet sheds on the heel that has crushed it." – Mark Twain

Forgiveness is a beautiful trait to possess. Of course we should never forget anything hurtful that has been inflicted upon us; we should certainly not allow ourselves to be taken advantage of again. However, being at peace with any intended harmful event can be a way of creating health and happiness within us. Being able to forgive someone means that we acknowledge that we have also been weak or imperfect. If we forgive others, then we can forgive ourselves if, and when, we act in ways that do not coincide with our own values. We must become centred again in order to restore harmony and synchronicity, and to develop that trust within ourselves again. Send positive wishes and energy towards wonderful people you may know, but especially for those who let you down or have previously hurt you: they are in fact hurting themselves by not being within your circle or troop, and they need support and guidance. The more destructive people are, the more embracing we must be. That does not mean that we encourage it; I am not advocating being friends with those who disrespect you, but be open enough not to wish ill-will and, instead, wish beautiful things for them, for they know not what they do (they do not know how to reach their highest selves). This will support them whilst giving us the positive energy and balance we all need to operate and function at our best and highest selves. We need peace more than ever before.

How can something that is so simple be so difficult to achieve? We live in a world of constant stimuli where people allow themselves to be constantly distracted, overloaded with information, and trapped within their faltering ego's desire for drama and quick gratification. It is very hard to control our feelings if we are never giving ourselves the time to really reflect. We must find time every single day to reflect: ponder our goals; contemplate our relationships, visualise a beautiful, exciting future; consider our current shortcomings; being proud of who we are and grateful for what we have. Peace and happiness are massively intertwined. Beautifully, it is something we can experience immediately. Where there is peace, there is detachment, space and mental clarity. When we have clarity, we are able to access our best thoughts, feelings and thus deliver with the best possible actions. This is all we can ever do. When we are at peace with who and how you are, we remove all of the tension. We create the freedom necessary to act at our best.

Inappropriately, we become so absorbed with getting ahead of everyone, with comparing ourselves to others, even trying to disparage others due to our own insecurities. We should never need to compare ourselves with someone else. Firstly, we are either comparing ourselves to someone who is not as adept as us, and therefore we are setting low standards for ourselves, or we are comparing ourselves with someone who is better than us, which can demoralise some if their ego is in full swing. It is both healthier and better to simply compare ourselves with our past selves. This is how we truly measure progress. We must be who we want to be regardless of how societal or familial ideologies and material fixations try to mould us. Do what feels right. Being virtuous and giving love will open all kinds of pathways and avenues for us. Whilst many people are highly intelligent, happiness is more closely linked to our emotional intelligence.

Emotional intelligence has been shown to be more important than our mental intelligence, and this has never been more pertinent today. The smartest people do not always get the position they desire. However, the person with the highest EQ will get the highest positions. It comes down to how we control our feelings. It is the ability to remain calm, in control of one's emotions and objective enough to consistently do the right thing. It is about being able to motivate oneself. It is about being professional and consistently turning up regardless of how we feel. It is about setting high standards and challenging ourselves to push beyond our limits when most would crumble due to them not having enough emotional strength. Moreover, EQ is also about knowing how other people operate. It is about being empathetic enough to comprehend what motivates other people. What is their why? What is important to them? How can we help them? It is about being able to experience from other people's perspectives, and to be in tune with these people's energies. It is about seeing the larger picture.

Health

"I believe that the greatest gift you can give your family and the world is a healthy you." – Joyce Meyer

Much of the happiness and success we experience comes down to our relationship with food. The more energy we have, the more open we are to experiencing positive, upbeat thoughts and feelings. It does not matter how intelligent we are, if we are fueling our bodies and brains with garbage, then we are crippling our ability to consistently perform at our best. Our eating lifestyle has a profound impact upon our serotonin levels and our general wellbeing. We are all humans, and so we all experience very similar emotions. Just because I am a positive and enlightened being, does not mean that I never experience a negative thought or emotion; the only difference is how this negative fabrication affects me. It never immobilises me. In fact, whenever experienced, it spurs me on and motivates me. A negative moment is just that: a moment. This massively relates to our emotional intelligence: the more quickly we are able to change and manipulate our state, the easier it is to take control of our experience and therefore do the best thing more often. Refuse to allow a detrimental thought or emotion to affect you for a longer period of time. We should never entertain something that has no value to us. On a different note, even the most positive and energetic person will experience lethargy. Whenever the mind or body is exhausted, then it is almost impossible to feel empowered and inspired. This is why eating properly is crucial for daily mental and physical optimisation. Consider your eating plan and evaluate whether you have a balance of essential macronutrients and micronutrients.

How do we know if we are living prosperously? Is it based upon the minimal moments of ecstasy experienced when we attain something, like a promotion, the birth of your child, fleeting intimate experiences with a partner? Is this how we evaluate success? Or do we attain happiness by having what others want and value such as mansions, sport's cars, a trophy wife or husband? True happiness is about maintaining energy and positivity on a daily basis for long periods such as months and years. It is what we feel during the most familiar processes of our daily lives. It is our base mood or default emotion. We can 'set' our default emotion (to be happy, peaceful or joyous) by consuming high-quality, healthy foods and drinks. The immediate experience is what determines if we feel happy, and to win the ultimate game of life is about being able to experience satisfaction and happiness every day for as long as possible. This can only be achieved through the energy that we have on a daily basis. In order to maintain this energy, eating well is mandatory.

Eating well and healthily is a way of cultivating success. One of the most important moments in my life was when I began to eat and take care of my body to the maximum. Joyfully, I noticed that I had a greater desire to learn things; I noticed that I was even more loving and giving to others; I became less anxious or stressed out with many diverse things. Thankfully, I decided to consume primarily earth-grown foods and drinks. Furthermore, I not only developed the discipline required to remain focused on what truly matters in life (family, friends, giving, health and wealth), but I was giving my mind and body what it needs to feel lighter and to think more clearly.

Really, eating and exercising require the same belief. It is all about focusing on one day at a time. Understandably, it is important to know how we want to eat and exercise in the long term, but the only way to stay on track is to focus on the next step. If we go for a run, and we are becoming increasingly exhausted, then all we need to do is focus on moving our legs for the very next step. If we are overly concerned with the entire run, then we may psyche ourselves out. Similarly, if we are looking at that cake, then all we need to do is focus on our very next move: bypass the cake and opt for the salad. Forget about thinking about your healthy eating for the rest of the day or the entire week; just avoid that moment of potential weakness and get through it. Interestingly, our desire for that cake will subside quite quickly once we move on. Only think about getting through that moment of impulsivity. It does not last long.

Exercise consistently both moderately and intensely to increase your energy. Stretch and move your body every day. Just turn up at the gym. It is half the battle. Aim to beat and overcome physical, and mental, aptitudes by setting goals and reflecting over your success. However, never let exercise weaken the mind. Overtraining can hinder any possible physical and/or mental gains. It can also lead to fatigue and wildly overeating. Listen to your body: if it is excessively sore, then rest. Otherwise you will stress the mind, as the mind will have to work harder to keep you on track. Incidentally, those who see themselves doing better than they actually did in an activity are more likely to continue partaking in that same activity. In contrast, those who evaluate themselves realistically do not exhibit the same amount of enthusiasm to continue with their efforts. It is better to be optimistic than to be realistic especially when embarking on new skills. Accentuate your strengths to yourself, and this will give you the boost to persist in an activity, such as exercising, so that you can develop the resilience needed to deal with adversity unwaveringly. Believe that you have the potential to be the best in your given field. See yourself performing slightly better than you actually did. Even if you know it is an exaggeration, it is still worthwhile because you manage to manipulate yourself masterfully. You begin to envision greater success and positive performances, which spurs more positive thinking, emotions and further actions. It maintains the belief that you can do even better, and that your qualities are limitless.

Be Yourself

"To be yourself in a world that is constantly trying to make you something else is the greatest accomplishment." – Ralph Waldo Emerson

You are more than enough just the way you are right now. I am sure that your future self will be even more successful, happy and powerful (otherwise you would not be reading this type of book), but you have enough within you now. As Tony Robbins says, "The ultimate resource is resourcefulness." We must simply be more resourceful with our internal resources! This means just working on creating a state where we can deliver at our best as the ability is already there. Relax, be who you are, and ironically enough, you will also receive more acceptance this way. We are most confident when fully expressive and ourselves. The more restrictions we mount on ourselves, however, the less confidence and more tense we shall be. If we feel like you have to speak a certain way, move a certain way or have a certain degree of formality, then we will invariably be less confident. It is not about pleasing others. It is quite the opposite: we must please ourselves, by being ourselves, and that is how we will inadvertently please others. There is a difference between being right and doing right. Those who are focused on being right will end up having lived the wrong life. It is subjective, but everyone would benefit from doing what they think is the right thing to do. Doing so creates a shift from an extreme ego (one of crippling stubbornness) to one of openness. If we give like we have everything, then we will attract everything. It is all about having an abundance mentality. Remain flexible, natural and therefore abundantly confident.

Keep it to Yourself

We should not speak of our achievements until they have actually been accomplished. It can lose its momentum and energy. We should keep our deep desires and plans to ourselves. There can be a kind of negative energy that occurs when we try to impress others by sharing what we are doing. This can trip us up, especially if we are sharing them with people who are unsupportive. Once we believe something is so, then it changes. The moment we think we are in great health, then we suddenly attract a cold. The moment we think we are going to get a promotion or that the interview went well, then other factors will change. Now, I do not mean that we should not be optimistic or positive, but we must remain detached and comprehend that there are other forces at play. Maybe we were not meant to get that new job. Maybe it is not in our future plans to settle down with a particular partner. We can benefit from holding our cards tightly to our chest, and only revealing the winning hand when it is a certainty.

Resilience

"The more you sweat in practice, the less you bleed in battle." – Unknown Author

Every single time we have to do something new or unfamiliar, we will meet resistance in the form of unhelpful negative thoughts. The key to circumventing this is proactivity and anticipation. We must be able to predict some of the thoughts and feelings we will evoke when encountering the unknown. If we are going to a job interview, we must anticipate that we will feel incapable or stressed at some point during the process, which is oftentimes in the lead up to the actual event: "I just don't think I have all the skills needed yet, so I should really just cancel the interview and attempt it when I am definitely ready." The problem is we will never be completely ready! If we are about to go on a first date, anticipate that we will feel like the date is not worth going to: "What is the point on going on the date today? I mean we might not even connect that well. Plus, there are things I need to do. We can go out another time." The problem is if we do not have the urgency to meet now, when feelings and information is fresh and interesting, then when will you actually meet? Be ready for your negative talk, and have positive affirmations ready to keep you on track.

Do not make promises to yourself, or others, if you know you cannot keep them. Every time we do not follow through with something we really want to do, or something we know we should do, we trust ourselves less and less, and we begin to doubt ourselves more and more. Not being able to live up to our promises in our area will pervade into us not believing ourselves when we want to save up money for an investment or stand up to a bully at work. It ruins the congruency within. The next time we genuinely think to ourselves, "Right, I have to start this diet today. Enough is enough!" we will have a subsequent thought that will say, "Who are you kidding. You never follow through." We now begin to identify ourselves as someone who talks, but does not execute. Think about what this does to our belief. This negativity then manifests itself within other areas of our lives as we have now created a limiting belief. The label, "I am someone who does not follow through" then rears its ugly head when we want to travel the world or start up a business or begin with an investment or create a work of art and so on.

"Everything you attract into your life is a reflection of the story you believe and keep telling yourself." – Farshad Asl

What we think about proliferates. What we say, and the kind of words we use internally will dictate our experience. We must focus on how emotive, extreme and hyperbolic our vocabulary is. For example, was that workout fun or onerous? Was your performance all right or spectacular? Was the event remarkable or decent? Are you feeling fine or incredible? This is never more important than when we face adversity. When in a pressurised, precarious or tense position, the language we use is vital. Was the environment hostile or uncomfortable? Was the argument vicious or insensitive? Was your partner unkind or brutal? The vocabulary we use cuts off our possibilities and limits our options. For instance, if we are losing in a competition, we could communicate with ourselves in many ways. Limiting and negative questions would be: "This is usually when we fall apart. Why does it always happen?" whereas promising and optimistic language sounds like: "We will keep moving forward because we are more talented than them. They will break." We can change how we respond in moments of uncertainty because of the beliefs that we have built about ourselves: "I never stop until I get the job done." "I always find a way." The more we repeat these with intense emotions, the more they become automatic whenever we are in difficult situations.

Clarity

"It's a lack of clarity that creates chaos and frustration. Those emotions are poison to any living goal." – Steve Maraboli

Whenever I forget something I want to recall, I always clear my mind, and believe that the answer is about to come to me, and guess what, it does. This is because our subconscious is still searching for the answer long after our conscious mind has given up trying to remember. When this happens, stop trying to force the answer to come; just continue doing what you would have done next, and then the answer will suddenly present itself. While this is true on this small scale, I believe it is true in a larger context. Simply program your mind to always ask yourself a massive question (you can set these as reminders on your phone for instance), and then you can choose to carry on your day as usual. Why? If you keep asking this open, specific question, then, over time, you condition your subconscious mind to constantly search for the answer. You do not have to remind yourself, and then sit there struggling to formulate an answer. Simply present it to yourself for a moment, and continue with your day. It could be questions such as: "How can I create more value for my clients?" "How can I do more for my family?" "How can I increase my passive income?" "What business should I create?" "How will I do better in my exam?" "How can I make my partner even happier?"

If our minds can be seen as a representation of our personal space (home), then we can link parts of this home to elements within the brain. Our loft/attic can be seen metaphorically as our unconscious. This is where our deepest emotions and memories lie. Why is it so often the least important and visited place in our 'home?' Focus on what we neglect. Many people do not take the time to condition their minds, to take control of their actions, thoughts and behaviours because we allow ourselves to be too involved in our external world: our visual, physical, yet faker world. Our inner world creates what we see externally.

Reduce Drama

"All the world's a stage and most of us are desperately unrehearsed." – Sean O'Casey

Do not get sucked into another person's games. Remain focused on your path. We want to avoid listening to people who constantly come up with excuses for not following through. Have a set time and place to catch up with friends and family on most occasions. Other than that, we will want to limit hearing about other people's problems and issues as they take away our energy in other areas. Even worse, refrain from getting into petty arguments and conflict with anyone. Again, this takes energy, and throws us off our path. Avoid conflict and problems on a smaller scale, and you will notice that you do not encounter really horrible confrontations because you are not looking for them unlike most people (who like to distract themselves and vent out their frustrations, which deep down are really with themselves).

We do not need to add things to our lives to be happy. We need to take things away, so that there is space for our natural ability, or unknown ability, to ascend. In writing this book, I began to separate myself from others. I was still just as giving and polite in all interactions, but I felt compelled to avoid distractions, and to ensure that my thoughts and story was not being compromised. Do you have something in your life that grips you like that? Can you immerse yourself in something meaningful for days on end? If we do not, then we must reflect on our passions and priorities. Start asking better quality questions. Become focused, driven and enchanted by the prospect of experiencing flow. When writing this book, it was as if space was being created for me to fill it with writing. You will notice that things work in your favour and you produce things even better when completely immersed in something for hours and days on end. As long as you have time to do other things, such as meditate, plan, see friends and family, then become immersed in something beautiful as it reduces negative talk, keeps you focused on positive things and makes you feel capable of completing something worthwhile.

Be thoughtful of what emotions you invest in. The more often we experience certain emotions, the more intense they become. They become more and more gripping unless we break them down to a granular level. Consider the emotions you experience daily, and seek to eradicate the more deleterious and negative ones where possible. What thoughts bring them on? Where are you when they occur? What did you think about previously before you felt this way? How can you shift your focus quickly when it comes back? The person who expends great negative emotional intensity, such as anger, will soon find himself or herself exhausted and unable to function effectively. The person surrounded by debilitating negative emotions and relationships will be too fatigued to produce something of value and excellence. We only have a certain amount of time and energy every day. Where do your emotions take you every day? Which ones drain you, and where does this source come from? How can you change or eliminate this source? What actions must you undertake? Think about how much this is costing you. We only live for so long…

One of the reasons why religions are so poignant and omniscient to many is because of the order it creates in the mind. Whether something pleasant or disharmonious happens to us, we turn to our virtuous side and beliefs in a great power to help guide us. This is prominently known to exist in the form of prayer or meditation. The imagery within their stories and parables is majorly influential. This order in the mind can also be attained through repeating positive quotations by influential figures or by learning incantations/affirmations off by heart, which we turn to in similar situations. This turns chaos into order, enabling us to think more clearly. It invaluably provides control and direction within our unpredictable situations.

The Sun and The Clouds

What can prevent us from shining? Becoming more successful is not having or manufacturing a better sun. It is removing the clouds that are in the way, so that the sun can shine. We all have a sun within us; we all have natural and developing talents; we all have a longing to be the best we can possibly be, but the clouds (intrusions and obstacles) inhibit our ability to realise our true potential. If we want shine, then we must remove the drama and mental chaos that is always waiting to cloud our judgement. We must stay strong, keep our eyes on the right path, and move toward it steadily.

Abundance

"Abundance is not something we acquire. It is something we tune into." - Wayne Dyer

There is always enough of everything, and we can always attract what we desire. However, we cannot experience more success and happiness unless we can already deal with what we currently have. If money was spread equally to everyone all over the world, we would all have more than enough. There is no shortage of money; there is only a shortage of wisdom. We do not need to compete with others in any respect. We should not perceive it as though having money ourselves means that others do not and vice versa. Metaphorically speaking, people live in two different worlds, and interestingly enough, they correlate in many different ways. For example, some believe in scarcity: they think that there is not enough money in the world; they think that there are not enough interesting people who will want them; they believe that there are not enough people out there who will like them for who they are etc. We attract what we think about most frequently, and we attract what we feel most frequently. All we need to do is remain focused on our goals, plan well and keep mentally and physically healthy to ensure efficacy.

In stark contrast, there are those who believe in abundance: they believe that they can attract as much money, potential partners and friends as they wish. Whatever you truly believe to be the truth, will become your reality, so why not just choose to believe in the best possible things? This mentality must be cultivated. If we want to attract anything we want into our lives, then the shift must take place across all areas. There is enough of everything that we want in the world, and if we believe otherwise, then we have been falsely conditioned. We must be congruent with our beliefs. Begin to cultivate the belief that you can have whatever you desire.

High Standards

"Set high standards and few limitations for yourself." – Anthony J. D'Angelo

Expect the best, but be prepared for the worst. This way we remain positive and optimistic whilst being prepared to appropriately deal with a difficult circumstance. We must have a strong blueprint as to what can be achieved, and what we expect our current, and future lives, to be like in all respects: love, finances, hobbies, appearance and so on. Consistent small actions and steps will bring about drastic change. Every day should be even better than the previous. It might just take a small tweak in order to completely implement a new habit that can positively change the course of our direction. Sometimes we may positively change a sequence (thought, subsequent emotion and action), but the benefits of this change may not be noticeable until years later. We may think that something lucky just happened to us, but it could have been a direct result of a small change, or many small changes, that we made a long time ago. Think about the golf analogy: when playing golf, we come to understand that the most nuanced change in our strike can instigate the most profound change in the course of the golf ball in the air and ultimately where it lands. The same applies to our daily lives: small, useful changes build up incrementally. We can start the transformation now.

We need to be authentic with ourselves. This means ensuring that there is congruency between our thoughts, feelings and behaviours. Being aligned and balanced will allow us to truly focus on what we want. Things will work in your favour more if our thoughts, emotions and actions work synchronistically together. It is all about creating the right kind of energy around us. Someone who is imbalanced in one important area will often be imbalanced in another significant area. If someone wants to be healthy, yet he or she is emotionally attached to food, then they will have conflicting emotions and will thus be incongruent within themselves: they are angry and want to change their mind and body, yet they receive instant pleasure and immediate joy when eating addictive foods that are unhealthy. Another example is someone who wants to be wealthy, yet is doing the best he or she can to avoid doing any work, and whose actions tend to be seeking quick ways of making lots of money, which is almost impossible without studying, learning and hard work. A third example is someone who wants to get married to a reliable, family-oriented person, yet loves to date exciting, spontaneous people he or she would never settle down with, and so they treat the right person wrongly and the wrong person rightly. It is like completing a puzzle: we need the right pieces in order for everything to fit. What we focus on (our thoughts) must coincide with how we feel about its attainment (our attitude), and we must take the necessary actions to make it all happen.

Setting high standards relate to being very focused on one thing at a time as this is the only way we can execute at the highest level. In order to be fully immersed in important experiences, we must condition ourselves to be fully in the moment and focused even during seemingly innocuous situations. The same applies to the quality of our inner dialogue: we want our inner dialogue to be fully focused on what is happening right in front of us rather than being within a certain context yet at the same time be thinking about something totally unrelated. This lack of focus often results in unsupportive thinking. We can change this by firstly changing how we are on a smaller scale. For example, if you are watching a film, stay off your phone. If you are having a detailed conversation with someone important to you, remain focused on what they are saying, and not on what you will be doing later. If you are doing work, refrain from having a conversation with someone. If we improve our focus and inner talk during these moments, then we will perform much better when delivering presentations or working on a business deal and so on because we are fully committed to the immediate experience that is happening right in front of us. It is all about conditioning.

In order to motivate ourselves, we must know that we have something that is missing or lacking in our lives. This is often referred to as known incompetence. It is not necessarily a bad thing. Feeling that we could improve and do better is beautiful. People often feel motivated because they feel insufficient. However, it is better to be self-motivated by simply knowing you have everything you need, but want to give and be even more. Most people would rather keep their hundred pounds (in money) than gain a hundred pounds. The fear of loss is more powerful to most than the pleasure of gaining. If we are to be extremely powerful, happy and successful, then we must change this mentality. Take calculated risks. We must make sure that we go for what we really want. Instead of chasing what we can never catch, however, we must have quality habits in place, and simply allow things to come to us. When it comes to motivation, we have what is known as toward and away from motivation. Toward motivation is when we want to move closer to something: "I work hard because I want to buy a nice car." Away from motivation is when we do something in order to move further away from something: "I will not ask him out because I do not want to get hurt." Interestingly, we can experience both when thinking about the same thing: "I want to have complete freedom in my life, but I also want to have my own family." This can lead to a lot of frustration, hopelessness and incongruence. We will want to make a choice between whether we want to move closer or further away and develop affirmations whenever we are thinking about this thing in order to keep us focused. The predominant motivation will soon work its way into our subconscious.

Love to Learn

"Live as if you were to die tomorrow. Learn as if you were to live forever." – Mahatma Gandhi

A love of learning is invaluable. It fills our lives with great joy. It serves to massively reduce moments of boredom and sadness whilst keeping our brains active and challenged. If we love to learn, then we can always occupy our minds when alone or bored. There is always something to do. It is a healthy mindset that keeps us away from negative, decadent habits. Nonetheless, we must choose to learn topics that are important, and not just learning for the sake of learning. Research and study what interests you. It is always beneficial to research and explore key fundamental areas such as how relationships work (communication, rapport and psychology), health (what fuels us and supports the brain's function) and wealth (forms of active and passive income).

Learning any new skill or information can be easier if we have the right mindset. Approach it as though it is a simple concept or skill, and we will learn it more quickly. Some people may think, "I am about to learn something new, but it takes me ages to learn new things." What we say about ourselves is what we are. Never say that we cannot do something, because that is the narrative we are painting for ourselves; we literally put up walls around us that prevent us from learning. The phrase, "takes me ages," sets in stone exactly how we absorb meaning. Furthermore, some people say things like, "I could never be a doctor," or "I am just not physically coordinated." Take the words "I can't" out of our vocabulary. What we believe is our reality. Make sure that we are in the right state to learn: sit upright, be positive and optimistic, focus on the present moment. In addition, we must remove any clutter in the mind; the clearer our thoughts, the easier it is to literally store and retain information in our long-term memory.

Ensure that we act upon the material we have just learnt. Make changes quickly after we have learned this new information. Take what we have learned, and kinesthetically and physically do something to embed this new information. Start the momentum. See if we can apply this newfound knowledge within different contexts. See if we can make connections between topics and skills that we know very well, and whatever it is that is now being learnt. Moreover, make some kind of personal or emotional connection with the material we are learning. Unfortunately, many people hear or see something interesting, yet they say things like, "I'll get to that," or "it's great that I've learnt that" (without even putting it into practice yet), or "I should definitely try this one day." The problem with these phrases is that they create distance between their new felt thoughts, emotions and actions. They have logically understood that something is great and beneficial, but they leave it so long that their emotions have not been engaged deep enough, and thus no action will follow suit down the line. We think, feel and take in so much information every single day that it is hard to simply pluck things out and embed them in the mind permanently. This freshly instilled knowledge (and subsequent action) must be exercised frequently to ensure that enough energy and emotion has been invested into its worth. The more we revisit information, the more it becomes embedded into our long-term memory.

One of the keys to unlocking the door to happiness is knowing who we are and how we function. This level of meta-cognition and self-comprehension is crucial. Understanding what we like, and what we dislike allows us to be more efficient with our time. If we know how we learn best, then we most efficiently learn new material: what space do you learn best in? Do you like to independently study on the computer? Do you prefer discussing key topics with friends etc.? When at work, how do you perform at your best? In terms of your relationship, what mindset enables you to get the most out of yourself?

Take the time to learn from our experiences and that of others. Value learning otherwise the apathy and indifference sustained over time will come back to us in harsher and more painful ways. A painful experience is a chance to reflect and learn. By not reflecting and learning a lesson, the same lesson will come back twofold. This 'compound pain' repeats itself until we break the habit, and attack the source of the problem: usually us. If we think about it, everything compounds. Just like compound interest, we invest something (our money for instance), and then we reinvest again whilst keeping the original sum. This is why people get more devastated every time they incur a meaningful setback. Their affliction compounds. The same works in the positive realm. Invest time and energy into the creation of something, and then our next creation will have the success from the previous one along with whatever new skills we have now developed. This is oftentimes why most people fail with their first business venture. They learn from the previous errors, and have accumulated massive strengths, lessons and resources.

Complacency

"Success breeds complacency. Complacency breeds failure. Only the paranoid survive." –
Andy Grove

Complacency is incredibly precarious. Complacency happens when we only choose to stay within our comfort zone, but if we only stay there, then there is no growth. Where there is no growth, there is no challenge. Where there is no challenge, there is boredom. Where there is boredom, there is laziness and a lack of energy. Where there is no energy, there is sadness. Where there is continual sadness, there is depression. And where there is depression, there is despondence. This is a vicious cycle. It becomes habitual, and it can seem inescapable, but there is a way out: have a big enough *why* in order to change our circumstance. Complacency infiltrates our very being until we fear change. Think of complacency as slowly shrinking our box: the more comfortable we become, the less we want to do. If we want success, power and respect, then we must become more flexible. Flexibility derives from being open minded, dealing effectively with change and learning from other people's brilliance. Our way is not always the right way. We must understand that our weaknesses empower us; refusing to accept weakness weakens us further. What was once positive becomes familiar, and the familiar becomes a weakness. Grow and develop in all aspects even if they are your current strengths.

"When you stop being nervous is when you should retire. I'm always a little nervous for

anything I do because when complacency sets in, that's when I feel it's time to move on to something else." – Chris Jericho

Staying within your comfort zone is a recipe for true failure, as it does not allow us to live up to our true potential. Living within our comfort zones is one of the most selfish things we can do. We prevent ourselves from learning, growing, becoming wiser, and thus not influencing the lives of others more positively or powerfully. Attacking small challenges is the perfect way to gradually dip our feet into the waters of the unknown. If we attempt something too difficult, then we will put ourselves off attempting anything new in the future. We will mildly traumatise ourselves, and every time we want to attempt something new, this experience will be our reference point, deterring us from stretching and growing. When we gradually increase the level of tension (stress) we experience, then we develop mental and emotional stamina. We then create a foundation of successful experiences that we can refer to when beginning a new challenging experience. It is all about momentum. It is all about convincing ourselves to show up, and let whatever happen take place. We need faith.

"There is more than meets the eye and unless you are willing to experience new things, you'll never realize your full potential." – Wim Hof

The Perfect Pair

The wishful man wanted the perfect pair of shoes. Dismally, he walked passed the prestigious store weekly to see if the price had dropped. If so, the beautiful pair would be worthy enough of purchasing and enjoying. Months went by excruciatingly, and he continued to pace passed the shoes admiringly yet disappointedly. Shortly after, the man obsessively walked passed the store, only to hear that the shoes had sold out… The story holds truth in that we should not wait to get what we want in life. The shoes is a metaphor for going for what you want in life as things are always changing, and time is never promised to us. If you desire something, then do what is necessary to take it.

If we dread or fear working on something, then we can utilise the contrast principle. This means working on something that is even harder than what we originally found challenging. We all have a stress and challenge threshold in terms of what we can handle. If we have something we must do, which is nerve-racking or onerous, then do something that is even more intimidating and challenging. We will find that we handle the original challenge much better as it does not seem as daunting now. For example, if you are fearful of talking to a member of the opposite sex randomly, then organise something harder such as presenting in front of a larger audience at work; if you are more fearful of that, then go on the scariest roller coaster ride imaginable, and if you find that too scary, then organise a mixed martial arts' fight for charity and so on. The aim is to frequently step outside of our comfort zone because that is when we truly grow, and realise that there really is not much to be fearful of really.

No single action acts alone. Our daily behaviours work together to produce who we are. If we want to change a specific behaviour, then the entire spectrum of associated actions must be altered to compensate for the necessary change: we cannot take out a rectangular brick from a fully built house, and replace it with a squared brick. There is a domino effect taking place, even between our behaviours. The same applies to our daily routines: in order to take out one energy source, we will need to be flexible in our lifestyle. There is a sequence of thoughts, emotions and actions that results in an action that we do not like. If we want to change an action, we must trace backwards and comprehend what feelings we felt, and then what thoughts preceded that led to those feelings. For example, firstly, we may want to stop biting our nails (the action). Secondly, we will need to understand the feelings that led to this: anxiety or excitement or fear (the emotions). Thirdly, we need to consider the thoughts that led to these feelings: "There is no way I can complete this project on time." "I cannot believe I said that, how embarrassing!" "I do not think my job is certain." All of these thoughts are undesirably phrased. They all make us focus on something negative. Now, these thoughts are inevitable; no one can actually stop these from manifesting in our minds. However, we must be able to calm ourselves down by engraining more positive thoughts within as soon as possible. For example, after we think to ourselves, "I cannot believe I said that, how embarrassing!" we must be able to immediately overwhelm this thought with something positive and beneficial: "Well it has happened now. I know that I need to be more careful next time, but there is nothing I can do now." After this more supportive statement, it is important that we take a deep breath. It may even be beneficial to think, "I am ready to let that moment go, and move on with my life."

Love and Relationships

"Love is of all passions the strongest, for it attacks simultaneously the head, the heart and the senses." – Lao Tzu

We absolutely must love ourselves. We must love our strengths, our weaknesses, who we are and what we can become. It is one of the most giving things that we can possibly do for others. Obviously we must not love ourselves egotistically, but in a manner where we accept ourselves for who we are. If we do not do something as well as we desire, then refrain from any punitive thoughts or behaviours. Instead, we must appreciate our strengths and weaknesses, and use these to spur better outcomes. Love for oneself is akin to our self-esteem. The higher our self-esteem, the more accepting and respectful we become of others and ourselves.

Love is a spell. Love is a weakness, yet a strength. It is the most beautiful weakness that there is. When people turn away from love, they turn away from the essence of who they are: ultimately weak, fragile, emotional human beings. If death is our ultimate fear, then love is our ultimate antidote. Is it possible that we can combat our fears with love? Powerful poet, Ralph Waldo Emerson, poignantly portrays love as actually being God. When we experience love, we are experiencing God. When we experience flow, we are experiencing God. Could it be that when we are giving, powerful and loving, then we are in fact God ourselves? Our beliefs are irrelevant at this moment: by referring to God here, we are simply referring to a greater power, and that may be the greater power we have within ourselves. If someone asks if we are religious or spiritual, we may respond with, "yes, I believe in love."

We must understand that we are complete just as we are right now. We do not need anyone or anything. Yes, externals can enhance us, making us feel loved and significant. When we buy things, we try to buy feelings: buying an amazing car makes us feel joyful (for the moment); purchasing a stunning dress or suit makes us feel secure and attractive and so on. Can it be that the more we look to buy feelings, the less likely we are to generate those feelings naturally within us? We should never need something external. The way we are now is the way our lives has been guided, and our current path is, at this moment in time, set to teach us the lessons we need to encounter to reach our destinies. If we love and respect ourselves enough, then we do not need a thing.

When we truly love someone, he or she enchants us. Being in someone's mind frequently is a spell. Having our behaviours influenced or dictated by someone indicates how enchanted we are. We will do anything for them; we think about them; we are always there for them. They exist within us, and can guide our actions, even though they may not be physically there with us. Take a moment to think about the people who influence what you do. Are these empowering and beneficial habits that they have indoctrinated? Keep them if they are. However, if they are not, then we will want to mitigate the effects of this 'spell.'

Technological advancements allow us to connect with more people, but potentially at the expense of having fewer quality relationships. We are constantly on the phone, social networking, researching things and sometimes we do this in the presence of our loved ones way too much. In order to improve the quality of our relationships, decide to give people or a person a specific amount of time where there will be no interruptions where you can just focus on talking and fully being in the present moment together. This is invaluable. Communication is the most important part of any relationship. We are not responsible for anyone else's actions. We do not control another human being, and whilst we can influence and guide others, what they do is their prerogative. Effective parenting is about modelling quality behaviour, and providing opportunities for our children to emulate, become independent and follow their true passions. We do not want to be the parent who limits the soul of a child by guiding them into what we want them to be. They may come from us, but they are not ours.

It is debilitating to conceive a relationship as a battle or fight for power. Know how to influence others, but avoid using these strategies where possible. The best relationships simply flow. A successful relationship blossoms when replete with empathy, communication and the primary intention of supporting one another. If we want our partners to be happy being with us, then allow them to truly be themselves: whenever someone can say and do what they naturally want to do, the more confident they become. The more confident partners are, then the more willing they are to give and be more for us. The more we put into something, the more likely we are to commit to it. For example, the more time, energy and money we spend on a date, the more we will want to see that person again. If we won the lottery, we would be far more expansive and squandering of capital than if we became rich by struggling and persevering through effort, trial and error.

If you want someone to like you or stay with you, have him or her do things for you. Make them think about you. The more energy, time and money they invest in you, they will be more likely to commit whether it is a friendship or something more intimate. These can be small things, especially to begin with, as no sane person would commit massively to doing things for you because they would need to be severely depressed, desperate or lonely to do so. Small things make a difference. Have them pay for coffee if they offer? Have them drive for once? Have them meet you somewhere? Have them book or reserve dinner somewhere? Have them do the research when planning a holiday together? Why? The more they do for you, the more they say to themselves, "I must be doing these things for ...... because I like/love him or her." Of course be realistic with these advances. If you overstretch and become overzealous with your expectations and demands, then they may go the opposite direction. The person who does more in a friendship or relationship is unconsciously viewed as 'inferior' unfortunately. While it is not nice to believe this, it is reality. This is why the relationship must be balanced. This person has committed and struggled more because the other is more valued, precious and thus perceived as more significant. It is not necessarily important, or right, to manipulate others, but at least it is essential to know how this works, so that you can make small adjustments.

How can we strengthen a relationship? We should not only be fully committed to this relationship, but have him or her also go the extra mile for us. Regularly have them put more effort, time and money into us, as they will value us more by doing so. Unfortunately, many people harm their relationships because they deal with stress ineffectively. They have arguments. They develop a need to control and dominate. They are more prone to making others feel bad. They disparage others more. They are aggressive when driving. They are more likely to feed the disease that will lead to their demise. They have no real inner peace. They do not understand how their partner mentally and emotionally operates: what are their likes and dislikes? What are they passionate about? When do they get angry and why? When are they most happy with you? However, of course, we cannot help how others choose to feel, but we can take responsibility for what we say and do.

Moreover, our relationships are truly tested when things are not going well. Who turns up for you when you really need them? If you need someone to help you move, or if you need some extra money during a tough month, who is there to support you? These are great opportunities to learn who your true friends are, and who only turn up when they want to turn up. A relationship should never be evaluated when things are going well for both people, but when one or both people are struggling. When we do not feel good about what we do or are not doing, we make others, or try to make them, not feel good about what they are doing. Being a burden and being depressed is the most selfish thing we can be. Ruminate the people in your life who can have this kind of affect on you, and seek to minimise or exclude them from your life where possible. Additionally, we never know what someone is thinking and experiencing. Understand that everyone has their problems and struggles in life regardless of how successful and happy they are. Conversely, we must understand that many people are emotionally and/or mentally weak, and so their behaviours may not match what we expect. Remain on your path. Who cares about petty things and petty arguments? Know what is important, keep these in mind, and avoid or ignore the weak obstacles (people) you will encounter. They will not be in your life for long.

"People are like dirt. They can either nourish you and help you grow as a person or they can stunt your growth and make you wilt and die." - Plato

The key to a healthy relationship is to spot problems early, and to intervene as soon as possible. It is even better to be proactive, in all aspects of your life, but also in our relationships. If we have strong emotional intelligence, then we will understand how people operate. If we are aware of how our loved ones react to stress, unfamiliar situations, work etc., then we can predict their state, and thus change our approach to communicate with them most appropriately. Do not exacerbate a situation by viewing it as a power struggle. Negotiating in business and relationships is about learning how the other person is thinking, expressing our point of view and *working together* to make both parties satisfied. Incidentally, if you want to influence someone who is stubborn, then give him or her something to refuse, so that they believe they are in control. In order to influence someone, have him or her refuse something that appears important but is not. Distract them with one thing, so we can get the real thing we wanted.

If we find it hard to initiate a conversation with even a loved one or a friend, then it is because we are afraid of being rejected. We are vulnerable to not being spoken to at all or not being shown the same affection that we displayed. If we find it hard to say, "I love you," to kin, friend or family member, it is because we are afraid to learn that we are not loved back or are not loved as much in return. This sensitivity prevents us from taking risks, and putting our emotions on display as we worry that we will not be accepted and are unworthy of it in return. The underlying belief is simple: "I will not express myself because I fear that I am not enough." This self-fulfilling prophecy will show up in many ways until we have suffered enough to actually do something about it.

We will never really break through and achieve what we wish if we compare ourselves with others, and allow ourselves to be consumed with our reputations and how others perceive us. In the past, we may have thought about how much better the future would be; in the present, we may worry about how quickly our prime will disappear; in the future, we may sentimentally and regretfully look back and consider how we could have done things differently in retrospection. All relationships remain bright due to excitement and uncertainty. Bringing certainty to romance is like bringing water to fire. The same works in all of life's modalities. Once we know something for sure, then it has lost its power.

"Loneliness does not come from having no people around you, but from being unable to communicate the things that seem important to you." - Carl Jung

The key word is communication. Perhaps Jung's statement refers to all forms of communication: communication with others, yet even more so about being unable to communicate with ourselves effectively and openly. Many people are not totally honest with themselves about how they feel, and what they really want. It is this lack of clarity and honesty that prevent people from living their ideal lives.

Our Surroundings

"Surround yourself with only people who are going to lift you higher." – Oprah Winfrey

With whom do we surround ourselves? We must have positive role models around us. Are you more intelligent than your friends? Are you healthier than your friends? Are you more successful, financially or physically, than your friends? If the answer is yes, then you are letting yourself down dreadfully. We must ensure that we are stimulated, challenged and continuously progressing by spending time with successful and motivated people. If we are stronger than our peers in areas of great importance, then we are letting our egos get the better of us. This is detrimental. We must always learn and grow if we are to maximise our potential. We must be mindful of what we listen to. We will adopt many of the beliefs and thought patterns of those we are closest to, so be selective with whom we spend our time with and how often. Moreover, be conscious of the type of music that we listen to: aggressive music can make us more aggressive; depressing songs can make us feel sadder. Whilst I understand the need to play with our emotions (to experience variety), be cautious of the emotions we allow ourselves to experience each day. If they become addictive, then we search for them in other contexts.

In terms of our physical surroundings, ensure that your room, flat or house is consistently clean. Our physical surroundings are a direct reflection of our mentality. If writing or computer-based work is a priority, then ensure that your desk is clear and only equipped with essential stationery. If your family keeps you motivated, then have a picture of them in front of you when working, so that you turn to them in moments of challenge. The same applies to religious imagery or quotations if religious, and having pictures of our role models. You want the setting to give you most clarity and strength needed because this is where we shape our lives.

Focus on the positives; refrain from giving energy to things that are harmful. For example, if there is a colossal car accident on the motorway, then purposely choose not to look as you drive by because it is important not to focus on fatal things. Additionally, purposely avoid the news primarily because it focuses on negative, sad things; remember we search for the things we see and experience most often. Avoid spending time with dramatic people or people who are severely unlucky primarily because you wish to experience positive, supportive things. You will attract wonderful things because you are a loving, giving and friendly person. Know, deep down, that we deserve success. Know that by continuously improving, our happiness will not end because we achieved these beautiful things the right way. Give love because you are love. There is beauty in everything. See the wider picture, and act based upon positive thoughts and emotions: thoughts are more accurate and clear by its very nature whereas emotions are thoughts that are unquantifiable and indefinable. Thought occurs when we are proactive, and emotion occurs when we are reactive.

There are usually just a few moments in life when we really get to find out what we are like. It is easy to talk the talk, to think that we are a certain way, and that we know how we would react in certain situations, but many people would be surprised if they knew exactly how they would react if something really difficult happened. It is in these moments that we find out exactly who and what we are. We know who we are when faced with challenge and adversity.

Modelling

"We like to think of our champions and idols as superheroes who were born different from us. We don't like to think of them as relatively ordinary people who made themselves extraordinary." - Carol S. Dweck

A large part of becoming an expert within a specific field is to learn from the most successful and talented people within our area of interest. All we need to do is emulate their beliefs, thought patterns and emotions (to a certain extent). Pay attention to the way in which they carry themselves, the way they dress, how they look at people, how they charismatically draw others to them, how they speak of others and what their beliefs are. The more we adopt from these brilliant individuals, the more likely we are to attract some of their qualities. We begin to think and act more like them, and so we can attract the kind of great things that they attract. Naturally, people can only become masters within one or two fields (as it takes such dedication, effort and experience), but by studying them meticulously, we can also master, or come close to mastering, what they have done by simply taking on their perceptions and the things that they did successfully.

Ultimately, it is always better to be yourself, but there is nothing wrong with incorporating the qualities of some of the most successful people in the world. There is nothing wrong with exaggerating your current features, so that you become more like the strong, successful men and/or women that you appreciate. Whether it is someone's style, humour, ways of moving and so forth, take on their qualities, and you will have a powerful concoction of flair, style and charisma.

Obviously, learning from both their psychology and mechanics can be highly beneficial, but be more interested in their psychology (how they perceive things) rather than their mechanics (the things they actually do). What mindset and experiences led to their greatness? How do they think, and what do they do in terms of activities? What are their daily routines? What do they avoid doing? What were the key moments in their lives and why? Analyse and adopt the vocabulary they use. Let us explore some of the most incredibly successful, influential and powerful people who were able to rise to the top in their given field:

Steve Jobs

"Keep looking, don't settle." – Steve Jobs

Steve Jobs never graduated from college. Dropping out turned out to be one of his best decisions. What at first appeared a failure, opened opportunities in other avenues that led to the typography and multi-face of the mac. You have to trust that the dots will connect, and that it will lead you to where you want or should go. Live life on your terms. Stay hungry. Jobs frequently asked himself, "How can we better this?" This is an excellent, simple question to use whenever you want to develop something. It ensures continual improvement and reflection. It is an open question that challenges the brain to search for positive solutions. Do what you love. Be passionate. Have a strong and clear vision. Jobs stated, "Any rational person can give up." Persevere by loving what you do. Go for something with clarity, fervour and be obstinate in your journey. This is the only way to maintain motivation and to ensure longevity in what you do. Will power alone will not suffice. Find your passion, and then find a way of making it as lucrative and useful for others as possible.

Make things as simple as possible. Simplify your life as best you can. Steve Jobs took this to an extreme as he would wear the same outfit all of the time (washing it often of course). It reduced complexity, and saved mental and physical energy, which helped him to concentrate on more important creative tasks. Think about ways where you can be more efficient. How can you conserve your energy on the low-impact activities you do, and increase your output for the more substantial daily activities? Kick-start your brain by doing something new! Think differently, and have a vision. Be innovative. Just because it has not been done before, does not mean it cannot be done now or in the future.

Sir Richard Branson

"What I like most about my life is that I'm learning all the time." - Sir Richard Branson

You create your own luck. Learn something powerful and meaningful every single day. If you do not have time to read, then listen to an audiobook or meet with your mentor or successful friend and pick their mind. Success is determined by your hunger to acquire more knowledge. An unrelenting desire to learn comes from your overall energy for life. You can always get better no matter how successful or happy you are. Why? Knowledge and success are immeasurable. Your thirst for knowledge will keep you improving, thereby avoiding stagnation and its subsequent friend: depression. If you want to avoid depression and negativity, then get busy and learn. Learning and challenging your brain keeps it strong and sharp. This philosophy will keep your mentality healthy as we continue to age.

Michael Jordan

"Failure gave me strength" – Michael Jordan

Michael Jordan was the first person to show up at practice and the last person to leave. He had a beautiful mindset especially when it came to failure: "I will not let the opportunity of failure stop me from doing something that I truly enjoy doing." "I can surpass any expectations I ever made for myself." Both Tyson and Jordan believed that they could be even better than their already extremely high expectations. They had no barriers and no limitations. For Jordan, challenging himself was a must, as he knew this is the only way to grow: "I had to challenge myself." We must find a way of keeping motivated when doing repetitive training. This is a man who appreciated his failures: "A thousand failures bring major success." "Limits like fears are often just an illusion." In addition, Michael Jordan was also extremely competitive. He would hate to lose a game at anything even if it was not within his specialty: basketball. He was a pure winner who set the highest standards of himself. He took responsibility whether his team won or lost. One of the biggest lessons we can learn from Michael Jordan is the need to take responsibility.

Muhammad Ali

"If my mind can conceive it, and my heart can believe it – then I can achieve it." – Muhammad Ali

One of the most beautiful things about Mohammad Ali was his self-belief. While Ali exaggerated much of his communication with the public through rhetoric and poetry even for humour and publicity, his self-talk is evident and indicative of his thoughts about his aptitude. He claimed to be the best way before he actually was. He put that potentiality out into the universe, and gradually moved toward it until it became his reality. He is one of the few people who talked a big game, yet backed it up magnificently. Mystically, he would often predict the round in which he would win, and he even had the audacity at times to predict how he would win! He was a man who was poetic in his words as well as his movement. A man who seemingly had it all: he was a handsome, confident, athletic, highly opinionated and unpredictable champion. Furthermore, Ali was also very courageous and opinionated. He will forever go down as the greatest boxer of all time because of the qualities he displayed inside and outside of the ring.

Mike Tyson

"In order to be great, you have to be prepared to fail greatly as well...it's all about how you handle the failures." – Mike Tyson

Some superstars can teach you what not to do rather than what you should do, and so you can learn much from the naturally impregnable and impervious Mike Tyson who could not develop his emotional intelligence at the same rate as his muscles and movement. Arguably the greatest physical specimen of all time, Mike Tyson, had it all and lost it. Why? He had a poor person's beliefs, and he did not love himself: he had low self-esteem. He is fascinating to listen to, as he epitomises how you should not speak of yourself: "I don't like Mike Tyson." "I never respected women, maybe because I've never respected myself." Tyson always felt unworthy, and even when he had woman after woman, he lost respect for them because he did not respect himself. "I've being doing boxing for 20 or 25 years and I haven't received and dignity from it." "It made me not like Mike Tyson no more. When you show me love I hate you because I don't like myself... I'm not happy with myself. I don't care if I live and die. I don't care about any of you but I do." "I am whatever they want me to be."

In stark contrast, he spoke highly of himself, but only in the form of metaphors, which we can utilise, by comparing himself alongside other greats: "I am impregnable. I'm Sonny Liston. I'm Jack Dempsey… There's nobody who can match me." While Tyson can certainly be self-hating, he displays great discipline: "I can do what I hate to do, but do it like I love it." "I keep doubt. Doubt is a saviour. The doubt makes me perform better. A person who is totally secure in their position is in a position to lose it." "I had to look at myself greater than I actually was and believe that I was greater than I actually was." Setting frighteningly high standards, and conceiving an exaggerated and proficient version of your true self can be empowering and at times understandable or necessary.

On a positive note, Tyson built some very powerful habits in his training: he ran in the early hours of the morning when he knew his opponent would be sleeping. He knew that this gave him a competitive edge. Tyson's audience, the world, created the monster known as Mike Tyson. We encouraged the beast, and then were outraged by the beast's nature. Sympathetically, all he ever wanted was to be accepted. Even though he was the most devastating and exciting fighter of all time, he needed externals, which indicated a massive weakness. Women were his downfall. He did not receive love as a child, and so he learned to cover up his emotions by chasing material goods. What you do not deal with in life, will end up dealing with you. Trying to take short cuts by skipping things will trip us up at some point. We are tested when things do not go according to plan, yet we are also tested when we attain success and finally get a break because this is when we must continue to push the boundaries of success once again: success after success. Our results coincide to create a chain of events.

Will Smith

"I have a great time with my life, and I want to share it." – Will Smith

Firstly, this quotation, and especially the preposition, "with," instead of 'in' shows how Will Smith is detached from his life in order to accurately and effectively make the adjustments necessary to progress. "This is what I believe and I'm willing to die for it." "We make the situation more complex than it has to be…it can't be that easy." "Where I excel is ridiculous sickening work ethic. While the other guy is sleeping, I'm working. When the other guy is sleeping, I'm working." Lay one brick at a time perfectly, and work on our craft daily. Refuse to let resistance and procrastination stop us from working toward our goals. We have to visualise the big picture (your greatest possible success), but it is the small actions that compound into the cultivation of bigger successes.

We must take control of our lives if we are to flourish. However, this can only happen when we take responsibility for everything that we do: how we react; how we frame events and happenstances to ourselves, and to never allow ourselves to be a victim in any sense as this is a disempowering excuse that builds up helplessness when it is never the case. Take responsibility for what we eat, what time we wake, how we dress, how we interact with others, what we think and represent and so forth. We have to believe that change can happen, and it can happen at an extraordinary speed. Refuse to do what others consider the norm. Refuse to be realistic. We must remain focused on our intention, to do better for ourselves, and, in turn, the universe. We can help other human beings through our core gifts. As Will Smith states, "There's a flow of the universe that I've grown to know just how to go with it." We can only do our best; everything other than that must be embraced and taken within our stride. Will Smith interestingly exclaims that he "started attacking things that (he) I was scared of." Whatever we fear, we must move toward. Not only is this defeating that specific issue head on, but we broaden our ability to be resilient in other avenues too.

Oprah Winfrey

"Be thankful for what you have; you'll end up having more. If you concentrate on what you don't have, you will never, ever have enough." - Oprah Winfrey

What a truly remarkable woman. Oprah Winfrey withstood the most crippling childhood: having been raped and molested at a young age; losing her siblings due to different circumstances, and having to deal with losing her child due to complications. In this situation, it would be very easy for most people to claim to be a victim for the rest of their lives, but she did not. Oprah wonderfully illustrates how we can turn our "wounds into wisdom." Fortunately, she demonstrated incredible perseverance and dedication to become the most inspirational talk show host. She took responsibility for her situation, and refused to allow her painful story to dictate the rest of her journey. She had every reason to fail, and live a despondent life, but she knew that she could give and be more. Think about your story. How can you use the good and bad experiences of your past to propel you into prosperity? There can be no excuses. It is not easy to become successful, but it is more painful to live a lackluster life.

Chapter 6 - Leadership

"A leader is best when people barely know he exists...when his work is done, his aim fulfilled, they will all say: We did it ourselves." – Lao-Tzu

Leadership is such a massive section within this book because it crosses over into all three areas: feeling powerful, feeling happy and feeling successful. Leadership is all about being able to influence ourselves, and then being able to influence others. True leaders are able to influence people so profoundly that employees, family or friends will always set high standards for themselves even when the leader is not physically there with them. If the leader is not at work, then the employee will still arrive early, put in a shift, behave professionally and they will feel empowered to do their job brilliantly. If the leader is not with their friends, then his or her friends will still speak highly of the leader when the leader is not around; they have the leader's back, and will defend the leader if another person does not speak well of him or her. If the leader is not with his or her child, then the child will do the right thing and will avoid rebelling and doing scandalous things because the child values himself or herself and wants to represent the family well.

Leaders and winners always find a way to get the job done! So how does the brain work when tackling something challenging or arduous such as completing a project at work, writing a book, completing a painting, preparing for a presentation, persevering with a partner, preparing for a competitive event etc.? We tend to go through the same sort of cycle when doing things that are taxing and tough: potentially we usually start things well (because of our enthusiasm, and the novelty of what is being done), and then we reach a moment where it suddenly becomes really hard (mostly because something dawns on us that we did not expect, or something was harder than we thought it would be); during this moment, we start to question the activity, and ourselves, more: "I don't know if I have enough time to finish this today," "There are too many stages to this, and I may need something new in order to finish this, which could take a while." The interesting thing is that if we somehow manage to be resilient in these moments (by calming ourselves down; mustering enough mental and physical energy to continue and so on), then we will notice that the 'hardest part' (especially nearer the end of the hardest part) suddenly becomes a lot easier, and we end up finishing the task sooner than we thought. There are many aspects that make a great leader, which will now be explored.

"People who are truly strong lift others up. People who are truly powerful bring others together." – Michelle Obama

1. Responsibility

"You cannot escape the responsibility of tomorrow by evading it today." – Abraham Lincoln

Leaders always take responsibility whether things are going well or badly or whether they win or lose. Leaders never claim to be the helpless victim. Leaders always have options and choices because they are versatile and manage to create a new way if their prepared notions are not going according to plan. The person who refuses to take responsibility will suffer from the 'victim syndrome.' We are powerful human beings who always manage to manifest the energy within ourselves to step up whether we feel like it or not. We must believe that we are responsible for our actions and our destiny.

Once we take responsibility for our actions, behaviours, routines and reactions, then we begin to make personal improvements. Leaders know that they always have a choice. We choose where we direct our energy and focus. When we take responsibility, we feel empowered and in control. The externals should never dictate our intrinsic beliefs, and the way we should live our lives. External things are never to blame for our situations as we must be strong enough to dictate our own journeys. When we blame externals, we communicate that we are not in charge, and other people and events can dictate our life's journey. This is a destructive and pessimistic viewpoint. Resist the decadent urge to blame society, politics, our spouse, siblings or friends. This is taking the easy way out. Nothing worth living for is easy. We must be intrinsically impregnable, and always look inward rather than outward if something does not go our way.

2. Decision-Making

"Inability to make decisions is one of the principle reasons executives fail. Deficiency in decision-making ranks much higher than lack of specific knowledge or technical know-how as an indicator of leadership failure." – John C. Maxwell

The more quickly we follow our intuition when deciding upon something, the more efficiently and clearly our brains will operate. The more we hesitate, the more uncertain we become in other areas. The more we question something, the weaker it becomes. If we want to develop this ability, then, as with everything, we must start small. When making small-scale decisions, such as what to eat today, or what to wear, we must condition ourselves to make the decision immediately. People overthink and spend way too much time contemplating things that are insignificant. We also teach the brain to never be assertive and decisive whenever we do this. They psych themselves out. They prevent any opportunity to experience flow, which is all about minimising our conscious mind, and allowing our unconscious qualities and mechanics to come out magnificently.

Intuition should surmount overthinking. Our intuition is our gut feeling, which involves our subconscious perceptions. Follow this every single time. A general rule of thumb is to make up our minds within ten seconds, regardless of how monumental the decision. Leaders are decisive, and we want to lead our lives with confidence. Yes, it can be beneficial to write down the pros and cons of our options, but people are capable of making quality decisions rapidly. It just takes practice and conditioning. Here are some things to practice before embarking on bigger decisions: what do you want to eat for breakfast tomorrow? Decide in ten seconds. How much fat do you want to lose by December? Decide in ten seconds. What outfit do you want to wear for your next night out? Decide in ten seconds. Power comes from being certain and decisive.

3. Goal Setting

"If you don't design your own life plan, chances are you'll fall into someone else's plan. And guess what they have planned for you? Not much." - Jim Rohn

We must know where we want to go in life. If we do not know where we are heading, then how will we get there? How will we know if we are on track? We could spend all our time labouring and gathering resources for the journey, but if the destination is right next to us then what was the point? We must write out our long-term goals, and break them down into smaller, actionable, simpler steps that make our quality goals appear more easily surmountable. What will we need to learn to get the next promotion? What social networking might we need to do to increase our client base? How much money do we need to save if planning on having X amount of children?

It is absolutely crucial to set goals for ourselves (short-term, medium-term and long-term goals) because they will keep us focused and disciplined. We live in a world where we are bombarded with so much information that it is hard to stay focused on absolutely anything for a sustained period of time, let alone something every day. We are so accustomed to incessantly checking our phones, and having our immediate attention taken by various marketing tools, that we can get lost in a world of other people's wants, and, thus, we lose focus on the things that we want! We need to have a result in mind; most importantly we need to know *why* we want to achieve something, and we need an action plan to ensure that we get it for a specific date (whether it is our best creation or not).

"A goal is a dream with a deadline." - Napoleon Hill

We are more likely to achieve what we want if we focus on it and remain driven. We want to make it habitual. We will want to write out our goals daily or at the very least weekly. Be as specific as possible when setting goals. What makes a goal more powerful? Firstly, we can phrase it positively by using the strong, modal verb, 'will.' Secondly, we must outline the specific things that we want. Thirdly, we have to set a deadline for this goal, which makes us more accountable as we know things will have to happen (taking action in different ways) for us to achieve this goal. It can be even more powerful to phrase this as though it is already happening. Assuming that we already have what we want can subconsciously trick our minds into thinking that it is already there. We attract what we truly believe in.

We should have at least three important goals in our lives. It could be our health, relationships and wealth for example. What do we do every day to transform these wishes into our reality? We should remind ourselves of our goals daily, and feel grateful for the opportunity to pursue them. Little things combined result in the accomplishment of monumental things. What ways of thinking and actions can we introduce today to achieve our goals, desires and dreams? If we believe our destiny is to create a gigantic business that provides great satisfaction to millions of clients whilst attracting exponential lucrative gains, then what can we do today to bring ourselves a step closer to this vision? Whom could we converse with to inspire or provide essential knowledge? What research could we conduct about our business? What seminars could we attend? Why not sign up to it today? What books, from people who have achieved in this field, could we read? Who are our role models in this field? How can we learn about their aptitudes and experiences as a way of motivating and modelling?

If one of our goals is to create a loving and harmonious relationship with our spouse, lover, child or parent, then what can we do today to surprise them? It could be a spontaneous message. It could simply be the way we hug them. We could research something that they love and hold dearly to convey our understanding of them. If we are not improving something, its strength will decline and weaken day by day. Routines that are outdated need to be reexamined. Exciting and thrilling our partners will restore lost, suppressed feelings, and rekindle what once was. Inadequate attention to their thoughts and feelings over time will weaken our bonds. Treat our partners as though we have just fallen in love with them. It does not matter if we have been in a relationship with them for a few years or several decades. Every fire can be reignited. What was once passionate can be passionate again. What was once alive can exist again. We cannot measure love, yet we can take action to enhance the fire that keeps it eternal.

If we want to, or need to, improve our health, then what could we do today to support our energy and longevity? The Internet provides great copious information as it relates to health and fitness. What grocery stores do you go to? What is your standard shopping list? What is stored inside your fridge? How active are you every week? Sometimes we just need to stop reflecting and just do. Nothing is holding us back. We do not need all of the latest gym equipment or health shakes. All we need to do is invest in our health in order to do what is necessary. We should invest our time, energy and resources into our health. Without our health, everything else is meaningless and can capitulate as a result.

If we want to improve our wealth, then what can we do today to gain a better understating of the different forms or active and passive income available to us? Who would be a great mentor for us? How can we improve efficiency within our business? What does the stock market look like at the moment? Is it a good time to buy or sell? How can you profit from your passion? Wealth creation requires a great deal of action and experience. Timing is crucial. There are so many different tools available to us, and yes we need a diversified portfolio, but when is it the best time to purchase commodities, stocks, property, bonds etc.? Continuously learn about different investments, attend courses, and surround yourself with like-minded people.

Always have another goal in place, and that you are already working towards, just before you achieve your original goal in order to sustain your drive. It keeps your momentum going when you accomplish your original goal. This means beginning a new project before the current one is even finished. If you get promoted, begin learning the skillset for the position above what you just received the promotion for. This does not mean you should not celebrate where you are now, but already have the motions set in place for the next step. You should always be content and happy with where you are, but it is highly beneficial to know your next endeavour. Move towards your blueprint with intensity, and refuse to allow anything to compromise its cultivation.

Everything in life is connected. Our lifestyle is a reflection of our beliefs. Our lifestyle determines our path: if we eat garbage, see our friends for too long, do too many things that are urgent but unimportant, then it is clear that it will take us a long time to accomplish a goal let alone many goals. If we want to accelerate the process, then we must become more productive, judicious and disciplined every single day. Whatever we think about manifests into our lives (but only if action is taken). We find what we look for. Unfortunately, people have conditioned themselves to either look for the wrong things or wander around looking for anything. Have you ever bought a car, and then all of a sudden you saw that car seemingly everywhere? We attract what we focus on. Therefore, we must do our utmost to remain focused on things that support us. Those who wander and meander through life are the ones who fall into other people's plans; they are the ones who get sidetracked, caught up in petty squabbles and drama. Good things may show up, but will we be opportunistic enough to take advantage of them? Will we react flexibly, and with clarity in thought and movement? There are openings and opportunities around us every day, but we must have the mental clarity to conceive them.

Visualisation

"A picture is worth a thousand words." – Napoleon Hill

Visualisation can be a magnificent tool. Some people say they are not creative, but this just means that they have limiting beliefs regarding their imagination. We have to be able to imagine getting what we want. If we can visualise things in our minds, then they can be manifested into reality. One must be able to visualise, and believe in the possibility of such a thing coming true. Without conceiving the possibility, our thoughts, feeling and actions will never work congruently to achieve our desires. NLP (Neuro-linguistic programming) cofounders,

Richard Bandler and John Grinder, teach how to visualise in the most potent of ways, so please look into their work. Some sub-modalities of visualisation involve making the picture we want to materialise brighter and clearer, viewing it as though it is right in front of us (seen through your eyes) with movement and sound as opposed to seeing it within a 'frame' like the kind of frame around a portrait.

These strong sub-modalities will serve to motivate us further, as the mind finds it hard to distinguish between what is real and what is imagined. If you imagine it vividly enough and often enough, then the mind will act as though it is already here, and so we will act in ways that will naturally create such beautiful things. We must be able to imagine its success, and use the techniques of NLP along with incantations to drive it into the subconscious. However, to materialise this desire, we must follow our intuition, and take action quickly rather than delaying or hesitating. The ability to imagine oneself being successful at something is crucial. It can be challenging to distinguish dreams from reality at times; therefore, being able to imagine success signals to the brain that it can be achieved. The brain is unable to distinguish the difference between something that is visually constructed and that which is a real visual moment. We can, therefore, use this to our advantage by playing them out more favourably in our minds. Nothing exists in reality unless it was once imagined. Life has a very interesting way of bringing things into our lives if we know exactly what it is we want, and, of course, if we take massive pertinent action.

"Imagination is more important than knowledge." – Albert Einstein

Imagination can be more profound than knowledge as it relates to bringing our goals into realisation. Our imagination holds incredible power, yet many people do not take the time to visualise what they want in their lives. They fail to coerce their own mind into conceiving a promising future. Why? It is deemed unconventional, outlandish and thus weird. I do not know about you, but I would rather be bizarre and happy rather than normal and depressed. This visual impetus can help in creating a shift; it creates the possibility of a compelling future, and gives us the motivation to take pertinent actions to manifest the life we want. Visualisation and affirmations alone will not magically gift us the life that we want. However, it can begin to set positive outcomes in motion. Visualisation develops the confidence required to continue taking action even when things might not be going according to plan, or if things still seem so far away. As William Blake once proclaimed, "What is now proved was once only imagined." Therefore, we may never have the life we want if we have never imagined its possibility in meticulous, vivid detail. We can only create what we can imagine. We give life to what we imagine. Moreover, what we think about before and after sleep is pivotal as these ideas accentuate and perpetuate our beliefs. What we read, study or visualise before and after sleep become more deeply embedded within our long-term memory and subconscious.

"What is now proved was once only imagined." – William Blake

4. Daily Routines

"The secret of your future is hidden in your daily routine." – Mike Murdock

We empower ourselves by incorporating uplifting and inspiring daily routines and habits. Consider your daily schedule. Which of these habits drain you, and which of these, even though it requires energy, actually creates more energy and enthusiasm? Establish supportive morning and bedtime routines as it will make you feel in control of your thoughts, emotions and actions throughout the day. Look to supplant your more unhelpful habits with those that add to the quality of your life. Start and finish the day in control. Begin the day with momentum. Please read, *Miracle Morning* by Hal Elrod. Each day should begin with a morning routine. Now, let us look at what creates a fantastic start to the day. The way we start something sets a precedent for the rest of the day. Upon waking, we should get out of bed within five seconds. No snoozing, no excuses, no playing about on your phone. Get up, drink a big glass of water, brush your teeth, wash your face, and then begin the following activities: silence (meditation or deep breathing to provide clarity); affirmations (self-talk); write down what you want to achieve (short-term, medium-term, long-term goals); visualisation (imagine what you want in your life); exercise (it reduces stress, boosts energy and ensures mental sharpness); reading (study things that are important to you); write (this can be notes, writing up a to-do-list, writing in your journal, writing a book, writing down what you are grateful for in your life etc.) Take the first two hours of your day very seriously. You will notice that you become so much more productive.

Moreover, establish a quality nighttime routine. Not only is it really good for you health wise, but it makes us feel more in control of our day: our thoughts, emotions and actions. Finishing the day with a nice routine prepares the mind for a restful sleep. It also builds consistency and trust within you. So what is a great nighttime routine? Start with a shower (preferably alternating with hot and cold water), and apply a quality shower gel to nourish your skin and thus your mind. Then apply a nutrient-dense lotion all over the body. Next, apply a nighttime face moisturiser. After that, brush your teeth thoughtfully. Subsequently, plan the tasks and short-term goals for the following day as this enables you to start the next day with clarity and direction. You may even mull over these tasks whilst you sleep! The penultimate thing you may wish to do is read over anything imperative that you need to memorise or remember. Before you get into bed, you may want to take essential supplements such as vitamin D3, magnesium and fish oils, so that they provide your body with key nutrients whilst you sleep and recover. You may even want to sip apple cider vinegar as it is healthy and supports quality sleep. There we have it. A brilliant start and end to a productive day. It ends with you feeling physically and mentally stronger. This will create the kind of discipline and power needed to go for what you want. Improve the quality of your overall life, and watch the beautiful things open up to you in a plethora of ways. Something tells me you will be sleeping even better now.

We must use our time effectively. We should understand when our brain and body work best during the day, and dedicate that time to complete the most meaningful tasks. Whatever takes precedence needs to be given the right time and thus energy. For example, if you are a morning person, then set aside the pertinent time required in the morning to get these most difficult and challenging tasks done, and vice versa. Attack these tasks when one has most energy and enthusiasm.

"Think in the morning. Act in the noon. Eat in the evening. Sleep in the night." – William Blake

5. Building Rapport

"Rapport is the ability to enter someone else's world, to make him feel that you understand him, that you have a strong common bond" – Tony Robbins

All leaders, not managers, are likeable and capable of winning many people over. They pay attention to details, they value their employees' opinions, and they do their best to empower others. Leaders know the importance of growing leaders, and they know the importance of creating a talented team. Leaders understand that they cannot do everything on their own, and so they delegate important tasks to develop those within their organisation, family or peers. Leaders know that quality communication is compulsory in order to get the most out of their team. They listen to others, and show, by their actions, that they have listened to their team.

Leaders do not micromanage. They model quality behaviours, empower others, and step back to watch their teammates develop whilst stepping in only if appropriate. As leaders, we must believe in our vision and ourselves if we are to get others to buy into our vision and us. Trust is mandatory if others are to allow themselves to be influenced by us. If we do not trust anyone, then we do not trust ourselves. If we do not trust anyone, then we are untrustworthy. If we do not respect anyone, then we do not respect ourselves. If we do not respect anyone, then we are unworthy of respect.

Before we can influence someone, we first need to build rapport. In many ways, our overall happiness is down to the quality of rapport built with people, and subsequently to what degree we can influence them. We need these skills everywhere: to influence our partners, to influence our children, to influence our peers and friends, to influence our colleagues or employees etc. Building rapport can be improved in a multitude of ways. We can develop rapport by showing that we share similar interests and passions with others. We can develop rapport by showcasing excellent speaking and listening skills. We can develop rapport by mirroring the body language, gestures, vocabulary, tonality and even breathing of others. We can develop rapport by showing that we care about the wellbeing and happiness of others. Interestingly, people are stronger and more united when they have a common enemy or problem. Countries can be brought closer together by having a shared enemy; families can be brought closer together by having a shared enemy. Why not attack a problem that you both want to overcome and share a more connected and united existence?

6. Prioritise

"The key is not to prioritize what's on your schedule, but to schedule your priorities." – Stephen Covey

Whilst it is important to build upon our successes, we should always have one thing that takes precedence, for a certain period of time, because this is how we master a skill. Alternate when to prioritise different things. This is when timing is crucial. Know when to put marketing first; know when to put exercise and healthy eating first; know when to put your investments first. Also, know what to always keep as a secondary focus point: something that is beneficial, but should never be a priority. Our hobbies and interests are secondary. Our family, health and finances are primary focus areas.

Do what is important first, and not what is urgent. If urgent things pop up frequently, then we are probably being too reactive and not proactive enough. We must be able to anticipate what issues might come up, and have time and systems set up to deal with its apparition. Things that are important are usually long-term activities. Things that are urgent and that do not hold great significance are short-term things that take up our present moments. Aim not to give substantial time to what is urgent. There is a massive difference between what is important and what is urgent. We can greatly reduce what is urgent by being more proactive. When we think about something, consider the next two or five steps needed; think of it like playing a chess match. Anticipate any issues that may pop up within our relationships, business interests etc. It is very easy to be distracted by what is urgent, but if we have a schedule, then we can still focus a lot of our time on the things that are important, so that urgent matters never drastically ruin our priorities. We must know when we are most productive during the day (when we have most energy), whether in the morning, during the day or at night, and we must consistently dedicate this time to what is important. If we give our best to things that are only urgent, then it will take us much longer to accomplish our long-term goals.

Make time every single day for your priorities.

People get stressed because of an accumulation of things. When we allow ourselves to be overwhelmed, we end up not doing anything at all. This is when the mind wanders, and this is when we procrastinate. What is the worst part? Many people are so busy doing things that they do not want to do, that they spend little time on things that mean a lot to them. They have not taken care of themselves first, and are putting other people's needs above their own, which indicates a lack of self-esteem. This results in long-term insufficient fulfillment. However, some people use it as an excuse to not do more meaningful things because of some form of fear. Others get stressed and indignant as a result of never completing what they really want, and thus never feel fully actualised. This is also why many do not achieve what Maslow calls self-actualisation. We simply cannot experience the blissful state of self-actualisation if we have not fulfilled the preceding human needs first…

Firstly, let us focus on our physiological needs. Yes, we all understand that we need to stay warm, sheltered, fed, rested and so on. Unfortunately, business oriented and stressed individuals often neglect this basic stage because they are so obsessed with the later stages. Regrettably, this is unsustainable in the long-term. We need to develop and embed regular patterns for these basic needs, so that we do not have to think about them, and thus detract focus from more meaningful things: we must have regular sleeping patterns; we must have specific eating schedules, and preferably certain, simple, repetitive meals in place (unless others cook for us) and so on.

Secondly, we all need to feel safe. Whilst this stage can refer to physical safety (and this is true), we must appropriately interpret this stage as referring to our mindset. Do you feel in control of your life? Do you feel stable? Do you feel like you are certain about what your future will be like? Once we feel mentally and physically safe, we can then look outward. Consider your limiting beliefs and where they developed. We will want to address them at this stage healthily if we are to progress onto the other stages more effectively and robustly.

Thirdly, we all have the desire to feel loved or at least connected to others. Our inner chimp (our primitive brain) will never allow us to be self-actualised unless we feel part of a troop. Many people are too nice, and they feel as though everyone in society should be part of our troop. This is ignorantly perilous. There are only a few people who should form part of our troop (our closest family members and friends). These are the only people who we should want to impress because these are the people who realistically give us, or should give us, unconditional love. We should care much less about what others think about us however. Our loved ones support us, motivate us, and, therefore, we have the desire to excel financially and in our careers. Consider the people you would trust with all your money. Consider the people with whom you would risk your life for. These are the people who are part of your inner circle. Choosing unwisely can lead to a lot of pain, trauma and thus psychological problems.

Fourthly, we have esteem needs. Once we feel appreciated and loved, then we are able to thrive and feel significant. This need is all about flourishing. We have the foundations in place: we feel physically and mentally strong and safe. We know that we are loved, and people are there to catch us if we fall, and so we have the inner strength to really go for what we want. We look to become the master in our given field at this point. We want to prove ourselves to the world. We want to feel significant. We turn our attention to what completes, inspires and drives us on our journey to freedom.

Fifthly, we have finally arrived. This is the pinnacle. This is where we should all want to be. We now shift from being obsessed and preoccupied with ourselves, and we now think about giving to others. Firstly, we wish to help and love our troop. We then desire to positively affect as many people as we can. This can be in the form of giving products and services for free, or being philanthropic, or supporting others who have great altruistic intentions. Not everyone makes it to this stage, but this is the stage that contains the most peace and satisfaction. This is the stage where we feel as though it is not about us anymore. We have accumulated all the toys and material goods we always wanted. This is where we get bored of all our material luxuries, and we look for greater meaning and depth in our later years.

Let us perceive Maslow's hierarchy of needs as a kind of force field around us. It is really all about the quality and quantity of energy we have and share. When we are working on our basic needs (physiological and safety), our energies, our bubbles if you will, are only within us. We are unstable, insecure, vulnerable, and thus we cannot support anyone or anything else. When we move onto our psychological needs (the love and esteem areas) our 'bubbles' become bigger, and our energies shift to our friends, family and those who benefit in terms of clients, colleagues and employees. At the self-fulfillment stage, we are so strong and successful that we now give for the sake of giving, and our bubble is unlimited. We no longer focus on ourselves, and our main drive is to change communities, countries or maybe even the world.

Chapter 7 – Peak Performance

"Empty your mind, be formless. Shapeless, like water." – Bruce Lee

Regardless of what we do for a living, ensuring that we perform at our best when it really matters is vital if we are to lead successful lives. Whether we are athletes, artists, business professionals and so on, the ability to instantly change our state, so that we can perform at our highest potential consistently will ascertain not only how well we do, but how much we enjoy these activities. Underachieving is never about not being enough, it is about not being resourceful enough. Have you ever been in a poor state where you could not perform basic things that you would often do effortlessly? Of course you have. This is because of the poor state you were in at the time. Being in an unhelpful state does not allow your brain, body and energy to apply everything it knows. Fortunately, we can access this state if we know how it works, and if we know what we can do to perform at our best.

Flow

"Flow is being completely involved in an activity for its own sake. The ego falls away. Time flies. Every action, movement, and thought follows inevitably from the previous one, like playing jazz." – Mihaly Csikszentmihalyi

Firstly, please read, *Flow* by Mihaly Csikszentmihalyi, as it brilliantly breaks down the constituents that enable the state known as flow. Let us explore the diverse elements that must occur for us to experience flow, and, thus, enjoy things to the maximum (not only significant activities such as creating, performing and presenting).

Experiencing flow occurs when we are so immersed in what we are doing that nothing else matters or disturbs our thought. This hyperbolic phrase emphasises the type of focus, drive and clarity necessary to achieve flow. In these moments, we do not allow any intrusions to deter our thoughts, feelings and actions. We are so in tune with the present moment that we are unable to question ourselves. During this experience, it is common for people to view themselves from outside of the box, and to think of the bigger picture, our roles in this universe, who feels our energy vibrations and how this might this transcend into other people's relationships. When people are performing at their best, and when they are experiencing flow, they explain the experience as though it is not them who is doing it. They feel as though they are watching themselves, almost like they are playing a computer game.

The less you think, the better you perform.

The subconscious is in full swing whenever we experience a state of flow. Our conscious can often get in the way even though it is only trying to protect us sometimes. If we master a skill, then whenever we perform this skill, we will want to remove our conscious thinking as much as possible. The removal of our conscious thoughts will enable flow. During flow, there is no thought; there is only fluid action. To experience flow, we must be so competent and focused on something that we are in a positive trance. We enter a hypnotic state when we experience flow. This is when the subconscious is allowed to run the show, and our habitual skills are capable of flourishing. We lose this extraordinary experience when we begin thinking about what we are doing.

Internal talk must cease. Even positive self-talk does not help as much when wanting to access flow. Any hesitation of thought, and the moment of magic becomes lost in translation. A frail, older woman was able to lift a car to save her child who was caught under the wheel. How? There was no thought. Her subconscious took control in its most instinctive way. If there was a moment where her conscious intervened and took hold of this circumstance, then that child may not have survived. If for a moment she thought, "There's no way I can lift this car," or "I cannot save my son," then she would have fatally faltered. Pure love and focus dictated action and belief. She refused to allow any externality to prevent such heroism. In moments of success, we do not need to think; we do not need to *try* or force anything. We just allow ourselves to let go, because we trust ourselves enough to let go in these moments, and we will naturally know what to say or how to move. To experience flow, we cannot think things through; we must simply allow the mind and body to do what come naturally.

Flow is all about achieving the perfect harmony between our subconscious mind and body. If our mind is truly relaxed, totally clear, then we will achieve flow more easily. This is why yoga, mediation, and conditioning the mind to be free of thought, or close to, will result in operating fluidly and smoothly. It is like driving a car on a bumpy road: we can never really relax if we have to be aware of all of the bumps in the road. These bumps are our thoughts intruding upon our mental clarity, and, thus, our ability to access flow. Every thought and action flows interchangeably. There is no room for doubt or hesitation if we want to access our best state: flow. The more we simplify our lives, the more mental clarity we have, and the more clarity and peace we have, the more readily we can access flow. Flow inducing activities must be appropriately challenging in order to demand complete focus. It must not be overly familiar (too easy), and it must not be overly novel (too hard). This is why we must build up the level of complexity and challenge gradually, so that we stay within flow.

In order to access flow, we must be able to hypnotise ourselves. We are still aware of things, but it is the difference between being the person who is playing the computer game (being detached and in flow), or being the character in the game (too close to the action and unable to experience flow as thoughts and emotions intrude too much). Think and do as you would when you experience these positive and empowering states. We are most confident when we feel like we can be ourselves. Utmost confidence is displayed when people experience flow, as they do not allow any hesitation or self-consciousness to disenable their aptitude. We can relax, and literally allow the actions to unfold in front of us. We must do what feels natural to us in that moment.

Peak State

"It's not knowing what to do; it's doing what you know." – Tony Robbins

Our state is determined by our internal representations such as what we focus on and our physiology. We want to project ourselves confidently, not necessarily to others, but as a way of evoking our most helpful thoughts and emotions. Our physiology and gestures can teach the mind how we want it to think and feel because the subconscious knows what body language and gestures we use when feeling sad, or angry, or motivated or confident etc. This not only refers to physical appearance, but also how we carry ourselves. How do we walk? Is our head always high and looking into the distance, or do we look to the floor (accessing our emotions and feelings more) and look narrowly (not taking in the things nearer the sides of our eyes' vision that is still observable)? Is our body language closed off, arms folded, covering our core (heart, and main organs) with your arms or an object? Our physiology shapes our thoughts and feelings. When we look down, we access our emotions and thoughts.

Looking above eye level allows us to access the imagination where we can be more open, flexible and creative.

To break a state, we need to interrupt the pattern. One aspect of excelling in an activity is to change our state and experience as quickly as we can when we feel fear, anxiety, stress or psychic entropy encroaching insidiously. How quickly can we change this experience? Immediately. We can change how we think and feel instantly. Breaking the pattern means doing something that is totally unexpected, not the norm for us, as a way of breaking the chain of events that result in an unhelpful state. All we have to do is change what we focus on and how you interpret the immediate experience.

What we focus on is massively important when determining how well we perform an activity. We must have one sole thing or purpose in mind if we are to perform it magnificently. We cannot be thinking about what we will be doing later that day, or what time our favourite show is on, or what other people may be thinking of us. We must be so focused and so immersed in the immediate experience that it is as though nothing else matters. It is just you and the activity (the audience, our peers, even the opponent does not matter). We must be focused on what we want to achieve throughout the experience, and move naturally in order to achieve it.

Incantations and Anchoring

"NOW I AM THE VOICE. I WILL LEAD NOT FOLLOW. I WILL BELIEVE, NOT DOUBT. I WILL CREATE, NOT DESTROY. I AM A FORCE FOR GOOD. I AM A FORCE FOR GOD. I AM A LEADER. DEFY THE ODDS. SET A NEW STANDARD. STEP UP!" - Tony Robbins

We must be able to use affirmations (repeating an idea or belief to get a certain result) and incantations (using our physical movements and gestures along with saying these ideas or beliefs intensely to get a certain result) whenever we want to create a powerful state. We must embed powerful sayings within us that we turn to such as, "I am stronger than this," or "I know this trick, and I will stay on the right path," or "I am in charge." Have a select few statements that you can memorise and use whenever you feel that you must change your state.

Incantations are extremely powerful in generating the level of focus, intensity and peak states that we require. We can condition ourselves (anchoring) to feel a certain way immediately because of what we associate mentally and emotionally to a physical action. If we repetitiously say something powerful intensely enough whilst we carry out the same physical action, then we can learn to trigger an automatic response (an anchor) at will. This tool is invaluable. It will keep you on track in moments of uncertainty and poor-quality states. It can trigger positivity and power within, so that we consistently make the right choices.

We can condition ourselves to access powerful, uplifting and supportive states. What can you do as your action? It depends on what you want to feel. Do you want to feel calmer? Do you want to feel stronger? Do you want to feel passionate? What do you do whenever you win at something, or whenever you want to get your focus back on track? Do you click your fingers? Do you smack your chest? Do you make a fist and shout "yes?" Do you smile and laugh? Do you pray? Your action can actually be far less obvious especially if it is inappropriate to do some of these actions in the workplace for instance! For example, you can just hold your right wrist with your left hand more tightly, or you can covertly just tug on your ear. If you have chosen a rather active move, then you can always perform this in your office or in the restroom etc. Decide on your action now.

Consider what you want to say to yourself when doing this maneuver. Keep it short, concise, use emotive words and include an "I am" that is positively phrased. For example, "I am ready to deliver at the highest level," or "I am ready to give myself to you Lord/Allah to do what I must with all my strength," or "I am a winner," or "I am deserving of any and all magnificent things that are about to happen." It is also worth considering your breathing in these states. How do you want to breathe? This goes back to what state you want to create. If you want to feel passionate and intense, then take fast and ferocious breaths. If you want to remain calm, then take deep inhales and even deeper exhales. Additionally, here are some other variables to consider: Where do you look, and how do you look? What are you thinking about when in these states? Do you think more or less? What kind of voice are you hearing in your head during these moments? Is it loud and powerful or clear and calm? What are your internal representations?

Lastly, we may even want to visualise either how we want to look or be. We can also remember past experiences where we did things brilliantly or when we were proud of our accomplishments. Once we have chosen a specific action (anchor), saying (affirmation) and visualisation, then we must practice it over and over again until the pattern is engrained within us. Whenever we perform it, however, we must do so with absolute belief and commitment. Really go for it. This creates the kind of energy and fortitude to really communicate things to yourself, and thus others, with the enthusiasm, passion and determination we need.

Physiology

"We convince by our presence, and to convince others we need to convince ourselves." – Amy Cuddy

Our mind and body will go into the mode it has been conditioned and attuned to go into. We can change our physiology, and the way we talk to ourselves to recondition our automatic response and patterns. We can only change a behaviour best once in the moment of that experience. For instance, if we want to communicate an idea most passionately when presenting in front of a group, then yes we can rehearse out of the actual context, but the actual transformation, and the internal changes, will happen most potently when in the actual experience: when presenting.

Our thoughts influence our physiology, but it is conceivable that changing your physiology can enhance or detract from quality states of mind. We can cultivate the physical life we want with our minds. Why does my hair not look great today when I made it look great yesterday? Why did I look great in the mirror last night, but terrible this morning? Much of this really comes down to our state of mind in that specific moment. Is it possible that what we say to ourselves when we look in the mirror can change our physical appearance over time? It can certainly begin the process. We should be very careful what we say and communicate to ourselves about ourselves! Interestingly, when we look down, we access our emotions and inner thoughts. When we look up, we imagine and visualise things. Therefore, if we are unhappy with what we are thinking, then we simply need to lift our chin and look above eye level and vice versa.

Breathe

"If you want to conquer the anxiety of life, live in the moment, live in the breath." – Amit Ray

Starting your day with conscious breathing enables you to take control of the day. We set the tone for the rest of the day. By starting the day controlling our inner workings, our breathing in this instance, then we teach the mind that we will be in control of ourselves no matter what unfolds during the day. Conscious breathing teaches us to be in the present moment. We can change our breathing patterns whenever we feel like we crave something unhealthy. It can change our state, allowing us to stay calm and emotionally detached from making unhelpful choices.

It may sound rather simplistic, but breathing is a fundamental component that cannot be overlooked. We can change our states and thoughts by manipulating our breathing. Breathing in different tempos, exertions, rhythms, and so on, can drastically change our states. In terms of forming a more serene and tranquil state, we will want to breath in for at least four seconds, through the stomach and not the chest, and then hold our breath for at least six seconds, and then we will want to exhale for at least eight seconds. You can build our tolerance over time, so there is no need to push yourself and make yourself uncomfortable. This form of breathing improves clarity, and relaxes us, enabling us to put things into perspective: not taking things too seriously as we see them for what they really are, which is a small problem in comparison to much larger concerns.

Breathing and cold therapy expert, Wim Hof, teaches a similar deep breathing method that is even more intense and profound. When lying down, with your back against the bed, simply practice breathing in and taking in as much oxygen as you possibly can. Even when you think you have breathed in as much as you can, then you can still take in some more gulps of air through your mouth and nose until you have fully maximised the space within. We will feel like a balloon that has be blown up to the maximum at this stage. Once we have done this, then we can begin to exhale, but we should only exhale the usual amount (not as though we are trying to drain every bit of oxygen out of our bodies). We should do this ten times, and then that is a breathing set completed. Complete as many sets as you wish.

Whilst we can inhale and exhale deeply to relax us, we can also inhale and exhale more quickly and profusely, thereby dramatically changing our state and energy levels due to the high amount of oxygen being pumped in and the carbon dioxide being pushed out. This rapid form of breathing changes the body's and mind's rhythm and circulation. Also, it can be a great way of eliminating toxins within the body. This form of breathing can dramatically alter our states, and make us feel light headed, so be cautious and refrain from breathing like this when working with machinery or when driving etc.

The fitter we are, the more slowly we tend to breathe when resting generally, and the more slowly we breathe, the more relaxed we feel. Fitter individuals therefore feel more relaxed when doing their usual day-to-day tasks. Think about what this does to our stress levels and daily energy. Unhealthier individuals tend to breathe more fiercely and loudly when in more relaxed states (like they are struggling almost), which is a clear indicator that their lungs are not operating as efficiently as they could. Fitness levels are linked to calmness. Consider the following questions: How do you usually breathe? How do you breathe when you are totally confident and feeling powerful? How do you breathe when apprehensive? How do you breathe when you are with a good friend? How do you breathe when you read? Learn to be more conscious of your breathing throughout the day, as a way of manipulating your states and stress levels.

Breathing is so significant that we can actually develop more rapport with someone by harnessing the power of breathing harmoniously with that person. If we match our breathing with others when interacting, then it can function to build greater rapport. Observe how and when the person's shoulders, chest or stomach rises and falls when breathing. It can be tremendously powerful if we adopt the person's breathing pattern. People can feel absolutely connected to us when we breathe in the same rhythm as them. When people talk, they are slowly exhaling, and so we can exhale slowly also when another person is talking to us, if we wish be to be harmonious with them. We should notice our breathing patterns when around different people. Always remember to breathe deeply. Many people tend to hold their breath when they are intimidated, fearful or anxious. For example, we might hold our breath when we see someone we find extremely attractive or if we see someone we find intimidating. We might breathe more quickly when in the presence of someone we dislike. We should always pay attention to our breathing, as this will influence our physiology.

Partaking in yoga can also be very beneficial for changing how we breathe generally. When we are moving and stretching during yoga, ensure that we breathe deeply with every movement we make. If we match our breaths with our movements, then we create physical and mental synchronicity. We want our internal processes (breathing) to be congruent with our externals (movements). This keeps us aligned. It makes us feel more centred, more in control and therefore more ready to effectively deal with the day's challenges and inevitable stresses. Meditation can also be wonderful. It is a great opportunity to practice positive thinking or to clear our minds. This sets a wonderful tone for the rest of the day.

Less is More

"The less I have, the freer I am to do whatever I want to do." – Lauryn Hill

Now that we have explored what we can do during the actual moments leading up to and during important activities, we should also explore the other lifestyle changes we can make, so that we are abler to access quality states for often.

Socrates once said, "The only true wisdom is in knowing that you know nothing." We strive to know as much as we can, and we allow ourselves to be inundated with futile and lackluster thoughts and ideas. Instead, doing less can oftentimes enable us to access more. We must appreciate that we cannot actually capture or keep anything in life. It is within this humble and gracious knowing that we ironically feel most complete, and thus more open to different ways of perceiving and allowing.

The more materialistic we are, the more fake we become. The more inauthentic we are, the more pain we will endure. Being materialistic is a way of hiding; essentially it is like make-up covering our true selves and essence.

We are pressured to have the latest brands and fashions. We are pressured to be what others want us to be. The more we try to please others, the less we live for ourselves, and thus the unhappier we shall be. There is nothing wrong with enjoying the finer things in life, but they should never outweigh the qualities we have inside. Unfortunately, many people's outside is much more impressive than what is inside.

We must acknowledge that we are complete. We do not need lots of tattoos, make-up, piercings etc. to make us feel more complete. We do not *need* anyone or anything. Yes, externals can enhance us, making us feel loved and supported, but we should never need something additional. We *decide* how we think, feel and act. It is all within us. If we support a sport's team, and our team loses, does it ruin our day? If the driver on the motorway is aggressive and disrespectful, does it anger and hurt us? If a member of the opposite sex, whom we like, does not return our call or text, are we frustrated? Why do we need these? If we love and respect ourselves enough, then we do not need a thing. Unfortunately, our egos can hold us back. It keeps us rigid. Spirituality and higher thinking creates fluidity and flexibility in thought. It releases us from judging and labeling, and so we will not feel as judged and labeled in return. We will also attract people who do not judge or label as a result, thereby attracting like-minded people to support us and vice versa.

The more valuables we accumulate, the more we take away from the invisible: the spirit, soul and unconscious. Maybe, just maybe, the more we generate, the less we have of our higher self. Think of it like a seesaw. The more we have, the greedier we might become. The more we live in the physical, the less we live in the spiritual. The higher the wall we create, through materialistic paradigms, the more we drown the soul. Now this is not to say that we are malevolent, unsophisticated or less self-actualised if we would like to buy a stunning watch or suit. However, the moment we give material goods precedence over our intrinsic qualities, the more we decline in terms of character and quality. We become preoccupied with what is never ours, and we prioritise what we will one day lose. Instead, give precedence to our thoughts and feelings, as these are far more likely to live with us forever.

Establishments thrive on making citizens feel insecure, weak and setting unrealistic expectations as a way to make us buy their products and services. People buy things with emotion, and justify with logic. They make people feel like they are in desperate need, so they can profit from us. I call it the 'deficiency syndrome.' The media and societal ideologies project deficiency, foregrounding that we need this and that. It can make us feel as though we are not enough, and potentially ostracised, if we are different and do not adhere to social norms. The grass is *not* always greener.

The way we physically look is largely a result of our thoughts. The way we physically look is largely a result of what we focus on. We will creep our way into the blueprints we have for ourselves. If we believe we are unattractive, for whatever reason, we will act accordingly and make choices that support this belief: unhealthy food choices, taking drugs that make us look uglier, living an acidic lifestyle that ruins our insides and thus our outsides. Now I am not including things like surgery, enhancements, and detractions. We are referring to how our faces subtly morph over the years; obviously there is nothing we can do when we reach the life's later years. Our choices of clothing, accessories, teeth, nails, skin clarity etc. are a result of our thoughts and choices. Focus on changing the roots not the fruits.

Simplicity

"There is no greatness where there is no simplicity, goodness and truth." – Leo Tolstoy

We must look to create simplicity in our lives. Be childlike and natural. Most people have their inner child suppressed because they need to 'grow up.' They are taught in the workforce to be professional, accept things as they are and adhere to the business' cultural etiquette. We all have an inner child… it is the part within us that just wants to laugh, be expressive, say how we really feel and chase the dreams we have. Instead, most people become physically and mentally rigid. They lose the spring in their step. They become accustomed to low energy, low vibrations and mediocre relationships. Are you restricted in life? How and why? How can this be changed? Why must this be changed?

It comes down to how we were raised, and how people have conditioned us. Unless we are mindful, people can knowingly or unknowingly try to make us feel insufficient and as though we are lacking in an area. It is a weak, insecure tactic to try and wield power over us, and it works on many. This is so they get what they want by making us feel insecure, but the self-actualised human being does not care for this. The self-actualised among us are never coaxed by this game, and they are fully aware that they are in charge of how they think and feel about themselves. If we believe that we *need* anything, apart from survival reasons, then we have been influenced and manipulated. Who is it that judges adeptness and ineptitude anyway? We hold the power.

The unexpected will arrive when we are unprepared. If we have made life simple for ourselves (by deciding upon things more quickly, reducing drama, reducing how many urgent things we must do etc.), then we will be well equipped to handle wonderful or horrendous surprises that are inevitable. The issues most individuals have is that they become so self-absorbed and involved in the 'rat-race,' that they develop the 'inadequacy syndrome' or 'progression complex.' We get too drawn into the game of doing 'better' than others within our fields that we lose touch with the bigger focus: abundance in all avenues. We also lose touch with what is fundamentally important and natural: kindness, giving and acceptance. We judge and criticise ourselves, and others, based on questionable means.

Live a beautiful life by not being attached to anything. There is no need to fully belong to a specific friendship group, cult or organisation. We do not have to pick one thing and elicit hatred for anything different. We are complex and beautiful creations. We may love to read, yet love to practice martial arts. We may love to speak philosophy and psychology, yet love to listen to silly and crude stand-up comedy. We may value silence, and recognise its therapeutic effects, yet value the sharing showcased from socialising. Things are not black and white. We do not have to believe that we must choose a select few things, and label ourselves and others based on these alone. We must appreciate our diverse nature and interests. It keeps us balanced. We should love all that we do, yet become separated from such things and still be exhilarated and active. Being indefinable is a sensational feeling. We can feel emancipated to take up any activity, and feel as though we can both belong to and learn from its teachings.

There is a clear connection between our inner and outer worlds. They go hand in hand in many ways. If we want a clearer mind, then we should clear and organise our physical space whether that be our offices, our bedrooms, our homes etc. Physical clutter creates mental clutter and vice versa. Clear out what we do not need, and replace old, archaic things with newer more useful things. If we want to change our lives, then we must change our surroundings. The more we have, the more complicated and stressed our minds function. There is a reason why Steve Jobs wore the same outfit every day. Look at everything we do, and we should ask ourselves, how can we make this simpler? Simplicity brings clarity and focus. Ironically enough, the easiest options can give us the better results. Many people think that the more they acquire, the happier they will be. So they hoard what they have, and keep adding to the pile, inadvertently and unwittingly creating their future downfall. These things, thoughts or overzealous opulence, build up over time.

They limit the options available to us, and consequently derail and hinder progress. Why? Because we become so inundated with what we perceive to be good for us, but that which holds us back. We become restricted in our ability to move forward because we fear the changes and what we might lose.

Concentrate on quality over quantity. Focus on acquiring beautiful and meaningful possessions that we will use frequently as opposed to purchasing overwhelmingly copious things that clutters space and thus our minds. This is why people naturally love ceilings that are high up, and large open spaces, as they condition the mind to think more openly and abundantly. The sky is the limit. We are our private environments. Moreover, many people inundate their lives with endless, often unimportant tasks. A lack of patience, along with the consequent shorter temper, has made it harder than ever to simply sit in silence and think in solitude. This lack of being with oneself in the truest sense has led us to be tenser and disconnected. Only when the mind is silent will the muse be more likely to show. Only when the mind is quiet can we experience flow and clarity. This is necessary to develop precision, meticulous thinking, and, thus, achieve greatness. This is why a clogged up mind will choke and fail to rise to the occasion. Abstain from taking in nonsensical and futile information.

Humour me, and conceive a plastic bag as a metaphor for our minds. The more we put inside a 'bag,' the less space we have to add and progress. If we fill the bag too much, it will rip and capitulate. One of the limiting beliefs people have is that life is hard, and that complexity brings success. We could make our lives as complicated and busy as we want, but that may not lead to success in any department at all. Simplifying where possible ensures that we have the energy, instinctive brilliance and wherewithal to rise to the occasion when something truly challenging arrives. This is where simplicity creates abundance. The noisiest people, things and lives often hold the least strength and power. As the saying goes, the emptiest can makes the most noise. Claude Debussy fascinatingly expressed that, "Music is the silence between the notes." View the notes as being what our senses experience (our external world), and view the silence between the notes as being our inner world.

Chapter 8 – Energy

"Everything around is made up of energy. To attract positive things in your life, start by giving off positive energy." - Anonymous

It is wise to espouse the philosophy that everything happens for a reason. What happens to us is a culmination of the type of energy we bring forward, and the energy of other people's thoughts and feelings about us. This is why we must seek to find only good things coming into our lives. I am sure you have had moments where you randomly thought about someone with whom you used to know a long time ago, and suddenly you bumped into him or her shortly after. Perhaps our thoughts and energy crosses over for different reasons and purposes.

Sometimes the energy surrounding the materialisation of something is not aligned. Whether it is our energy, or the energies within others, the synergy overall dictates the happenstance, and it can be why we have not yet achieved something in particular. Things may or may not be in harmony with each other for that action to take place. These events, whether wonderful or undesirable, are guiding us down the path most suited for us right now. There is no right or wrong path. We certainly control our own overall destiny. We just need to steady the ship if things are not going well for many people around us. If we listen and feel enough positivity, then we can act in positive ways to get us out of pernicious predicaments. Of course we can affect the direction and experiences in our lives. However, we must view the wider picture, and not become disheartened if we are not where we currently wish to be. Energies have not been brought together yet.

"Energy is contagious, positive and negative alike. I will forever be mindful of what and who I am allowing into my space." - Alex Elle

The man who was injured in an accident eventually returns home and appreciates what he has. He kisses his wife and children, and shares a beautiful moment with them. The next day, his wife makes a donation to a charity to support others. Subsequently, the supported disabled child receives the love and care he needed to recover. That boy grows up indebted and grateful to a stranger (the wife), or strangers for their warmth and care. He then goes on to excel and one day, for some strange reason, decides to look after a man who was inured in an accident. Okay, so the story was not meant to be likely. However, I am sure you comprehend the domino effect that our actions and happenstance can have on others!

This is how we attract what happens in our lives. Another example of energy coinciding is when we are messaging someone, and he or she seems to be messaging us at the exact same time. What intangible element is at play when different human beings, in vastly different locations, think of us and reply at that precise moment? Perhaps the energy others give us is a factor involved in what we attract. The more pleasant looks we receive from the opposite sex not only increases the quality of how we think, feel and act, but sexual interest from others will increase exponentially as a result. Look after yourself, your mind and body, and the world will look after you. Despise and loath yourself, and the world will despise and loathe you. Attracting and planning nice things to happen to us are important, but there is more to it than that. We must also undertake the necessary action to accomplish our goals. We must be willing to meet the universe half way.

We all have our own individual energy force. The area we inhabit has some sort of metaphorical circle around us that exudes our energy. When we encounter someone, we are interacting with his or her energy. These vibrations can be highly contagious. Have you ever met someone, and for some weird reason you had a sense of exactly how they are for better or worse? Have you ever looked somewhere and caught someone staring at you? What was that? Your antenna was instinctively aware that someone else's gaze and focus was on you. Does it stop here? Are there other energetic fields available to access, which we simply cannot detect? There is a sort of invisible detection that we all have. Perhaps women posses this skill more inherently and greatly: they must be mindful of what kind of man is around them for safety reasons. Regardless, it is worth considering what kind of energy we have, what it attracts, and what types of people (energies) we interact with daily. Low vibrations will reduce the quality of our vibrations; high, powerful, loving vibrations can uplift and inspire our energy and vice versa. Maybe there is something to the saying, fake it until we make it. If we act as though we have everything that we desire, which we all should feel anyway, then we will be in a place to attract like-minded people who have the skills, resources and experience we can learn from.

We have looked at people's positive and negative energy, but in order to be positive, we must have great actual energy. Positive thoughts occur more often when we have great mental and physical energy; negative thoughts creep up on us when we are most tired. These moments can be greatly reduced, but, to a degree, they are also inevitable: what comes up must come down. Fortunately, we can live our lives generally with great energy, depending upon how we live and what habits we employ daily. Boredom and tiredness are intertwined, which reveals the power of being in flow as much as possible. Do you ever sometimes have strong energy, but when it dawns on you that you have to complete a laborious task, suddenly you lack that physical and mental capacity? Fortunately, we know some techniques to apply now to change our state. We also understand how our minds work better now, and so we can preempt that we will suddenly get tired when we get to our desk etc. We know how our own minds try to trick us.

"Without passion you don't have energy, and without energy you have nothing." - Donald Trump

Instead, we can use our disappointment to make ourselves even better. They can ignite our desire to get better, stronger, smarter, sexier and thus, ironically, more self-assured. Life comes down to how much fight we have in us. This is why we all love the story of the underdog who ends up winning: we know that it can be done if we just apply ourselves and believe in ourselves. If we are to fight in life, we must have enough energy to drive us through challenging moments. We die and pass on when we eventually lose the fight in this dimension. The happiest and most successful people in life are those who see abundance and opportunity everywhere. It is mightily significant to have high self-esteem. Self-esteem and confidence are different: confidence refers to knowing our ability and strengths within a given activity whereas self-esteem refers to how much love and appreciation we have for ourselves generally (whether we are doing well or 'badly' at something). We will attract the type of partner we want primarily by focusing on bettering ourselves and sending the right energy out there. How can we build self-esteem? Love how we are now. Yes, we can always get better at things, but know that we are enough just the way we are right now. Everyone is imperfect, and the more we seek perfection (unless we are humble in our pursuit), then the more imbalanced and thus disturbed we will become.

There are three priorities we should all seek to constantly improve if we are to live balanced and incredible lives. Firstly, we must prioritise our health. We must continuously look to improve our health in a multitude of ways: ensure that we sleep well; reduce stress by partaking in our favourite activities often; eat quality, nutrient-dense foods 90% of the time; drink plenty of water; consume fundamental supplements (fish oils, vitamin D, zinc and magnesium); have sex often; be active (don't always look to park closest to your destination for instance; train at least three times per week); drink or eat greens! These health rules will make us feel lighter, more energetic, and we will not incur as much mental and physical pain as we grow older. The way we eat and drink now will be felt ten years from now. Secondly, our relationships should always take precedence. It is wise to only have a small circle of people with whom we trust with anything and everything. Make time for them! Share, communicate, laugh and give as much as we can with these wonderful people whether they are family or friends. Our relationships are often like muscles: if we do not put effort in, then our relationships will 'atrophy.' Thirdly, our wealth is key. Regardless of our beliefs, and how we perceive money, let us be honest. Money is very important to us all. We will incur problems whether we are rich or poor; it is easier to face our problems if we are a strong financial position. It is just the world we live in, and so it is a game we must learn to play well. Consistently reflect on your business, career and assets. Go on courses, research profusely, and take action! The animal kingdom is naturally determined by survival of the fittest; they rise to the top based on strength and size. Humans, however, are different. Our version of survival of the fittest is down to how much wealth we accrue.

Consistently reflect upon these three priorities. Monthly, give yourself a score out of ten for how well you are doing in each department (ten being incredible and zero being atrocious), and take certain actions depending on which one has been lacking recently. This ensures balance. If we are doing well in these three areas, then we tend to exude robust energy. We will attract more. Things are never as easy as they seem, and things are never as hard as they seem. Bare this in mind, and we will not incur as many disappointments or surprises in our lives. Once we think we know the answer, the question changes.

"As soon as beauty is known by the world as beautiful, it becomes ugly.
As soon as virtue is being known as something good, it becomes evil."
- Lao Tzu

Circumventing Inertia

"The real key is to live in an environment where the mind feels free to choose the right thing instead of being compelled by habit and inertia to choose the wrong thing." – Deepak Chopra

No one is powerful when tired. People simply cannot perform well, or even think positively, if they are tired. The more energy we have, the more positive and vibrant we feel. This is why it is so important to sleep, eat and exercise well. Here is a strategy to use when we feel exhausted. Firstly, we need to dramatically change our physiology, so we must literally do the opposite to what we do when we are exhausted: how do you prepare yourself mentally and physically before taking part in a competition? How do you stretch? Do you jump about? Do you beat your chest or make a fist with your hand? We associate these gestures with alertness and readiness. They instinctively have the same effect even if we are about to go into a meeting or start reading extensively. Secondly, we must focus on our breathing. What is its speed? How long and deep is our inhale and exhale? Again do the exact opposite. Take several vigorous breaths. Breathe inwards with velocity, and blow out every bit of breath with fervour and determination. Make your exhale last longer than the inhale. If we have an anchor set (a movement we have conditioned by associating feelings of power and confidence with that gesture), now would be a good time to use it. We should now feel more vigilant and active.

The Present Moment

"Do not dwell in the past, do not dream of the future, concentrate the mind on the present moment." - Buddha

Why spend time dwelling on the past when it is over? Why worry about the distant future when it is unknown? Instead, focus on the present moment, as this is the moment we can enjoy and make the most occur. Problems are continuous and never lacking. We will always have problems; even the most spiritual, peaceful and happy of us have problems. The key is how we deal with these problems, and what we associate with them. Some problems are necessary, healthy and good: how can we increase profits so that they are higher than last year's? This is a great problem! However, other problems are intoxicating, and they could poison us within if we allow its pervasive and insidious nature to pulse through our veins and literally destroy our cells through stress over time. Really, all we ever have is the present moment, and this, as we know, is constant and ever changing. Perceive every day as though it is a mini life: be productive; see or talk to the ones you love; make some time for your hobbies and interests; give to others (working on your business or career). Make every single day the most productive, giving and loving day of your life.

"If you abandon the present moment you cannot live the moments of your daily life deeply." – Thich Nhat Hanh

We must live primarily in the present moment. Many unhappy people are too busy focusing on their past especially things that went wrong or how good things were lost. Conversely, there are those who focus purely on the future. The only problem with that is that whilst our future will inevitably improve, we are never actually satisfied because we are not living in the present moment. The best approach is to alternate between thinking about the future (in the form of planning and setting goals, and thinking long-term about things) whilst also living in the present, so we can enjoy where we are now and really experience life in its most natural form: being present in the moment.

Our minds often work on autopilot. This is where the subconscious takes over. This is where learned routines in terms of thought and feelings circulate and continue our underlying belief systems: "How do I look?" "What do others think of me?" "Why do I make these mistakes?" "Why can't I meet someone amazing?" "I don't have enough money." "I need more friends and attention." The mind is left to wander, and it reverts to what it knows; it can be influenced by our deep desires and fears.

These can definitely be changed if we are self-reflective, persistent and catch ourselves when we are about to fall into the same trap. If we keep replaying things over and over again in our mind, then we will manifest the same result in a slightly different context.

Short-term thinkers tend to achieve the least in life. They do not put their rubbish away (because that takes effort); they don't start drawing that artwork because it takes too long (because it takes mental effort); they do not get out of bed early enough upon waking, even though they want to set up their own business (because that means no late-night fun). These people require and rely on luck to actually achieve anything. Playing the lottery and betting is for the short-term thinker. It is the game the lower, working and lower middle class plays because it is the easy way to acquire big money. They feel like the world owes them, and so they use their faith only to attract wealth. It seldom works.

We must believe that we are only as good as we are meant to be right now. It does not matter if we were once rich or famous or happy or driven. What are we like right now? This belief will ensure that we challenge ourselves, and live in the present moment as opposed to nostalgically dwelling on what once was. This is how people become depressed: they actually oscillate mentally between the past and their present helplessness rather than focusing on the present and planning their future optimistically.

Take Action

"An idea not coupled with action will never get any bigger than the brain cell it occupied." - Arnold Glasow

Bring certainty to the uncertainty otherwise uncertainty will pervade what was once a certainty! Have you ever worked for someone with whom you thought you were more skilled and talented than? Obviously there are different variables involved: age, luck, gender and so forth. However, if there were not these variables, why is that person more successful financially than you in terms of your occupation? It is most likely these two things: likeability and taking action. Stop talking, and just do what you need to do. Just make a start. You will notice that you talk less this way, and actually accomplish more. The thought of taking action deters many. It is the fear of the unknown; it is the fear of change; it is the fear of not being in control. Yes, it is imperative to think things through rather than to leap into danger ignorantly, yet there is a great deal of pain and resentfulness built over time by people who do not take action for what they need or want for themselves and their future. Unfortunately, they tend to blame others rather than take responsibility for their current circumstance.

Inopportunely, many people simply do not take action because they feel they are unequipped with the necessary skills to take the plunge. They fear that they will feel judged, criticised and disparaged if they make a mistake or fail. Failure is the only way to achieve success. To fail means we took a step forward. Coming up short is a sign that we must improve, so that we can become more adept and successful. How will we find this out unless we go for it? Why did I write this book? There are even more things I could have read, learned, incorporated, expanded upon and deciphered, but many works are left unfinished because of this obsession to make things perfect (which is of course unattainable). But I wrote. I put pen to paper, and I hope you are able to do your best, and just produce the best that you can.

Pleasure and Pain

"The secret of success is learning how to use pain and pleasure instead of having pain and pleasure use you. If you do that, you're in control of your life. If you don't, life controls you." – Tony Robbins

Our psychology, associations and beliefs dictate the course of our lives. Consider whether you associate more pleasure or pain to the following situations: do you feel more pleasure or pain when eating an unhealthy dessert? What about once you are finished? Do you feel more pleasure or pain when you go to the gym? What about once you are finished? Do you feel more pleasure or pain by waking up early in the morning to get hard work done? What about when the day is finished? Do you feel more pleasure or pain from reading? What about when you are finished? Everyone will have different answers especially before and during these activities, but more people will agree that they feel much better because they did the challenging activities. This is the key to succeeding in life. It is not about enjoying things before or during all of the time. It is about how you will feel once you have delivered.

Really the pleasure and pain principle is all about how we frame things to ourselves. We can easily change these perceptions if we generate enough leverage. For instance, if we said that there is more pleasure in eating an unhealthy dessert than pain, then we can easily manipulate this evaluation. We just need to find something more powerful than our current associations: eating too many of these foods can make us obese, suffer from diabetes, die earlier, and, thus, limit the time we have with our family in this realm; eating too many of these foods can stop us from attracting the kind of partner we really want or keeping him or her for that matter; eating too many of these foods can show how mentally and emotionally weak we are. If we use certain trigger words to anger us, then we can stop ourselves from falling into any of these negative choices. If we weigh things up, by thinking longer term, we will be able to generate enough leverage to change our pleasure and pain beliefs.

We cannot manifest anything into our lives if things are incongruent or contradictory in our thoughts and belief systems. For example, if we want the sexiest husband, but we are afraid of being cheated on, then these beliefs are in opposition, and so the mind will either release the cultivation of its manifestation altogether, or move toward the thought with the most emotion tied to it. So if we are more afraid of the possibility of their impending infidelity, more than our love for a gorgeous counterpart, then we may live a life single. If we want to start a successful business, but we also want to live a relaxed lifestyle, then these two forces oppose, and so you end up in the middle or with neither. No outcome is worse, but only different, and it is a choice.

Focus and Perception

"There is no truth. There is only perception." - Gustave Flaubert

There is something to be learned in every single thing that we experience. It all comes down to how we choose to view what we encounter. Whether we conceive things positively or negatively will determine our direction, and, ultimately, our degree of happiness. What we focus on proliferates. We think around 60, 000 thoughts every day, most of which are repeated and often negative unless we work hard to condition ourselves. If we have more negative than positive thoughts, then it is only natural that we will end up attaching more emotions to negative thoughts. If they have any significance to us, then our thoughts lead to feelings, which lead to us taking actions (whether good or bad). Our success and happiness in life depends on the emotions we choose to attach to our thoughts. This is why we must fully immerse ourselves in our positive thoughts, and take some form of action to support it as soon as possible.

We must give energy to things that empower us. If everyone looked into the sky, each individual would think of something distinct: "I wonder if that star still exists." "Why am I here?" "Should I marry him?" "Should I divorce her?" "What is man's potential?" The same image can evoke any thought or feeling. Every single person conjures his or her subjective energy, depending on his or her perspective and the influence of the ego. A perspective has infinite possibilities, yet we subjectively choose to think and feel a certain way. It is interesting how we can hear, see, feel, smell and taste the same things, yet interpret things differently depending on our mood at that moment, and how we link things together in our minds.

A relationship means to have a connection. We have relationships with people, but we also have relationships with everything: food, work, hobbies, nature, sex, death, religion etc. A relationship depends on all the thoughts and feelings you have towards something. In terms of our relationships with people, others in the same relationship with you may have totally different thoughts and feelings toward you and your connection. Consider the important relationships you have with people and significant things. Evaluate whether they bring you more joy or pain, and act accordingly.

It is not what happens to us, but how we react to things that ascertain our happiness. If we drop a cup, and it breaks, what are the possible causes? Nothing at all; maybe I should take it easy; I am an idiot; I must be tired; I was supposed to break that cup and so on. It all depends on what we say to ourselves. These effects can be impersonal (they place no real judgement on us), or they are personal (I dropped the cup because I always make mistakes, or I dropped the cup because I am clumsy). These personal effects have 'I am,' and, thus, identity attached to them, which can either be empowering or disempowering depending on the impositions suggested.

It is fascinating how our perceptions to things totally change throughout our lives. What was once hated can one day be loved. What was once feared can one day be relished. What was once a weakness can one day become strength. It is about not accepting that our current situation is permanent. These also change depending on our priorities and stage in life. Fire can work with us or against us depending on how, when and where we use it. The same applies to anything.

We believe what we see; we choose what we see; we see what we believe.

Our brain chooses key things to pay attention to every minute of every day depending on likes, desires, tasks, relationships and so on. What we have plugged into our subconscious is what dominates the majority of our day. There are so many things we do on a daily basis where we turn on our 'default' mode; we go on autopilot many times during the day especially when we do things we are familiar with. This is why it is so important to condition our minds, and to be vigilant regarding how we think and feel throughout the day. If we focus on the insects in the grass, we will miss the birds in the sky. If we focus on the pain in the world, we will miss the bliss and giving that is there.

Intrinsically the same applies: if we focus on what is lacking in our lives, then our feelings will be negative, and our actions will support or encourage our thoughts and attention. However, if we think about the amazing things in our lives or the positive things that are happening around us (most of which we probably take for granted), then that will expand. Our thoughts, which are created by both internal and external stimuli, affect our emotions, and our emotions determine our actions. These three processes circulate again and again, building momentum and increasing the stakes day-by-day. Sometimes in life, we simply do not get things if we force them or want them too much. Give everything we have to something worthwhile, but keep things in perspective.

Mind your own business! Wish well for others, but do not become entrenched with what others are doing, unless we can support them or learn from them. When we focus on another person meticulously, we trip ourselves up in the process, especially if we are focusing on their problems or mishaps. Avoid people who are immature or cannot put things into perspective. Great pain derives from being given things, and not having to work for them. These individuals' will and appreciation diminishes. They have only known easy times, and so do not develop the kind of discipline, dedication and drive to pursue greater accomplishments in every sense. The worst thing we can be is spoiled. Why? We have high expectations of ourselves, but no real substance to acquire them on our own. This results in low self-esteem eventually, and a victim mentality when we start thinking why things are not going our way. The spoilt, victim is a recipe for disaster.

We have all had an encounter with a friend, family member or colleague whereby they said something to us that stuck in our minds. The same image and words were, and possibly are, repeated frequently in our minds. We develop stronger and stronger associations, thoughts and feelings toward this moment by mentally reliving it again and again. If we want to change this, then we must change our associations. In order to change our associations, we must change our perceptions of the event. Was the argument something that ruined our relationship or thoughts about ourselves, or can it potentially be something that will enable us to grow or adapt? If we always have choice, which we do, then we must always choose the answer that brings out our best side. If we do not like the answer, then we can change the question until we get the answers we want. We must start searching for answers. It does not matter if amazing answers do not come to us! We condition our minds to constantly see the good in things. Our subconscious will soon take over, and we will find ourselves in more fortuitous circumstances. The art is in training the mind to look for what it wants, and to look away as soon as we come across a barrier (some form of negativity). Either avoid the obstacle or walk through it.

"Where attention goes, energy flows." - Tony Robbins

Chapter 9 – Your Highest Self

"Success, like happiness, cannot be pursued; it must ensue…as the unintended side-effect of one's personal dedication to a course greater than oneself." - Mihaly Csikszentmihalyi

We already have everything that we need. The way we are right now is perfect; it is the way we are supposed to be currently. The mindset required, however, is the deep desire for constant improvement. Imagine how much better we can, and should, be next year or three years later. Perhaps it is not that we need to know more, but that we may need to be more resourceful. We have all the answers within us already to make our next step. It is more about tapping into our genius, and that requires a focus on peak performance. When we are least ready it will come. What we need to do is be as best prepared as possible, as everyone's inevitable weaknesses will be exposed in life one way or another. We cannot hide these. We must accept, work hard to improve them, and keep moving forward.

Sometimes the more rigorously we chase something in life, with the ego's influence only, the more it runs away.

The more unattainable it becomes, like trying to keep hold of slippery soap. However, when we are open, loving and do not rush, beautiful things may open up to us: a fantastic job promotion; meeting an interesting person; an investment opportunity and so on. Carl Jung states how when we are young adults we are predominantly run by the ego: we are obsessed with our appearance. The next stage is when we chase monetary success, and we are consumed with status. The final stage is when people begin to reflect and focus on their impact on the world. Wouldn't it be beautiful if we had the mindset of the third stage when we were a lot younger? Ironically, the final state is the mindset required to actually achieve the mental clarity and wealth that we always chased.

Self-Reflection

"The unexamined life is not worth living." - Socrates

We want to build our metaphorical house by looking at it from the outside rather than the inside. If we are inside when building, then it is harder to see the problems and issues within the house, as we are too close to the experience. We must step back, build gradually, and step back frequently in order to preempt any issues, and to design it impeccably. The best in every field are those who are constantly stepping back, and returning to their work with new insight and perspectives. This requires a great deal of objectivity and detachment from the ego. Many people cannot be completely honest with themselves because they immerse themselves in their ego.

We must work incredibly hard in areas that we deem to be important to us, and we will become successful and satisfied in that avenue. However, the ability to step back and evaluate ourselves is fundamental. This is when we reassess, and make small adjustments to keep us on track most efficiently and effectively.

Living a life dominated by our egos is very painful. Our fall becomes that much more tragic and brutal. We all experience similar thoughts and emotions throughout our lives, yet there are some people who take action in spite of what is going on inside. Once we take action, our challenging thoughts and feelings about whatever is happening will change. Nature and fate will take its course if we do not take action, and we will encounter greater pain consequentially. The seemingly negative and painful things that happen to us, end up being the most substantial, essential and transformational events. However, we need to condition our reactions to what has happened, otherwise we can let these events get the better of us. We can either use our perceived failures to make us better, or we can allow them to break us. When someone fails at something, they do one of two things: despondent individuals will associate themselves, and define themselves by this result: "I failed," "I am a loser," "I am not good enough," "This is who I am," and this downtrodden person will visualise a lack of success every time they encounter similar situations, further associating themselves with failing visually; resilient, detached individuals react differently, saying things such as, "Oh it didn't work out this time," "I am going to come back stronger," "I am better than that," "This loss will only make me better," "I am more than this outcome." It is in our struggles and challenges where we learn most about who we are. When we win, we celebrate; when we lose, we ponder. Therefore, we learn and grow more when we 'lose' or 'fail.' The faster we 'fail,' the more quickly we will succeed. Fail intelligently.

Internal versus External

"Your inner beauty is more important than how people see you on the outside." – Emily Coussons

People believe that their outer world, the people they interact with, determines their inner world. The opposite is true. How we process things, how we think about ourselves, and how we react to things in life, our inner world, will create our outer existence. Our outer world is the result of our inner workings. If we want a better quality life, then we must work on ourselves first. Do not worry about all of the things we must do yet such as starting a business, or searching for our partners, or having children etc. These wonderful things will all come in time. We do not want to start these things necessarily unless we have control and quality internally. People rush into things because they want quick results. We must work on ourselves tremendously, and *then* we will see the results externally.

Approach every new situation as though it is a blank slate. Approach every interaction as though it is our first. Develop the habit of having undivided attention when working on tasks or talking with people. A distracted mind is an unbalanced mind. People do things poorly, not because of their ability, but because they are focused on the wrong things. We are taught to fixate on the outside. Yes, the outside and our externals hold great importance, but never at the expense of neglecting quality intrinsic development. What we have on the outside changes and becomes lost while the internal is eternal. Those who are primarily focused on the outside are short-term thinkers. Their minds will not get them through too much. Think about it. If we eat healthily (look after our insides), then we benefit externally. If we read often (learning is an internal process), then we benefit externally (in the form of a better career etc.) The same applies with our emotional intelligence: if we control how we feel, then we are more likely to attract better opportunities and people into our lives.

It is absolutely fine to enjoy watching sports. Favouring a certain team or individual is natural, but we cannot let the result of a match dictate our mood or how the rest of our day will unfold. Refuse to let an external factor (a sporting event in this instance), something we cannot control, determine our thoughts, feelings (mood) and subsequent actions. The enlightened experience is about not needing externals, or reducing them drastically at the very least, as a way of reaching euphoria and emancipation.

There is nothing wrong with enjoying externals, but there is great freedom and beauty in not needing it or not as often at least. We want to train ourselves to not need praise or encouragement the way we once did. We do not need anyone's attention. We live in a world where many people need excessive amounts of things, and it creates the illusion that we need more and more, and ironically, we feel like we have less and less. There is a massive difference. We do not need to eat that much, and yet we can still feel highly functional, fit and motivated. We do not need constant attention from the opposite (or same) sex as we once did. We do not need to look at or use our phones as much as we do. Many people feel like they are missing out on things, but this is an illusion. The event does not make the people; the people make the event. We are not missing out on anything; all we need is within us. Become more peaceful, less needy and have an inner knowing that all is and will be great. Ironically, this mentality will actually attract even more events and qualities, but we can choose what we want to indulge in rather than being addictively swayed. There is no need to allow our moods and actions to be dictated by another person or thing.

Becoming overly attached to anything external jeopardises or compromises how we think and feel about ourselves. If we are, then our actions will be preponderantly to make others happy, and, therefore, we are communicating to ourselves that others are more important and we are less deserving. Corporations exploit people though media forums everywhere: the clothes never make the person; it is the person who makes the clothes. Small things like this appear worthless, but nothing colossal occurs instantly: we accomplish small things, and thus, over time, achieve monumental things. Adopt the mentality that our internal strength is the most important thing because that is the only way that we will be able support others.

"Your pleasure is a result of your thinking, not of your possessions." - Wayne Dyer

Introvert versus Extrovert

"Introverts are capable of acting like extroverts for the sake of work they consider important, people they love, or anything they value highly." – Susan Cain

Personality psychologist, Brian Little, explains that, *"Extroverts like to stand close, make eye contact, have a mutual gaze. When an extrovert meets [someone named] Charles, it rapidly becomes Charlie, Chuck, and Chuckles Baby. Introverts stay with Charles until they're given a pass to be more intimate."* Studies show that extroverts have more fun on average than introverts. Why? They break down boundaries more quickly; they relax others more quickly, which opens opportunities. Extroverts get away with more. So how can we become more extroverted? Talk to everyone. Become used to talking to different types of people in different contexts. Over time, the experience will feel natural to us. We will notice that people are friendlier than we think when we start to talk to different people in different situations. We never know who we are going to meet, and people are more likely to help others with whom they like. This is why it is good practice to just talk to people randomly at social gatherings. It creates a positive aura around us. People just seem to like extroverts more. Extroverts are far more charismatic, confident and capable of dealing with things better in most social interactions. Part of being successful in terms of careers and occupation is being likeable. We must be able to communicate effectively. Communication indicates care. It can go a long way.

It is possible, and better, if we actually have elements of being both introverted and extroverted. Introverts tend to be more thoughtful, studious, reflective and happy with their own company (all things needed in leadership), yet it is equally imperative to be extroverted in order to form quality relationships, build partnerships and to increase our client base. However, some people can be wasteful with their extroverted nature. Many people overload their days with ineffective activeness: talking too long to people where the conversation does not really lead to anything, going here, going there, breaking things and then fixing things. While it is pleasant to keep active, take action, talk with someone, anyone, people often keep themselves moving to avoid being alone and doing the important things. People think being alone conveys sadness and loneliness, but the ability to sit, think, recondition, and persist with structuring our thoughts is quite possibly the most beneficial thing we could ever do.

Being an extrovert possesses many beautiful attributes. However, extroverts are constantly out, amongst friends and away from silence or their own company. These people tend to be the same people who hate being single; they need a partner in order to feel complete. Unfortunately for them, it is in our silence where we learn most about the self. The more we learn about the self, the more enlightened and knowledgeable we are. By knowledge we are referring to our identity, relationships, spirit, psychology and philosophy: the most fundamental and omnipresent notions we could possibly have. Of course we learn much from socialising, sharing diverse perspectives and learning about one another, and ourselves, to an extent, but many people avoid sitting alone because of fear. If we do not put the time in to think deeply, then we will incur many devastating emotions through the events and philosophies we fail to contemplate. The happiest people I know are those who love to fluctuate between both worlds: they can be gregarious, playful, talkative one moment, and then become totally engrossed in their own company. Both personality types are incredibly important, and we need both to be a well-balanced and happy person.

Our Reactions

"A positive attitude causes a chain reaction of positive thoughts, events and outcomes. It is a catalyst and it sparks extraordinary results." –
Wade Boggs

If we are washing the dishes, and we smash a glass, what is our reaction? While this seems trivial and fruitless, it actually demonstrates our natural emotions when things do not go our way, and when we have made a mistake. How do we respond? "Why am I so clumsy?" "Why am I so stupid?" "See, this is what happens when my wife stresses me out!" Hopefully you have a more appeasing response: "It happens sometimes." "We aren't perfect." "Well if that's the worst thing that happens to me this month, then I am fortuitous." One person begins to shout and blame others or themselves while another remains serene. One says, "This happened because no one helps me" while the other says, "What a shame, I guess I better slow down" or "That was my mistake; I better take it easy for now." This all comes down to how we treat ourselves. It reflects our self-esteem. It reveals whether we are a 'victim,' or if we take responsibility.

Do we take responsibility for our actions, or do we use an external force as our excuse? A controversial moment such as this may appear innocuous, but this reaction enhances an emotion, and it can have a domino effect on how many other events unfold during the day. A simple thought ("I am stupid" or "It is all right; I forgive myself"), influences our emotions (feeling angry or loving), which then results in a behavioural change (not taking part in such useful activities for fear of failure, or an appreciation that sometimes things do not go our way, but we will keep doing our best). This seemingly insignificant pattern, over time, leads to a greater scenario with larger ramifications: making an error at work; having an argument with a loved one; even how we react when approaching someone of the opposite sex for the first time. Even if the context is different, the pattern is the same! These reactions and patterns not only determine our destiny, they also deeply affect how we interact and share emotions with others. We not only set up positive or negative structures within ourselves, but we also embed these in others (that is if they choose to agree with us or disassociate themselves).

Our reactions to externals are indicative of our internal representations, whether we have healthy and positive reactions or painful, defensive and negative ones. The external influences the internal, and the internal influences the external. This back and forth cycle ascertains how we perceive and interpret things. Listen to the following words; what image, thought or emotion comes to mind when you hear them? Depression... Rich... Pain... Interest... Love... The first image, thought or emotion that comes to mind must be analysed and evaluated. This is the connection that we make to the word at this present moment. If we are unhappy with the result, and can see the negative connotations that we make, do not be disheartened. This can be changed. We simply have to practise reconditioning the image and word interconnections. Here is another example: is there a particular song that reminds you of a past or present lover? This association can be changed if we wish. It is all about running the song over and over again, but thinking of something completely different with great emotional intensity. This is one way of mitigating our current associations to things. We must understand ourselves well enough, and in a way, plan our reactions to things just in case we have to go through that experience. The more prepared we are, the more options we have. We not only need to stay one step ahead of our competition; we also need to stay one step ahead of ourselves.

Breakthrough

"He who desires but acts not breeds pestilence." - William Blake

We will never change and take control of our lives unless we have built enough emotional strength to be resilient. Change can happen in an instant. It only takes one moment or event to push us pass our threshold: when we have had enough of something, and we know we must make a change. The intensity of this emotion has broken our patterns, and we are ready to perceive anew. Something switches inside. Our internal language patterns change, our feelings change and a new belief (new found certainty) is set in motion. These changes not only affect how we are in relation to that specific activity, but it pervades into other elements. Everything is connected in one way or another.

Unfortunately, many people have different thresholds, which are linked to their blueprints. For example, one person may only need to gain four pounds of fat in order to think that enough is enough, and they must regain their focus and lose weight whereas another person will need to gain say twenty pounds of fat in order to reach their threshold. We have thresholds for everything in life, and the quality of our lives in based on the standards we set: the quality of our blueprint. The higher our blueprints are, the shorter our thresholds become. We can flip the switch (threshold) more quickly, and change when problems start early rather than waiting, coming up with excuses and then struggling even more because we are so far behind. Consider the blueprints you have as it relates to your relationships, your health and your wealth. Could these be set higher? What is your threshold until you look to improve a relationship or your health or your wealth? What has to happen? Now is the time to recondition yourself, and breakthrough to the next level.

Suffer and Succeed

"Suffer now and live the rest of your life as a champion." – Muhammad Ali

Nothing will change unless a person has suffered enough. The harder we work for something, the more we appreciate it. The more time we invest in helping our siblings, the more we love them, and want to give them (especially if it is appreciated). The more money we spend on healthy products and services, the more we value our health. The more energy we give our partners, the more we value them. Consider your life patterns. Think about how much time, money and energy we give to feeding awful habits, and think about how little we give to areas in our lives that are actually important. The more we struggle and give now, the better our futures will be. The more comfortable we feel in the uncomfortable, the more successful we shall be. Nothing is meaningful, valuable and desirable unless we have invested sufficient energy and time into it. We must work hard at something to feel a true sense of accomplishment. Without hardship, adversity, persistence, challenge and so on, we will not exhibit lasting change. These feelings do not derive from inheriting things, pure luck or charity of some sort. We only truly appreciate something if we fought and thought for its attainment.

There is a balance to everything: the more we struggle for something, the more we will be rewarded by it. If we suffer for something, then we will experience great happiness in the future. However, we must be tenacious enough to stick with it. People often give up right before they would have begun to see the benefits. If we have been heartbroken and devastated, a beautiful and loving relationship is on the horizon. If we exercise and expend a great deal of energy, we will later be exhausted yet fulfilled. If we train intensely and suffer physically, our muscles will develop. Our muscles expand due to intense demand and excruciating pain. The harder we work for something, the more rewarding it shall be. Conquer challenges and build momentum in everything we believe to be worthwhile. Short-term discomfort leads to long-term happiness. Inertia leads to long-term affliction.

Success, as it relates to our minds, bodies, relationships, finances, careers and so on, requires a great deal of affliction. If the road to marriage was too easy, then the road to divorce would be just as easy. There is no need to unnecessarily create barriers or challenges, but we must work on what we want! We must invest in our relationships. People get married, and then they take their foot off the pedal. They stop working on themselves. They stop supporting each other. They believe they have accomplished what they set out to do. Wrong. If we are not learning or investing our energy into any important relationship (with people or priorities), then it is slowly deteriorating. Fact. If we think that our partners are just going to live contently the way he or she is now, then we are wrong. If it is not progressing, it is declining, and we will suffer greatly as a result. Incidentally, one of the reasons why a significantly high percentage of lottery winners lose their entire winnings is because they did not earn it. It was given to them. They neither appreciate it the same way, nor do they know what to do with it. Why? They never invested substantial time, money and energy into its cultivation. We return to our blueprints.

The more we suffer for something, the more we love it. The more energy we invest in something, the more we value it. This is why it is necessary to suffer for our children; this is the problem with many wealthy families who delegate all parental responsibilities to a nanny for instance. There will inevitably be a disconnect between parent and child. Why do we think childbirth is so painful? Think about the things we suffer for, and consider if we value these things more than other things that just happen easily for us. If we are spoilt as a child, we do not grow up to value money. If we are used to winning all the time, then we do not learn and grow from these experiences. If we do not struggle for the physical body we want, then we will not experience the bliss of our struggles. Earn it; enjoy it.

Our Patterns

"Patterns of repetition govern each day, week, year, and lifetime... But I say these habits are sacred because they give deliberate structure to our lives. Structure gives us a sense of security. And that sense of security is the ground of meaning." – Robert Fulghum

What things do we do repetitiously every day? What do we think about when we physically do them? The more we think about something when in mild trance-like states (exercising, washing dishes, cleaning the house, reading, playing computer games etc.), the stronger the association becomes. If we brush our teeth, and think about how difficult our day will be, then do not be surprised why we do not enjoy brushing our teeth! If we experience mental entropy and negative thoughts whilst driving, then we will not enjoy the process of driving in the future. If we talk about negative and depressing issues, then we give power and energy to them. Become conscious of your thoughts, and how topics move from one to the next in your mind and why. See if you can understand the psychological connections you make. For example, we may go from thinking about our ex partner to thinking about a boss we hated to then thinking about the business we are thinking of launching. Firstly, what connection is there? We have linked them all to failure or pain. Secondly, we have presupposed that the possible business would be damaging to us, and a complete failure. It can be very revealing. We must be mindful of what we think about when we are physically doing things. With repetition this becomes powerful and strengthened. Firstly, we can change negative trances by installing a more positive method of mental relaxation: exercise, yoga, sport, reading, writing, playing music and so on. Secondly, we can also consciously work on rewiring our associations by using enough intense positive and powerful statements and questions to uplift, motivate and overwhelm the negative, biological voice that operates within all of us. Our habits condition our daily lives, which reinforces our identity. Sometimes we need a different experience to trigger new patterns: the link between our thoughts, emotions and actions.

Our Reality

"You know you're in love when you can't fall asleep because reality is finally better than your dreams." – Dr. Seuss

What we believe will become our reality. If we believe in Islamic practices, then we are right. If we believe in Christianity, then we are right. If we believe in trust, then we are right. Whatever we believe to be the truth, the core of our existence, then we are right. Our internalisation is our truth. We create our energy, our divinity, and our effects on others. Our energy infects others, and meshes with the universe's energy to affect others one way or another. If we believe it, so it shall be. Unfortunately, or fortunately, people become rigid and stubborn in their thoughts and beliefs, which is harmful and perilous to the self: we limit what we can think, experience and share. We can only see from our eyes this way, and even if we believe in a wider cause, it is the ego that rears its ugly face whenever we undermine or belittle another's beliefs. The paradox is that we are always complete, yet whenever we stop learning and challenging ourselves, we metaphorically and spiritually die. We must be flexible in our beliefs, not necessarily docile and malleable, but capable of change. Anyone who remains the same no longer fits in today's ever-changing world. If we are inflexible, we will not progress. We must be like water. Do not work against what is natural. We all have a purpose, and an ability to profoundly affect others. We must decide what our ideal selves are, and make decisions based on these promising self-prototypes.

Physical muscles grow when they are pushed. The same exact principle applies to the mind and our willpower. To break through we must become uncomfortable. Unfortunately, this is often when people stop, and they feel helpless. It is because no character is being built when people do not break through. A weak character is a consequence of weak thoughts and weak standards. How do we know when we have broken through a metaphorical barrier? What is it that we always, or frequently, say to ourselves when we reach the peak of something difficult? "I can't swim another lap." "If I fail, I'll look stupid." "I've never been able to do it before." "I'm just not good at it." "This is enough for me." In these instances, the key words are obvious: "Can't," "stupid," "never," "not good" and so on. We must condition ourselves, so that when we reach these points, we say something more inspiring and uplifting. The powerful words, "I am" must be followed with whatever positive phrases we want. Now that we are conscious of what we say when in these situations, we must apply a vibrant image of success in our minds, and affirm using this chosen positive phrase over and over: "I am successful." "I am going to accomplish this" or even better, "I have already accomplished this." "I deserve this." All we need to focus on is taking just one step at a time.

If we are struggling to tackle something challenging, then we should begin something even harder than what we already have as a barrier to our progression. Doing something even more dangerous or challenging brilliantly utilises the power of contrast. The other task does not seem as daunting. Even so, things always have a way of working out, if we can learn to have faith and work on what we value. Yes, we can dictate our life's journey, but to achieve this poetically, we must accept all that happens in our lives. Things can always have a beautiful spin to them (context reframing) if we so choose to give it one.

We all have thresholds for different things. Some thresholds are higher than others. The way to grow is to always place demands on these thresholds, always pushing slightly more each time until our previous threshold is no longer a barrier, and we can push further, experience newer, and, thus, be happier. Happiness is achieved by continuous growth in areas that we value. Happiness is not something we will attain one day, like a possession. Even if we think we will be permanently happy if we just retired early, and never had to work again, we would be wrong. Boredom, complacency and the subsequent negative thoughts will soon seep into our extra freedom unless we find new inspiring activities. We must constantly challenge and break barriers to sustain true contentment and inner peace.

Think about the physical journey we most often make: usually to a workplace, relative or friend. What we will notice is that our minds go on autopilot due to the familiarity of the scenery and routine. This creates comfort and relaxation, but will rarely ever fill us with new thoughts. However, when we explore an 'unfamiliar journey,' our minds operate differently, often with chaos and randomness, and a whole range of extreme thoughts and emotions may pervade our fluency. Where there is chaos, there is a chance to create something new: a new belief. A challenge to customary thinking begins. This analogy is just how we live our own lives. We become complacent and unnecessarily comfortable. It is impossible to grow, progress and experience anew unless we travel down a different path (both physically and mentally).

The Mirror Effect

"We can only give away what we have inside." - Wayne Dyer

How we treat others will determine how others will treat us. The aggressor will soon be treated aggressively. The criminal will one day become the victim, even though they are practically victims to begin with. The player will one day be played. The pretentious will one day be humbled. The taker will one day be taken from. The giver will one day be given. The way we treat others is also the way we treat ourselves. Becoming angry easily with others foregrounds that we are angry with ourselves. Being harsh on others means that we are harsh on ourselves. Being loving and empathetic with others foregrounds that we love and appreciate ourselves. If we are impatient with others, it foregrounds that we do not take the time needed for ourselves. Unfortunately, individuals look for weaknesses within others; if we focus on other people's flaws, then we focus on our own too much.

The state of being depressed is very selfish. If we want to reduce the stress and tension in our lives, then be less narcissistic. What are some fears that most people feel or once felt? Our finances: growing our business is all about adding value to our clients. Focus on them, and we shall consequently increase our profits. Public speaking: speakers become nervous when they are focused on themselves: How do I look? I better not make a mistake etc. Instead, we should focus on communicating our ideas clearly, and we will become more satisfied and less pressured when we speak. Infidelity: instead of worrying if our partners are cheating on us, we should focus on making our partners happier by giving more and communicating better. Aim to focus more on others, and on what they need. Ironically, it will positively affect us in a multitude of ways.

Purposefulness

"He who has a why to live for can bear almost any how." - **Friedrich Nietzsche**

The loss of significance and purpose is the main reason why people perish. A way to always feel purposeful is to flow from one objective, goal or activity to another without any considerable break. This ensures purpose and clarity over our direction. It provides meaning for people. Boredom leads to negative thinking, which leads to depression. The mother who feels she is no longer needed will feel depressed and lonesome; the elderly husband who loses his wife may soon pass away due to lack of meaning and continuation; the incredible musician who loses her talent, will soon be filled with chaos and uncertainty over her future role in life.

What is your purpose? What are you happy about? Is it your career? Motherhood? Being a writer? Working for a charity? What is your calling, and how can you prolong the beauty and greatness within you? Professional athletes often face this issue. Many American football stars lose their zest and energy for life once their professional careers are over. They have an incredible start to life, filled with success, winning, admiration and acceptance, but then they lose the immense significance they once felt. Many end up broke, in debt, addicted to negative habits such as drugs and gambling, and so life's spiral leads them deep into depression and despondence. Brain damage is also a factor of course. Think about your purpose in the world, what your role is, and how everything happens to you for a specific reason.

The workings within our physical body are a reflection of our external reality and vice versa. There are more living organisms and bacteria within us than people in the world! How the atoms within our body interact with one another is how we conduct ourselves in our relationships and interactions. An atom that misses an electron is known as a free radical. This damaged molecule seeks support, another atom, to be paired with, and so it collides into healthy atoms, and in turn, ruins other healthy atoms. This collision breaks the healthy paired atoms apart, thus spreading the illness and disease amongst more atoms. These molecules are then isolated, and in need of support. The vibrations that the pernicious free radicals generate, creates a continuum of ill cells. This process proliferates. The antioxidants that we eat, provides stability and help for these free radicals, which in turn, maintains the perfect health of other paired atoms, and so the disease is greatly reduced. Our beliefs change our molecules and cells. It changes the chemical reactions in our bodies.

This can metaphorically represent how we live our lives: the vibrations and energy we bring forward will ascertain our existence. This can be how our energy works when it interacts with other people's energy. This is how our subconscious works when it interacts with other people's subconscious. Do your best to control your energy, keep yourself healthy, remain focused on your goals, and spread positive vibes and avoid awful 'atoms.' Therefore, the need to avoid harmful 'free-radicals' is pertinent to our ability to live healthy, positive and blissful lives. Living a happy and peaceful life is a talent to some, and a nightmare to attain for those ignorant and incapable of controlling their mind, emotions and body. Our body goes through copious chemical reactions that alter our moods. The feeling we have on a frightening rollercoaster ride may be indiscernible from our bodily chemical reactions when say public speaking or having a physical fight. That gut-wrenching feeling within the stomach manifests itself whenever the mind sends these signals to our organs. We can change these states by shifting our focus, and remaining detached from the outcome.

Timing and Precision

"Precision beats power and timing beats speed."
– Conor McGregor

It is not what we do that counts; it is when we do it. Everyone has the potential to do the right thing: we know that we have to shoot in order to score; we know the tasks we need to do at work; we know that we need to talk to our boss or employees, but the key is *when* we choose to do these things. Timing is crucial. We understand the mechanics involved to achieve something. As Tony Robbins proclaims, "eighty percent is psychology; twenty percent is mechanics." The mindset we have going into what we want to do will determine whether we succeed. Being perceptive and paying attention to subtleties will determine our precision and quality of decision-making. Most fanatics and observers will know how Tiger Woods hits the golf-ball, but he knows how to do it and when. Most people know what Donald Trump does in his business transactions, but he knows how to do it and when. Most people know the combinations Mike Tyson threw and the techniques required for every punch, but he knew how and when to throw them. Most know the lyrics to Whitney Houston's songs, but she knew how to deliver them and when to change her tone. People who rely on their power and speed are used to bulldozing their way pass their challenges. This strategy might work when facing many problems in life, but at the highest level, it is not enough. To be the best we can possibly be, we must improve our technique in life, which means learning new life-based strategies, becoming wiser, knowing when to invest in something, and when to cut your losses sooner. This is applicable in every avenue. Technique, accuracy and timing are the skills of the expert whereas power and speed are the only strengths of the novice.

Improving Adeptness

"The future belongs to those who learn more skills and combine them in creative ways." – Robert Greene

Here is a simple yet effective strategy to use that will enhance our motivation and feelings of competence. We can use metaphors when we want to perform at a high level at anything. One of the ways we can encourage positive thinking and high performance is by saying two things. Firstly, we can say that we are the person who is the best at whatever we are doing. So, for instance, if we are training boxing, we could think to ourselves that, "I am Mike Tyson." If we are delivering a speech or inspiring another, we might say that, "I am Lesley Brown or Tony Robbins." If we want to come across as charismatic, we would say that, "I am Muhammad Ali" or "I am Dwayne Johnson." The list can go on and on. Secondly, we can ask ourselves another question: "How would this person be? What would they be thinking? How would they move? What would they say? How would they react?" These interrogative sentences encourage high quality performance. It improves confidence as we begin to dissect these brilliant people's thoughts, feelings and actions, enabling us to mimic and model from the best in a given field.

We could also find a coach or mentor depending on our experience and level at something. This is a direct way of learning their thoughts and actions. Teaching a skill to others will also make us work even harder to learn the material and skills needed to excel within a given topic, so we must put ourselves out there and look to share our knowledge and expertise. Furthermore, immersion is also massively influential. Dabbling in and out of something is not the best way to improve in an area. It is hard to experience a state of flow when this happens. Instead, give yourself an entire weekend or week to only focus on that information and task. The more we focus on something, the more easily details and notions flow to us.

Think of something that you do very well. What do you do to ensure you are in the proper state? How can these affirmations, movements, behavioural patterns be replicated to allow the subconscious to shine when you are in a different context where you want a successful performance? For example, think about how you feel before and when you are doing something that you are brilliant at doing. Transfer the same thoughts, feelings and physiology into an area where you want to be more confident. Write these down. Make them apparent and explicit to yourself. Replicate and reinforce the process or adjust them in ways that ensure you are in a peak state. The more we do what we love, the more we progress in core areas of our lives. Doing what we are passionate about increases serotonin and pleasure, which gives us the energy and divinity necessary to push forward and attain what we want. This momentum creates a shift.

The Train

We have to decide how to guide our 'trains.' We can view our lives through this metaphor. People will come into our lives, onto our trains, at different stops, and they all have their own goals; they know, or should know, when to get off or stay on our trains. We must understand that people will be on our trains for varying lengths, and they will all influence the direction of our trains diversely. We must be careful with whom we allow onto our trains! Most people live their lives without knowing the stops on their train. There is no plan. There is no end destination. Without knowing our journeys, how can we best prepare and control the course of our lives? Each metaphorical stop should be the attainment of one of our short-term goals. People around us will create the tracks for our 'trains' unless we take control: plan our goals, set realistic deadlines and work toward their attainment with all the energy, focus and the belief that we have. The juice is worth the squeeze. Allowing others (our employers, parents or society's ideologies) to dictate our journeys will lead merely to mediocrity, disappointment and unfulfilled lives. It will end with us thinking about what could have been. How did we get here? Where did it all go wrong? Take control. We must recondition our minds and correct the tracks, so that our 'trains' can travel where we want to go.

Momentum

"A positive attitude causes a chain reaction of positive thoughts, events and outcomes. It is a catalyst and it sparks extraordinary results." – *Wade Boggs*

When we want to be successful at something, we must also continue to improve upon our current strengths, as our successes in these existing avenues can positively affect our current weaknesses also. Things may seem unrelated, but as with much in life, they are oftentimes interconnected. If we want to increase our success at work, then we can take the pressure off by performing well in the gym; if we want to improve the quality of our relationships, then we can improve one of our interests whether it is art, writing, sports and so on. Build success upon success. Develop that winning mentality. We must develop the belief that we will always find a way to succeed. This builds character. Set up another business or do work in a totally different profession. This even works with hobbies: if we give great devotion to an interest, such as swimming, then we can diversify our exercise regime by incorporating martial arts or football or golf. The change in perception allows us to take a step back from our main goal, in this instance swimming, whilst allowing us to enjoy another similarly related interest. It can take the form of an enjoyable distraction, and take away any tension associated with what we initially want to take precedence.

There is no particular correct way of doing things in life. We all have our different paths and admirable qualities whether discernible or latent. The key to success is momentum. Momentum is the ability to transfer the passion and enthusiasm generated from one success into another. We can use this positivity and success as leverage. Unfortunately, there are all types of obstacles waiting to destroy this momentum such as a jealous friend, a stressful spouse, noisy and needy children, the monotony of a suppressing job and so forth. We must be proactive enough to understand that obstacles will arise; we must anticipate them, and have a positive comeback ready when they eventually appear.

Chapter 10 – The Shift

"It is not the strongest of the species that survives, nor the most intelligent that survives. It is the one that is most adaptable to change." - **Charles Darwin**

The baby bear was linked with a rope to an immovable tree ever since the bear was little. Sadly, he had minimal room to move freely. As expected, the baby bear soon grew bigger and more powerful. However, the misfortunate bear was now strapped with a rope to a small tree that the bear could easily break, and then do as he wished. However, the hapless bear could not escape. Astonishingly, the conditioned bear believed that the tiny tree was always immovable, and so the bear was mentally stuck permanently until the bear's master removed the rope. Whilst we find this story amusing, and we pity the bear's ignorance and helplessness, we can relate to the bear's story. We are also conditioned, and we oftentimes give up even when there is no need. Why? What is the correlation between the bear's and our limiting nature? We stop asking quality questions. We stop trying. We come up with distractions and excuses that prevent us from facing our deep desires and fears, which are often intertwined. Maybe it is about time we escape from our own rope and live freely.

Self-development author, Brian Tracy, teaches how the formative years of a child's development are crucial. Unconditional love is essential for a child to grow, develop and feel accepted by the child's parents. They learn that whenever their parents discipline and reprimand them, they feel in need of approval and acceptance, which continues into later life, and it manifests itself in many ways. The baby receives unconditional love when it is born, but then the baby must adapt to societal and familial rules. Perplexedly, the child, now a toddler, begins to be reprimanded and told not to do certain things. This is very startling as the youngster who was used to doing and getting whatever the baby wanted. During this stage, the child will attempt many different tactics in order to get his or her way and their parents' attention. Desperately, the toddler yearns to be loved and accepted. Fearfully, the child may become naughty and scream and shout whenever the child wants his or her way: if the toddler consistently gets his or her way when behaving naughtily, then the child will continue to behave this way into later life. A new habit is born, and the child's fate is set in place: "If I go crazy and get angry when I want something, then I can get what I want." Conversely, the child might only get attention when he or she looks gorgeous or does something cute. In this case, a new belief (habit) is created, and the child's future path underscored: "If I look physically beautiful and cute, then I will get what I want in life." If a young child only gets attention when funny and silly, then no wonder why the child will become a comedian later in life. If a young child gets attention when being smart and studious, then the child has been emotionally conditioned to study for the rest of his or her life. We all need to feel accepted in life, but perhaps, as we become adults, it is more about accepting ourselves rather than being accepted by others, which was necessary for survival when we were babies.

We cannot make a shift unless we are first aware of whatever it is we wish to change. Some people cannot even positively change because they do not know what they want or where they want to go. Ask the right questions, and the right answers will appear.

Why do people find change incredibly hard? Firstly, we can only do what we know and have known up until now. Secondly, people fear the unknown, and they are afraid to change their ways for fear of even worse: judgement, hardship, effort, low self-esteem and so on. Not only are we more susceptible to acquiring the diseases of our predecessors, but we can also inherit similar fundamental psychological patterns from our ancestors. Yes, these can be changed with effort as with everything in life. However, the self-actualised among us appreciate change, and we are flexible enough to incorporate change ceaselessly. We have an open mindset and growth mindset as taught by Carol Dweck.

How does one become a master at something? Small actions and changes enable massive change. We must tackle things one at a time if we are to avoid being overwhelmed. This is how we build momentum, and develop the resilience needed to complete things. If we are not progressing, we are transgressing. We often experience moments of pressure, a challenge or a test that we either defeat or resist. Pain's longevity derives from not stepping forward in these difficult moments. The key is to have positive thoughts outweigh the negative. Yes, we do attempt, and sometimes naturally think positively. However, many more negative and suppressing ones usually contaminate these positive intentions and thoughts. "I feel so good today that I am going to go for that run. But if I run I could hurt my knee or ankle or I might forget to record my show, or it could give me a stomach ache, and then if I run I won't have the energy to complete the afternoon's tasks." How many times was this positive thought, and potential action, battered and bruised by the negatives? One positive shift incurred several self-defeating excuses and reasons to remain inert.

We all think negatively at times. In fact, every single human being will have negative thoughts every day. It is just the way it is. Some negative thinking has uses in that it can protect us. It is a biological creation to prevent people from grave danger when we were far more primitive and rudimentary. However, these days, rarely do we need to over-think and accept negativity, as we are not facing life or death situations on a daily basis! We can condition ourselves to adopt more positive than negative thoughts by incorporating powerful, supportive routines every day. Positive thoughts enhance energy in any avenue; every negative thought increases tiresome and inert behaviour. Negative thoughts are no longer prerequisites. We must work hard to override a negative thought with love and positivity as often as possible.

Stability

"So much of what is best in us is bound up in our love of family, that it remains the measure of our stability because it measures our sense of loyalty. All other pacts of love or fear derive from it and are modeled upon it." - Haniel Long

Stability is a fundamental feature that we all need in order to feel grounded. Stability fills us with total clarity and reassurance, so that we can really make the most of our potential. Strong ethics breed stability. Our rituals and belief systems drive stability. Stability is essential for us to have the foundations in place to thrive and be happy. Maslow's hierarchy of needs brilliantly exemplifies this. Firstly, according to Maslow, our physiological needs must be met (shelter, food, warmth, sleep etc.) if we are able to function properly at all. We simply cannot think straight if we need to go to the toilet. We cannot think straight if we are really hungry. We cannot think straight if we are massively sleep deprived. We must have these basic needs met, so that we have the energy and focus needed to excel.

Secondly, we must all feel safe. If we feel threatened emotionally or physically, whether in a specific moment or over a certain period of time, then we can never truly maximise our potential. We are excessively concerned about our health and wellbeing that we cannot press forward. The same applies if we have an illness. Feeling unsafe breeds psychic entropy. Thirdly, we need to feel a sense of belonging. We must feel connected to people, or at least ourselves, if we are to feel loved, appreciated and accepted. We must feel like we are part of a troop. Our main troop should always be our family. If we are not close with family, then we must seek this troop in the form of our closest friends. If this is not possible, then maybe we can build a troop at our workplace. By troop, we are referring to having absolute trust and unconditional love for the members within this close community.

Fourthly, only once we have stability in our lives, in the form of the previous three phases, then we can really develop our self-esteem. We can begin to explore new avenues, challenge our abilities and feel a sense of significance and power. This is when we wish to excel in terms of our careers. We feel successful at this stage. Fifthly, we can become self-actualised, which is all about giving and growing as a person. We are so full inside that we wish to teach, share and give what we have in terms of our knowledge, experiences, wealth and so on. Is it possible that we can skip steps? For example, if we act as though we are self-actualised (by giving in all of these various forms), then will that also develop our self-esteem, which can make us feel more loving and connected to others, which can make us feel safer, allowing us to cure our inner and physical ailments (to an extent), and thus feel physiologically safer because we have shifted our perspective? I think so. We should then look to add value, give and share as much as we can in all avenues if we are to truly feel powerful, happy and successful.

Have you ever given up on a goal? We all had something we wanted to achieve, but somewhere along the way our beliefs could only take us so far. We became distracted, we procrastinated and we lowered our expectations. We gave in, and we gave up. This is a natural human experience, but it should be unacceptable as of now. We are not victims regardless of what challenging or traumatic experiences we have endured. The moment we claim to be a victim is the moment we relinquish any form of responsibility. Leaders are responsible. Winners are responsible. The weak come up with excuses. The weak point at everyone apart from themselves. Every struggle encountered has been part of our journey. We all have our own destinies and purpose on earth. The most disappointing thing in life is that many of us do not manage to remove the dirt that covers the gold within us. We all have a light within us, yet, for many, our light goes unnoticed. It remains suppressed and subjugated for one reason or another: our upbringing and embedded limiting beliefs; our desire to fit in with our peers that has forced us to lower our standards; we have listened to negative stories from others about why and how we will never make it. However, it is us who *chose* to listen. We chose to restrict ourselves. Fortunately, this does not have to be the case.

As we grow older, changing our habits become increasingly more challenging, as we physically and mentally become more rigid and inflexible. We become more hopeless due to our overriding fear; we succumb to our forthcoming departure and many lose their sense of purpose. Simply accepting that we cannot change, however, illustrates that we have a fixed limiting belief. It is never too late to change. All we ever have is our present moments. Why choose to spend these present moments immersed in our worries and limited thoughts? Make a choice. I am reminded of a powerful ending of a renowned play: *The Death of Ivan Ilyich* by Tolstoy. The play is based on the protagonist's imminent death: he has lived a life of mediocrity; he has suffered from awful personal and financial matters as well as horrible relationships. In the final few moments of his life, he asks one spine-tingling question that provokes great thought. Ivan Ilyich says, "What *if my whole life* has been wrong?" We do not want to have any regrets when our time in this realm is over. This is why we must set high standards, hold ourselves to account and live by our own beliefs and not the crippling beliefs others thrust upon us.

Our House

Our foundations must be strong otherwise our 'house' or 'tree' can neither be built, nor can it grow to its maximum potential. We can still accomplish some magnificent things, but more often than not, these will be lost as a result of not having the foundations in place to keep us strong. A building is not strong because it looks unique or powerful; it is only strong if it was built properly from the bottom. A house (our lives) is not just built on top of land: builders must dig deep into the ground to ensure that the foundations are strong before any bricks become visible on top of the surface. Unfortunately, many people neglect the foundations of their lives because it is not pretty, or because it is the hardest part to work on (the mind). They prefer to see results quickly due to sheer impatience. We look at an athlete's impeccable body, and we focus only on what we see. We look at the wealth of the businesswoman, and focus purely on what she has. We do not see the unattractive things that these successful people must do in order to become outstanding in their fields.

As the saying goes, Rome was not built in a day. The impatient house owners jump ahead, and focus on the elaborate, luxurious furniture inside, the magnificent windows, the gigantic television and so on. One day the house will collapse. Why? The foundations were not strong enough to begin with. The structure of the building was neglected. Our buildings will not last if we think in the short term. Our buildings will not last if they are neglected. We must focus on what matters: our priorities. We may have beautiful and gorgeous things within the house, but these will be shattered if the entire building, our minds, collapses. Our belief systems are the roots of our 'garden's tree,' or the foundations of our 'house.' If we have any limiting beliefs, rigid fixations and traumatising memories from our childhoods that have not been dealt with, then there is no point concentrating purely on the future. We will all incur problems and obstacles in life, and we will not have the foundations in place to effectively deal with life's issues unless these underlying issues are addressed. We must make peace with our past. We must condition ourselves. Without a flexible mindset, integrated with strong, assertive belief systems, we will mentally break every time we face a real challenge.

Your Personal Balance Sheet

"Will you have been an asset or a liability on the world's balance sheet?" – Ryan Lilly

We must spend more time working on what we cannot see, and consequentially we will have incredible physical lives. The problem is most people chase what they can see (house, car, clothes, trophy partner etc.), and so these people often lack the emotional and mental fortitude needed to truly be content and happy. We must believe that we deserve more. We get what we consistently and congruently ask for in life. Now is a fantastic opportunity to reflect. Why do you deserve to be happier and to feel strong and successful? Why is it important to you? How will you feel when you achieve this goal? How will your mentality change when you are able to maintain this energy and inner power? What do you currently do very well? Where do you currently let yourself down? A traditional balance sheet is a statement of the assets, liabilities, and capital of a business. We should also have our own personal balance sheet, so that we can accurately evaluate what our current life looks like.

Firstly, let us look at our mental 'income.' What quality material do you have enter your mind every single day, week or month? What types of people do you regularly listen to? Who are your models and mentors when it comes to your happiness and success? Is it a family member, a trainer, someone inspirational with whom you listen to on YouTube etc.? If you do not have role models in these areas (people who are living your dreams), then you do not have quality, empowering knowledge entering your mind on a regular basis. How can you possibly expect to develop in an area where you do not regularly hear inspirational, brilliant notions and information around happiness and success? It is the same as wanting to be wealthy, yet only listening to poorer people all the time. It just does not make sense.

Secondly, what are your mental and emotional assets? Your assets are what make you rich (mentally and emotionally). What sources make you think and feel better? These are our musts. You must make time for these things. For example, what beliefs do you hold that make you a great person? What emotional states do you access in order to get the best out of yourself? Your beliefs will determine how you perceive physical goals, the mind and body connection, and what you are capable of achieving. Your 'income' (what you have enter your mind consistently) will infiltrate your assets and change your beliefs. We become what we consistently listen to and tell ourselves. Our assets (beliefs) must therefore support us. Here are some examples of quality assets: "I believe that I am in control of my actions." "I believe that my ideal body shape will make me a happier and more successful person in all avenues." "I believe that the body reflects the mind." "I am a constantly improving and determined person." "I am responsible for what I think and feel about myself." Your assets will serve to empower you, and keep you on the right track. Consider these and adapt where necessary.

Thirdly, we must ruminate over our expenses. These are the people we listen to every week or month who, in one way or another, detract from our happiness and success.

These are the people we listen to or people who affect our actions regularly. They are usually family members, friends, peers or society's ideologies. These people might directly say harmful things to us to demoralise us, or they may be people with whom we love who indirectly negatively affect us. Here are some examples of what expenses sound like: "You put too much pressure on yourself. Just chill out a little." "Your family has a history of depression, so there's no point listening to these self-help quacks." "Working on yourself is overrated. Don't you have important things to focus on?" We must ensure that our income outweighs our expenses.

Lastly, we have liabilities: negative beliefs that prevent us from breaking through. Our expenses will eventually pervade our liabilities over time, as we are only human, and we fall into detrimental patterns unless we condition ourselves. What are your mental and emotional liabilities? Your liabilities encapsulate where you leak; it is where you take away from your potential. What beliefs drain you of your energy, and your ability to generate positive momentum? Here are some examples of liabilities: "I believe that if I focus on myself too much, then I will not have the time to execute in real life." "I believe that bettering myself is selfish because I have loved ones who are already struggling more than me." "I just do not have the energy to constantly work on myself." We must ensure that our assets are stronger than our liabilities.

Our Inner Child

"Some day you will be old enough to start reading fairy tales again." – C.S. Lewis

We must keep the child within us alive. We must refrain from suppressing its cries for expression. Over time, we have our inquisitiveness, creativity and desire to do what we want taken away from us by our elders, society and the educational system. We learn to know our roles and fit in somewhere. However, in order to thrive in life, we need to be playful, fun and do what comes naturally to us, as this increases energy and enjoyment. We need these to remain flexible, to value ourselves and to think originally. The beauty of life is being natural. Unfortunately, this can be very challenging for some. As young children, we possess these skills. Children have a certain carelessness. They often do not care about how others perceive them; they desire complete freedom. This slowly and gradually gets taken from us. We enter the educational system where we are told exactly how to be, and we are criticised left, right and centre. The older we become, the more responsibilities we undertake; we must care for others more, and become increasingly mindful of how others perceive us. We wear suits, usually because we have to, and we learn that we must speak a certain way to appear appropriate and sophisticated, again usually to please others and fit in. We are told what we can and cannot do by our parents, siblings, teachers and elders. We become detrimentally moulded and broken down gradually until we fit into our own little box. Our dreams and desires are constantly facing limitations and restrictions. And so we learn to repress what we really want, which subsequently becomes engrained into our unconscious. This dying fire lays dormant. It is never too late to light the fire of freedom.

How to live an Exciting Life

"And yet, the only exciting life is the imaginary one." − Virginia Woolf

The key to true happiness in life is to surround ourselves with the people we love most, and to enjoy the process of achieving our deep desires and goals. We should frequently find the time to do the things we most enjoy. We can only make others happy when we are happy with ourselves. The most selfish people in the world view themselves as victims. Those who are depressed are often very selfish indeed. Why? They only perceive things from their perspectives. They are only viewing things from their own point of view. Depression is therefore a result of having an overactive ego. One-way out of depression is to help and support others. We must add value to the world otherwise others will not see value in us. By adding value, we mean developing your skills, talents, knowledge, wealth and so on, so that people benefit from us mentally, emotionally and thus physically.

An exciting life is all about constantly having something that we are immersed in because that is when we experience flow. We can benefit from working on more than one goal at a time because momentum takes over, and we will begin to improve in all of these facets. We must ensure that we are preparing for the next step even before we have accomplished our current goal. People fall into depression when they have experienced a massive high, and then they decide to step back. Think about the stereotypical athlete who has an exciting, rich yet short career, and then he or she ends up depressed and squandering his or her finances after. The same is for astronauts: they achieve something that not many people will ever experience, and so when they return, they have nothing that even comes close to making them feel happy. They then fall into depression. Even people who become rich after setting up and selling their business for example, will soon become depressed by just sitting around wasting their time. Boredom is a choice. Why do we experience boredom? We are bored because we either do not have enough energy to do things (poor lifestyle, eating habits, sleeping habits etc.), or we have not planned our lives well (we do not have meaningful goals or things that motivate us). Inertia and boredom are catalysts of depression. It is all about challenging ourselves, taking up new interests and expanding our current interests.

Spirituality

"I go to nature to be soothed and healed, and to have my senses put in order." – John Burroughs

We should recognise that our existence is not really real. The more afraid we are of death, the more we are controlled by our ego. The ego is a necessary component, but it must be kept in its place. We are on this earth, this dimension, for such a short period of time. We spend the majority of our lives fixated on the concept of time, especially the lack of it. Regardless of what happens once we pass, we must live the life we truly want for our friends, our family and ourselves. We must be giving to all, but attached to nothing. The ego, however, misleadingly pervades our existence, and all the limited creations around us distract us. Why let your employer anger you? You will not know him or her eternally, or even for substantial time. Why let the emotional scars of an ex-partner ruin your future relationship? He or she was just part of your life, for such a short period of time. We must always be able to see the bigger picture. We must be the director of our lives and not the actor or actress.

Sometimes we can take it all too seriously, resulting in rigidity (in mind and body), stubbornness, complacency, and overwhelming and immobilising fear. Seeing the folly of it all is a fantastic way of letting go of what holds us back: self-doubt, paralysis by analysis, taking limited action and caring too much about what others think about us. The ego falsely convinces us that we are all important and superior; an egotistical overdose keeps us from living an enlightened and self-actualised life where we appreciate all and believe in a never-ending existence in one way or another. The ego keeps us narcissistic and narrow-minded; spirituality keeps us afloat and detached, so that we can give more to others. It is all encompassing and detached from the material world. It would be preposterous to eradicate the ego completely. It has its uses. However, our spiritual side must always be allowed to run freely without the ego's rope to keep us at bay. As long as our faith and spirituality is stronger than our egos, then we will live happily. Our higher self must be the director; our ego must be an actor who is allowed expression at certain moments, so that our play can unfold as we want.

A Knowing

"Faith is the confidence, the assurance, the enforcing truth, the knowing." – Robert Collier

Whatever happens in our lives is in perfect accordance sequentially to guide us down our own paths. We must abide by our intuition and gut feeling where possible; go with what feels right and natural, as this will create harmony and congruency between events, which will align itself systematically for us. We believe that our actions and inner thoughts affect only ourselves, but it is all a part of the larger picture. All energy and decision-making coincide. People want to feel as though they are in control, and to some extent we are. The more knowledge and wisdom we accumulate, the less ignorant and more responsible we become. When we believe that we are both doing and being done to by something larger than ourselves, then we will learn to accept our circumstance.

We encourage everything through our thoughts, emotions and actions (our overall energy). Actions speak louder than words. Our thoughts (inner dialogue) start the process; our emotions prepare us to take the right or wrong course, and our actions epitomise our true nature. We choose what we focus on, but to have this power, we must be brutally honest with ourselves, and detach from our thoughts, so that we can change them at will. We should consider our initial reactions to things. These thoughts and chemical reactions within are our automatic responses to that particular given situation and any along the same lines. Yes, these preliminary thoughts can be changed with training. However, we must at first acknowledge both the thought and question its validity.

Everything happens for a reason, and yes we are capable of achieving anything. We just need to have the right reason. Just look at technological advancements as of late, and what we have accomplished medically over the last few decades. Paraphrasing Einstein, our technology has exceeded our humanity, but how can we make the world at large a more beautiful existence? You. Just focus on you, and what you send out into the universe, and how you interact with others. This is more than enough. If everyone in the world took responsibility for their own actions, then we would live in a much more successful, satisfied and loving community.

The more we chase, the faster it will run from us. The tighter we hold sand, the more we will lose. Sometimes when we want something so badly, and we take success too seriously, we send signals and energies that contradict, "If I don't get this promotion, I will look like a failure," or "Without this marriage, I will be lonely." We go from being positive and optimistic to being obsessive, and this obsession turns pure positivity into doubt, pressure and negative phrasing. The pressure will mount, and we may find ourselves either sabotaging our success, or making silly mistakes that we would not have made if we were relaxed and serene. Instead, it may be wiser to give a great deal of effort and energy to achieving something, but leaving it to the universe and a greater power to bring blessings into our lives. We fail to understand that we are all fragile; we can never have total control of our lives, how we will die, and the health and happiness of others. We are powerful and exceptional, yet it is pertinent to appease ourselves by leaving some power to the universe. Do not fight against the opposing, stronger force. The ego gets us into trouble, and it can blind us to what we need most. The ego functions to make us feel valued and subjective. However, objectivity is also a critical skill. It is vital to step back and view the wider picture, to consider other people in relation to their own motives and destinies, to see how we fit in the puzzle, and to appreciate our role and those with whom we can influence.

Of course we must work extremely hard at something we are passionate about. However, *trying* too hard to get what we want, such as chasing things and people, will not bring us long-term success. Know that everything happens for a reason. Have no regrets; everything that we have and will experience is the art of our unique and individual destinies. Simply learn from any 'mistakes.' We must give what we can without expecting anything in return, and then people and resplendent things will appear for us. Choose to spend time with others based on their energy, and not their appearance or circumstance. It can be hard for many because we are used to evaluating people based on their appearances or net worth etc. However, if we want to have an incredible life, we want to surround ourselves with positive, energetic, loving human beings who make us laugh, smile and grow.

Trust

"Faith is taking the first step even when you don't see the whole staircase." - Martin Luther King, Jr.

Chinese philosopher, Lao Tzu, in the *Tao Te Ching*, wisely teaches that once we think we know the answer, the question changes. Once we know something to be true, it becomes false. Perhaps this happens so often in life because it is the universe's way of correcting our egos. A belief is therefore linked to our egos. Whenever we think we know something for sure, we are oftentimes surprised when it changes. The athlete losing the contest, and everyone thinks it is over, will turn it around. Someone you thought was definitely interested in you turned out not seeing you the same way. The same happens when we label and stereotype. Always be careful about what you think you know for sure. The ego falls into this trap over and over again in different contexts, and the universe always laughs at us by presenting us with something new.

Getting something new can lead to something else not working or what I call a changing of the guards. Everything happens for a reason. For example, I have a perfectly good watch that I like. Quite literally, as soon as I bought a new watch, for purely frivolous reasons, the one I already possessed, that had been working just fine, mysteriously stopped working. It is almost as if synchronicity was at play as Carl Jung succinctly puts it. If we do not need something, then it is usually corrected one way or another, or there may be a sign that something needs to be corrected.

Where there is power, there is a struggle. On our journey, we will encounter many obstacles and problems, and these will oftentimes be people. If we are in powerful positions, then we will inevitably have people around us who try to encumber this. Some people may be jealous, negative and will look to deter us in different ways. Sometimes even close family and friends can negatively influence us, and whilst they love us, they may do this because they may fear losing us. They may want us to be more successful, but being too successful might make them uncomfortable.

Most people live life feeling as though they are always missing something; the grass is greener on the other side apparently. We can feel as though we are not making the most of things. This feeling of lacking something rears its ugly head in many areas. Children who are raised without ever experiencing struggle or challenge will have no appreciation and gratefulness. We may feel like our partner is not enough; we may feel that our job is not enough. The more we feel as though we do not have enough, then, ironically, there is no space to be open or to attract abundance. We must always know where we came from, and how fortunate we really are. We can subdue these harmful thoughts and feelings by appreciating what we have. Get out of your own way. Just let go and have faith. We must trust that we have more than enough within us to make others and ourselves happy.

Patience

"Patience, persistence and perspiration make an unbeatable combination for success." – Napoleon Hill

The information age is truly overwhelming yet incredible. Never before have we had the ability to share ideas, communicate and eradicate many problems in the world. While many wondrous things have arisen, there are also several problems that stem from today's innovative and flexible culture where things are changing exponentially and uncontrollably. Depression experienced by youngsters and adolescents are at an all-time high. People are accustomed to getting what they want at the click of a button. But with this, patience greatly suffers. People live busy, hectic lives where distractions are here, there and everywhere. People lose their concentration far too easily, and they give up on things more quickly simply because it takes too much time and energy. This could be one reason why we see such a high divorce rate: people lose their patience with their partners more readily, and it is incredibly easy to meet another partner these days. Amongst all of this chaos, it is down to us to remain in control. This can be achieved by greatly reducing the excessive news and drama both publicly and in our personal lives. Ensure that you have some time away from your phone and its distractions.

Overcoming obstacles in any facet provides clarity, optimism and resolve that all contribute to success and happiness. We are happy when we are progressing. Once we think that we have achieved it all, then boredom and complacency set in. We now know that depression is not far away either at this stage. We are never the finished article, and we should appreciate this. The more we reduce and control our fears, the more confident and impregnable we shall become. It is like searching for treasure. The more you *try* to achieve something, the harder it will be to attain. Everything must flow. Peace and harmony within will cultivate success. The earth orbits the sun and the moon orbits the earth. View your success as a natural transition.

Embracing Silence

"All of humanity's problems stem from man's inability to sit quietly in a room alone." - Blaise Pascal, Pensees

It has never been more important to utilise the power of silence. As previously stated, we are all inundated with copious information in the form of technology and marketing that silence is a true blessing. It is our responsibility to reduce the obstacles around us, and increase clarity and deeper thinking. Silence is where flow originates, but this is what people shy away from. If we do not condition ourselves to think positively and calmly in silence, then moments of forced silence (before sleeping, upon waking and when noise is inappropriate) will consist of copious negativity and trepidation. The self grows most in moments of silence. During these moments, the mind may wander, yet we develop the skill to focus on what we want by concentrating and keeping the mind centred.

Silence and meditation, in all its forms, harmoniously bring mind and body, and thought and action, together. If we are stressed and encounter negative thoughts about relationships and inept areas, then we reduce the ability to pump quality, positive thoughts into our subconscious.

"When you connect to the silence within you, that is when you can make sense of the disturbance going on around you." – Stephen Richards

People who dislike being on their own tend to dislike their inner dialogue. These are the people who would benefit most from sitting in silence with their thoughts, reflecting upon how they think and feel. They can change the negative wiring in their minds by appreciating what they have, focusing more on others and planning a beautiful future for themselves. Think of what you least want to do; this is the thing you need to do most. If you really want to know yourself, simply sit in silence and observe: what do you think about? How do your ideas and visuals interchange? What images come to mind and in what form? What does your inner dialogue encompass? Be very careful about how you communicate with yourself.

Silence is the sound of success. Why are yoga, fasting and exercise so potent? These activities convey just how appreciative and grateful we are to be alive: to breathe, feel and love. We get so absorbed in our lives over futile and nonsensical things: who has what? Who screwed whom over? How many things do you have? How many friends do you have? How beautiful am I? The three activities mentioned take us away from all of that. The focus shifts onto our basic physiological needs: I am hungry; my heart is thumping; my breathing is so slow; how long can I do this for? What's keeping me alive? So many existential questions come to mind. It takes us back to the basics, so that we can put things into perspective again: nothing is promised to us; we must make the most of our aliveness. We get to focus on things that are so fundamental; things that test us mentally and physically.

Without these therapeutic activities, we lose our ability to take a step back, to view ourselves from the outside, and to consider our true potential. Without them we become infused and consumed with all that is fake and superficial: the ego's pleasures. This is when people become greedy, malevolent and cynical. They become so consumed in competition and material needs, wanting to get one over the other, and to compare themselves with others in what is often a detrimental, unnecessary comparison. We must want to always improve and set high expectations for ourselves without the judgment and involvement of others. Developing the ability to think positively in moments of silence is one of the most important things we can ever master in life. It will improve our discipline, focus and self-esteem.

"Silence is a source of great strength." - Lao Tzu

A poem pertinently expresses the struggle for freedom and emancipation:

The Door That Was Never Opened

This door was not to be overlooked.
It was neither the most beautiful,

Nor was it the most majestic,
But it existed.

People would walk passed
Absorbed with their own issues.
Little did they know what they sought.
The door was gracious and resilient,
Yet the people gave this door no consideration,
For they were swamped in complexities.

They complained and complained,
"When will things get better?"
They wallowed in their self-pity,
And exchanged triumphant failure after failure.
Their helplessness and misery was apparent to all
especially the door for its omnipresent stature.

These people wept, argued and battled
Till the bitter end. Never changing their focus.
Lonely. Marooned. Beaten. Dejected.
But the door was always there.
Waiting to be opened.
Waiting to be noticed.

By Ali Niyazi

Sometimes the best things are right in front of us, and
because we are not ready for them, or we do not think it
will ever turn up, we miss glorious opportunities. Be open
minded, and pay attention to what you are attracting.

Accept and Appreciate

"Gratitude unlocks the fullness of life. It turns what we have into enough, and more. It turns denial into acceptance, chaos to order, confusion to clarity." – Melody Beattie

The loving father took his daughter to the ice-cream van. She shouted in joy that she wanted vanilla ice cream, and so the benevolent father got her two scoops of vanilla ice cream on a cone. As they were walking away, she dropped her ice cream on the floor. Uncontrollably, the little girl was moaning that it was heavy, and she lost her grip. Diligently, the father took her back to the van, and asked for one scoop of vanilla ice cream this time, but the child demanded that she wanted three scoops! Intelligently, the father firmly stated, "you could not handle two scoops, so why should we get you three scoops?" Adults can be like this in many ways (and sometimes still about ice-cream). We must love what we have currently manifested in our world, and only then can we come from a place of strength, so that we can handle our 'three scoops' when the time is right. When the student is ready, the teacher will arrive.

We cannot always be in control otherwise we would never experience anew. We would not grow or be flexible enough to react competently and with conviction. When we are grateful for what we have, then we can never be fearful. When people wear flashy things, they communicate less. When people look for a fight, they show true weakness. When people look to dominate others, they push others away. The loudest can is the emptiest. Create the visible by focusing on the invisible. All physical manifestations are a result of how we think, feel and act. When we begin to cultivate true gratefulness, we begin to strip away all of the unnecessary garbage that overwhelm us, enabling us to make better decisions. When we come from a place of strength and fullness, we no longer look to take anything and everything because we already feel abundant, and do not need to scavenge for things that are often unimportant.

Express love and gratefulness to others and yourself. Take a moment to look at yourself in the mirror, and, even though it may sound contradictory, focus on the part of your body that you least like. It could be a finger, your chest, hair (or lack of), your bottom or love handles. Anything. Stare at that area, and communicate to yourself that you are exactly the way you are supposed to be at this moment in time. For example, if you do not like your belly, look at it and say the following: "My belly is exactly how it is supposed to be right now. I accept myself in every way." We have been taught to be insecure and dwell on what is wrong with us. When we do this, we cannot focus on the wonderful things about us. I am not advocating that we ignore things that we want to improve, but we must not let these issues define or bother us. Just because we are saying we accept ourselves, it does not mean that we are still not driven to lose fat. It just means we do not need to approach fat loss from this angry, limited perspective. Make the necessary changes, and accept that you are this way presently for a reason.

The same can be done with other things we dislike such as our reactions or ways of thinking about something. For example, if you do not like that you sweat profusely when anxious, then repeat the following: "I appreciate how my body and nervous system reacts when in what appears to be a challenging situation. It shows exactly how I feel, and I accept how I react in these situations. Sweating is natural, and it is a beautiful response that my body chooses, as it does what is natural in this moment." The beauty of such self-accepting and self-loving behaviour is that, ironically, by accepting our flaws, our flaws will fade or dramatically reduce. Why? We give power to what we focus on. When we despise our flaws, we intensify its power (emotion), and we strengthen its response; we ooze hate, and manifest strong emotions that are counterproductive. Conversely, when we love our so-called flaws, we become detached from any self-defeating and limiting thoughts. This opens the possibility for change, and for letting go.

Flexibility

"Stay committed to your decisions, but stay flexible in your approach." – Tony Robbins

Our physical flexibility represents how flexible and open we are as people. Rigidity, in the physical form, is a representation of the mind's inability to simply go with things. Inflexibility can be linked to stubbornness, being closed minded and narrow-minded. The narrow mind limits experiences and ways of thinking. If we want to be open minded, and to feel like we can adapt well to various situations, then we should physically stretch and become nimble. A body that flows well, and moves well, is a mind that flows well and thinks well. The mind and body are incredibly intertwined. One is always influencing the other.

As it relates to relationships, Tony Robbins exclaims that in an interaction the person who is the more certain and mentally flexible will hold greater control and power. Why? They have greater resources to draw from. They have more options open to them. The most flexible person is the most powerful in any situation as they have unlimited ways of changing and adapting to be successful in the interaction. The most versatile person has the most control. The rigid and stubborn cannot adapt to any conversation and engage as well with many other people. The person with most choices available has the best chance of choosing one that is most helpful and supportive. Another analogy can help: the boxer will almost always lose a fight against the mixed martial artist. Why? The boxer is very skilled but one-dimensional whereas the martial artist has an array of attacks that bemuses and staggers the boxer into hesitation and mental chaos. The brilliant boxer will actually not be able to box as well because the boxer is so overwhelmed due to the opponent's ability to dictate the entire competition. This is how our interactions are with anyone and in any situation!

The Passenger

Whilst we have looked at so many diverse strategies that will make us even more powerful, happy and successful, arguably the most important thing to do is to live your life as though you are in the passenger's seat of the 'car.' The more detached you can be from what you are experiencing, the easier it is to make the correct choices. Have you ever sat in the passenger's seat, and felt differently to the person who was actually driving the car? Have you noticed how the actual driver tends to be more emotional, and tends to take things personally when driving and interacting with other drivers? Have you also noticed how the passenger always seems calmer and less agitated when other drivers, or things, exhibit negative and disrespectful behaviour?

We must live our lives as though we are passengers. Why? We will make fewer mistakes because we will be less emotionally engaged, and thus more logical, in all that is happening around us. We will be able to physically and metaphorically see more in terms of the overall picture because we are more focused on the journey than the mechanics of what is happening. We are more likely to experience flow because flow can be experienced more readily when the conscious mind is less involved. Take control of your life by omnisciently and objectively perceiving everything that unfolds inside and outside of your experience.

Give

"If we ask, we should also be prepared to give." -
Stephen Richards

We must give for the sake of giving. By doing so, we will cultivate many beautiful things in our lives. However, if we give to someone with the sole intention of getting something in return, then we shall find ourselves bitterly disappointed. The more we let go of the belief that we have to take from others, and suppress others to get ahead, the more capable we will be of manifesting abundance. One of the most beautiful things we can experience in life is giving to others. When we learn something powerful, do we keep it to ourselves, for fear of others growing, or do we look to enlighten and inspire others by extending our knowledge and wisdom? Why is this? Do we feel as though others will get ahead of us? This is obviously a limiting belief, and one that lacks abundant thinking. Are we afraid of being left behind? Well if that is the case, then it will happen. Do not ever feel as though a positive and polite act pulls us back in any sense. We are in charge of our destiny, and ultimately our happiness. The more we give, the fuller we become.

Conclusion

"We have to live life with a sense of urgency so not a minute is wasted." – Les Brown

Act with urgency in life. Life is short, and we all know how quickly time flies by. Achieve more now. Take action now. Love more now. We are on this earth, in our own specific and unique form, for a blink of an eye. We are in charge of what we think, feel and create around us. Feeling powerful, happy and successful are really determined by our level of self-esteem, and how many activities we partake in that either bring us great joy, or move us closer to achieving our major goals in life. The more loving and appreciative we are of others, and ourselves, the more we partake in activities with clarity, self-respect and without judgement. Our daily lives determine how happy we are.

In addition, we are looking for long-term happiness. Improving the quality of our lives is partly down to transferring more of our short-term actions into long-term actions. This means that we cannot class ourselves as happy individuals if we only feel this way a couple of weeks a year when we are on holiday or when we are celebrating people's birthdays etc. True happiness is about the emotions we experience daily, and whether we feel that our activities are taking us closer to where we want to be. Acquiring more and buying great things such as a new car, house, coat etc. will only make us happy for short glimpses. We are looking for something more meaningful, substantial and lasting. Being focused on short-term gratification will result in long-term pain. Short-term thinkers are most likely to become impatient, addicts and they are more likely struggle financially (rarely do get rich quick schemes ever work). Be a long-term thinker, but take action toward these long-term goals now!

Fortunately, we can free ourselves by never labeling and limiting ourselves. We are complex organisms with many talents. We have the ability to improve all our strengths and all of our weaknesses. We must have a growth mindset. Ask the right questions, and search for the right answers. We must treat our lives like a computer game. We want to be in control of what we do and when we do them as much as possible. We also want to remain detached regularly, so that we make better decisions more often rather than being swayed by the emotions of our egos. A balance between giving the ego expression, yet remaining detached from our experiences is essential. There is no need to force anything in life. All we need to do is develop our character, mentality and spirit, and watch how the seemingly impossible become possible.

We can liken success to the art of boxing. Problems and obstacles are always going to hit us. We simply cannot avoid some small and huge problems. No one is skilled enough to evade the punches that life will throw at us. However, people react in one of two ways when a problem is launched at them. Firstly, let us look at how not to take a punchy problem: the problems that knock us out are the ones that we do not see coming. We may be so blinded by our ego that we get caught off guard; we have been ignoring life's jabs (warnings) so often that we somehow allowed ourselves to get hit by the power shot. Life's punches also knock people flat when people brawl in life as opposed to developing technique and avoiding unnecessary punishment (problems). What do we mean by brawling? We mean just banking on being tough, and thinking that toughness is enough. Being a fighter will help you survive, but we are after the victory! Giving what we have and risking getting hit a lot is a recipe for disaster!

We can only take so many blows until the strength of our 'chin' diminishes. It then becomes easier for life to overwhelm us. There is only so much we can handle in life. We must play it smart. We must pick our moments. We must be patient. We must attack when the time is right. Since we cannot duck, slip and roll from all punches thrown at us, we need to learn how to roll with the punches. It means we must anticipate what problems might occur and when; we must be able to move our faces with the opponent's punch, so that we take some of the force off the punch. If we take a punch full on, then we will get hurt badly, which is what most reactive people feel: the short-term thinker. If we try to walk through the punch, then life's problems will catch up on us. If we see a punch coming, and yet we move toward it (focusing on the negatives in our lives), then the inevitable will happen. However, being proactive, and developing our defense, will keep us protected, so that we can pick our shots when opportunities present themselves.

Feeling powerful is more about feeling strong enough to tackle any obstacles that come our way, and so power is more about how much energy we have on a daily basis. No one feels powerful mentally, emotionally or physically if they are frequently exhausted. Therefore, if we want to feel more powerful, then we have to partake in daily activities that enable us to grow and move closer to achieving our goals. Some of these activities include meditation/yoga, incantations, writing out our goals, doing things that take us closer to achieving our goals, exercising, sex and pushing our boundaries. The more flow we experience on a daily basis, the more powerful we feel. Flow is power.

Our levels of joy and happiness are based upon our emotional intelligence. Being able to influence ourselves, and others, will greatly affect our levels of success most dramatically. Influencing ourselves means knowing how to get ourselves to take the action required consistently. It means knowing how to find the right kind of leverage to play with our own emotions in a way to get the best out of us, and this can happen in different ways depending on context. Being able to influence others is mandatory if we are to keep everyone at the right length, whether close or far, so that we can focus on our biggest life goals. As long as we feel as though we are moving closer to achieving our goals (progressing), then we will frequently experience happiness. We want to experience mostly positive feelings every day (happiness), and we want to have copious energy every day (power). Therefore, power is achieved when we experience both high energy levels, and when we think highly of ourselves regardless of our outcomes. Success occurs when both happiness (joyful feelings) and power (self-esteem) marry.

Energy (Power) + Progression (Happiness) = Success

Self-Esteem (Power) + Emotional Intelligence (Happiness) = Success

Power + Happiness = Success

We must believe that we deserve success. We must believe that we are enough just as we are now. We must believe that life will unfold the way we wish, as long as we keep pressing forward diligently. Lastly, we must be ourselves, and live abundantly: we must give more; we must love more and we must focus on what we want more. I wish you all the power, happiness and success that you deserve.

Bibliography

Hall, Michael. *Meta States: Mastering the Higher Levels of Your Mind.* Neuro-Semantic Publications. 2009.

Bandler, Richard. *Get the Life You Want: The Secrets to Quick & Lasting Life Change.* Harper Element. 2008.

Byrne, Rhonda. *The Secret.* Beyond Words Publishing. 2006.

Cialdini, Robert. *Influence: The Psychology of Persuasion.* Harper Business.1984.

Dweck, Carol. *Mindset: The New Psychology of Success.* Ballantine Books. 2006.

Elrod, Hal. *The Miracle Morning: The 6 Habits That Will Transform Your Life Before 8AM.* John Murray Learning. 2012.

Navarro, Joe. Marvin Karlins. *What Every BODY is Saying: An Ex-FBI Agent's Guide to Speed-Reading People: An Ex-FBI Agent's Guide to Speed-reading People*. HarperCollins. 2008.

Peters, Steve. *The Chimp Paradox: The Mind Management Programme to Help You Achieve Success, Confidence and Happiness*. Penguin Books. 2012.

Puttick, Elizabeth. *7 Personality Types: Discover Your True Role to Achieve Success and Happiness*. Hay House.2009.

Robbins, Anthony. *Unlimited Power: The New Science of Personal Achievement*. Pocket Books. 2001.

Tzu, Lao. *Tao Te Ching*. Hackett Classics. 1993.

Printed in Great Britain
by Amazon

36613964R00196